Key Stage 3 … port

Science

Ages 12–13

Bob McDuell and Graham Booth

survival GUIDE

Letts Educational
Chiswick Centre
414 Chiswick High Road
London W4 5TF
Tel: 020 8996 3333
Fax: 020 8996 8390
Email: mail@lettsed.co.uk
Website: www.letts-education.com

First published 2003

British Library Cataloging in Publication Data. A CIP record of this book is available from the British Library.

ISBN 1 84315 115 4

Letts Educational Limited is a division of Granada Learning Limited, part of the Granada Media Group.

Edited and typeset by Cambridge Publishing Management

Designed by Moondisks Limited

Science

Book 2 Ages 12-13

SURVIVAL SHEET 1

Research 4

Food and Digestion

Unit 1 A balanced diet 6

Unit 2 Mineral salts 8

Unit 3 Digestion .10

Respiration

Unit 4 Respiration in cells and plants . . .14

Unit 5 Lungs 16

Unit 6 Inhaled and exhaled air 18

Microbes and diseases

Unit 7 Bacteria and viruses 20

Ecological relationships

Unit 8 Carrying out a piece of fieldwork 24

Unit 9 Feeding relationships 25

SURVIVAL SHEET 2

Investigative skills 26

Materials – atoms and elements

Unit 10 Elements 28

Unit 11 Putting elements into groups 30

Unit 12 Patterns in elements 32

Materials – compounds and mixtures

Unit 13 Mixtures .34

Unit 14 Compounds 36

Geological changes (1)

Unit 15 Weathering 38

Unit 16 Rock 40

Geological changes (2)

Unit 17 Recycling 44

Unit 18 Uses of rocks 46

SURVIVAL SHEET 3

Drawing and using graphs 48

Heating and cooling

Unit 19 Moving energy around 50

Magnets and electromagnets

Unit 20 Magnetism 54

Unit 21 Electromagnetism 56

Light

Unit 22 How light travels 58

Unit 23 Mirrors .60

Unit 24 Changing speed 62

Unit 25 Colour 64

Sound and hearing

Unit 26 Sound production 66

Unit 27 Different sounds 68

Year 8 Test Paper 70

Answers 74

Jargon Buster 78

Index 80

1

Research

Nobody can be expected to know everything. Every year more things are found out and so the job gets more difficult!

We all have to look things up in books and encyclopaedias or find information from CD-ROMs and the Internet. The problems students can create for themselves when doing research may be caused by not being selective about what they actually need. They often copy out a whole article from a book or download a whole article from the Internet.

It is important to have a clear idea of what you want to find out. This comes if you narrow down your search to a manageable task. If you are using a search engine on the Internet think carefully about the words you are going to use.

When you find a suitable article, copy and paste only the relevant sections into a separate file. If you are using a book, copy out the relevant information onto a sheet of paper. When you have collected all the information, the job is to organise it into a relevant order. Before you finish, read out what you have found out and make sure it makes sense.

Research task

We now know that blood circulates around the body but people did not always know this.

Find out what you can about how scientists learned this. You should concentrate on what experiments, if any, they carried out and what conclusions they came to from their experiments.

If you type *circulation* into a search engine you might find 3 670 000 articles about circulation. The chance of finding a relevant article is remote.

If you type in *blood circulation* the number of articles drops to 592 000 and if you type in *human blood circulation* the total drops to 285 000. If you have found out that William Harvey was one of the scientists involved and type in *harvey human blood circulation* the total drops to 7390.

Four scientists should be studied in your research:
Michael Servetus   Galen of Pergamum   William Harvey   Vesalius.

If you need further help the website:
http://scienceworld.wolfram.com/biography is useful for finding biographies of scientists.

Alternatively you might look in an encyclopaedia for your information.

A balanced diet

A balanced diet provides:

- everything required for growth of the body
- everything required for repair of the body
- enough energy for the body's activities.

For good health the human diet must contain proteins, carbohydrates, fats, vitamins, minerals, fibre and water. A balanced diet contains just the right amounts of these.

The table gives information about these different food chemicals.

Food chemical	Benefit to the body	Source
Proteins	Provide amino acids for building and repairing the body. The body cannot store amino acids or proteins	Meat, fish, milk, cheese, nuts
Carbohydrates (including sugar and starch)	Provide energy	Bread, potatoes
Fats	Store energy	Butter, oil and margarine
Vitamins	Required in small quanitities for good health, e.g. vitamin C	Fruit, vegetables
Minerals	Required in small amounts for good health, e.g. iron	Fruit, green vegetables

In addition to the food chemicals in this table, the diet should contain water and dietary fibre (roughage).

Exercise 1

1 List the seven constituents of a healthy diet.

2 Why is it important to have a regular supply of protein foods?

3 Why do marathon runners eat large amounts of carbohydrate before running a race?

4 We are encouraged to eat a balanced diet. What is a balanced diet?

5 From the list pick out foods that provide high fibre.
butter sugar vegetables white bread
wholegrain cereals wholemeal bread

Vitamins

Each vitamin has a particular job controlling a vital process in the body. Only small amounts are required to ensure good health.

The table gives some of the common vitamins and the jobs they do.

Vitamin	Good source	Use
A	Green vegetables, butter, egg yolk, fish oils	Healthy skin and membranes
B complex	Yeast extract, liver, wholemeal bread	Various, particularly respiration
C	Citrus fruits, blackcurrants, vegetables	Healthy skin, strong capillaries
D	Butter, egg yolk, sunlight	Uptake and controlled use of calcium

We now know that eating fruit and vegetables that provide a source of Vitamin C is important. Scurvy was a disease that once affected sailors on long voyages. It was caused by a lack of vitamin C and led to bleeding gums, weakness of muscles and, ultimately, death. It was prevented by giving the sailors fruit juice to drink. Dr James Lind found this out in 1747. British ships going on a long journey took limes to prevent scurvy. This led to British sailors being called 'Limeys'.

The first vitamin to be identified was vitamin B1. In 1896 a Dutch doctor, Dr Eijkman, was looking for a cure for a disease called beriberi. He noticed that some chickens had a similar disease. He found that these chickens improved when their food was changed from polished rice (rice with the outer husks removed) to whole grain rice (which contained the husks). He concluded that it must be a chemical in the husk that prevented beriberi.

In 1906 he boiled up some husks in water and used the solution to cure a pigeon that was suffering from beriberi. In 1934 scientists identified the chemical in the husks and called it vitamin B1. By 1937 scientists were able to make vitamin B1 in the laboratory without having to extract it from rice husks.

Exercise 2

1 People buy vitamin capsules and tablets. Why is this not necessary if you eat a healthy diet?

2 Butter can provide two vitamins. Which two vitamins?

3 Margarine does not contain vitamins when it is made. Why are they added before it is sold?

Tactics

People buy vitamin and mineral supplements. Look at advertisements for these supplements. What vitamins and minerals do people buy?

ED Many people use the word diet wrongly. They associate the word with slimming and losing weight. Your diet is what you eat. ALERT

Mineral salts

A healthy diet must contain small amounts of mineral salts.

Minerals are chemical elements – either metals or non-metals.

The table gives some examples of mineral salts needed in the human body. Like vitamins, they are needed only in small amounts.

Element	Good source	Use in the body
Ca (calcium)	Cheese, milk	Bones and teeth
F (fluorine)	Toothpaste	Hardening tooth enamel
Fe (iron)	Liver, green vegetables	Part of haemoglobin in red blood cells
I (iodine)	Table salt additive, sea food	Thyroid gland
K (potassium)	Green vegetables	Nerve and muscle function
Na (sodium)	Table salt	Nerve and muscle function

Water is also an essential part of a healthy diet. Over 7% of the body is water. You need to have a regular supply of water.

Water has many functions in the body. It:

- acts as a solvent
- transports substances
- provides somewhere for reactions to take place.

Exercise 1

1 Why is it essential for children to have a regular supply of calcium?

2 Which foods are good sources of calcium?

3 Studies have shown that adding small amounts of fluorine, as fluoride, to tap water can reduce tooth decay, especially in children. Why does it do this? Why do some people object to fluoride being added to water?

4 Some people are anaemic which means they do not have enough red blood cells to transport oxygen around the body. They may be given iron tablets. What is the job of these tablets?

5 People might not eat enough iodine in their diet. What is done to ensure that iodine deficiency is not a problem?

Tactics

Read the labels on food products. It will tell you what is in the food.

Testing for proteins, carbohydrates and fats

You will probably carry out these food tests in the laboratory.

Testing for proteins

The biuret test is used to test for proteins.

The food is added to water. Then sodium hydroxide solution and copper sulphate solution are added.

A purple colour shows the presence of protein.

Testing for carbohydrates

There are two tests here – for starch and for simple sugars, such as glucose.

For starch

If iodine solution is added to a food containing starch, the solution goes dark blue-black.

For simple sugars

If Benedict's solution is added to a food containing a simple sugar and the mixture is heated, a red-brown solid is formed. Benedict's solution is a blue solution. It contains copper sulphate.

Testing for fats

Ethanol is added to the food being tested in a test tube. The test tube is shaken. The clear liquid is poured into distilled water. If the solution goes milky, a fat is present.

This happens because fat dissolves in ethanol but not in water.

Exercise 2

The table gives the results of food tests on three foods, A, B and C.

Test	A	B	C
Protein test	Blue solution	Purple colour	Blue solution
Starch test	Blue-black colour	No blue-black colour	Blue-black colour
Simple sugar test	Blue solution	Blue solution	Red-brown solid
Fat test	Clear	Clear	Milky white

What do these tests tell you about A, B and C?

RED ALERT Take care with dangerous chemicals like sodium hydroxide. RED ALERT RED

Digestion

Digestion is the breaking down of large insoluble food molecules into small molecules that the body can then absorb and use.

This takes place in the digestive system which is one long tube, called the gut, several metres long, starting at the mouth and finishing at the anus. At different places along the journey, food is treated in different ways to break it down and absorb it.

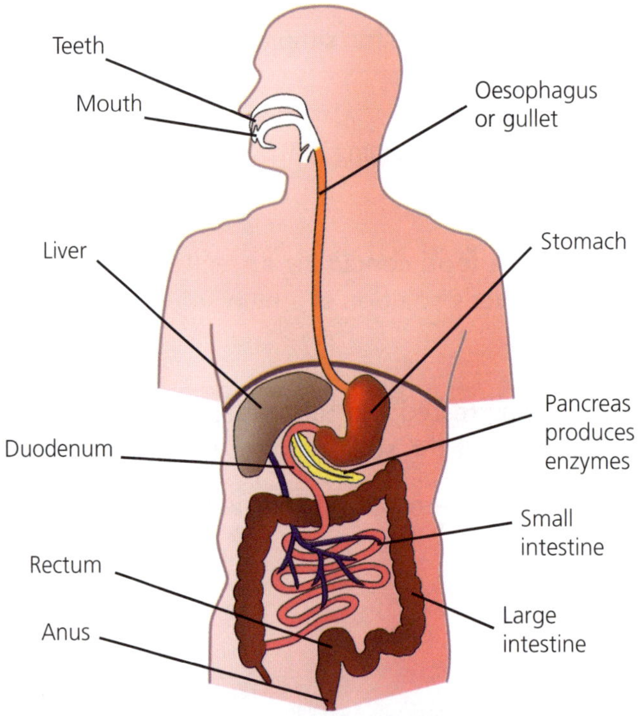

Exercise 1

The list gives some parts of the digestive system.

anus duodenum oesophagus large intestine mouth rectum small intestine stomach

1 Put these parts in the correct order starting with the mouth and finishing with the anus.

2 There are other parts of the system that have specific jobs. List the other parts not mentioned in question 1.

Tactics

Practise drawing and labelling the human digestive system.

RED ALERT Examiners often ask questions about digestion. RED

What happens in the digestive system?

The digestive process involves:

- a mechanical breaking down of food, e.g. by chewing
- a chemical breaking down using enzymes
- absorption of the small molecules produced.

The table shows what is happening at different places in the digestive system.

Place in the body	What is happening?
Mouth	Food chewed into small pieces for swallowing. It is mixed with saliva, which contains enzymes. Enzymes (carbohydrase) start to break down carbohydrates into glucose.
Oesophagus	The mixture of food and saliva pass down this tube from the mouth to the stomach.
Stomach	Food is stored for a few hours. Food is mixed with gastric juices. Hydrochloric acid kills most bacteria and gives the best conditions for enzymes (protease) to break down proteins.
Duodenum	The mixture is changed from acid to alkaline conditions.
Small intestine	Alkaline juices neutralise stomach acids and make ideal conditions for the breaking down of fats by enzymes (lipase). The food chemicals are absorbed into the bloodstream here.
Large intestine	Water is removed and reabsorbed into the blood. Unusable material becomes faeces.
Rectum	The faeces are stored here before egestion through the anus.

Exercise 2

1. Where is the food broken down into small pieces? This is called physical digestion.
2. Digestion uses enzymes to break down the food. Write down the names of the enzymes used to break down carbohydrates, proteins and fats.
3. The conditions in the stomach and the small intestine are very different. How are they different?
4. Where are the food chemicals absorbed into the bloodstream?
5. If you chew a piece of bread (carbohydrate) for a long time you will notice a sweet taste. Suggest why this is so.

Tactics

Having learned the parts in the digestive system, make sure you know the job of each of these organs.

Other organs are important in the digestive process

Liver

The liver has a number of functions. It:

- stores excess glucose produced in digestion as glycogen (a long chain carbohydrate). It can then be released when it is needed
- removes excess amino acids from the body and breaks them up (Remember amino acids cannot be stored.)
- produces some vitamins
- produces bile, which assists the breaking down of fats
- breaks down poisonous substances such as alcohol in the blood.

Gall bladder

Where the bile is stored before use in the digestive process.

Pancreas

This is a gland that produces enzymes, which speed up the breakdown of the food.

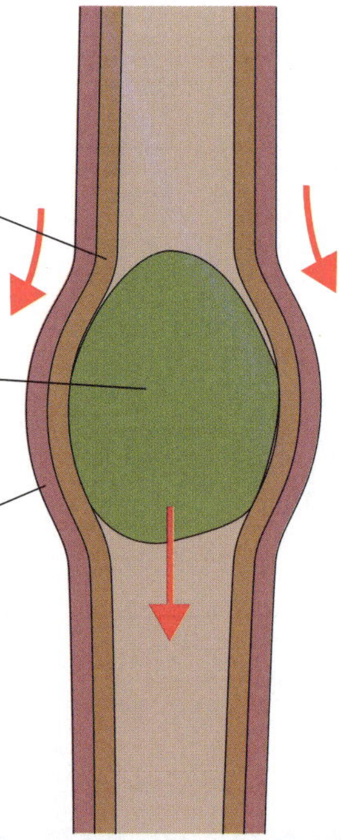

How does food pass along the gut?
Muscles of the gut contract and relax in a special way to squeeze food along the gut. This is called **peristalsis**.

Exercise 3

1 Other animals have digestive systems. Why do plants not need a digestive system?

2 Complete the table.

Large food molecule	Enzyme	Small molecule produced
Carbohydrate		
Protein		
Fat		and

RED ALERT Each of these organs has some role in digestion. RED A

Absorption

Absorption takes place in the small intestine. The food chemicals are absorbed into the bloodstream. The surface of this part of the small intestine, called the ileum, is folded with each square millimetre of the surface carrying a large number of finger-like projections called villi.

This produces a very large surface area, which is very efficient for absorption.

The diagram shows the cross-section of a single villus.

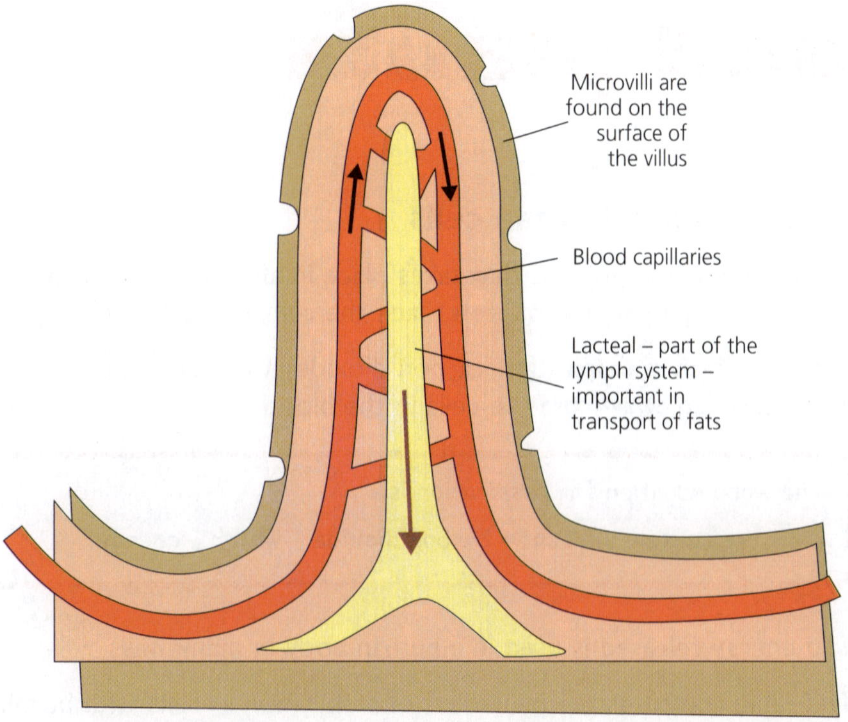

The wall is very thin and is permeable to small molecules such as glucose, amino acids, fatty acids and glycerol, which can pass through the wall into the blood capillaries. Blood from the capillaries joins the rest of the bloodstream.

Exercise 4

1 What is the plural of villus?

2 Why does the design of the ileum lead to good absorption?

3 Write down three materials absorbed into the bloodstream in the ileum.

Tactics

You should now understand the whole digestive process. Go back and re-read the whole process.

Respiration in cells and plants

Respiration in human cells

Respiration is the process that takes place in all cells to produce energy from glucose and oxygen. The glucose and oxygen reach the cells in the blood supply.

In the process of respiration, carbon dioxide, water and energy are produced. Carbon dioxide is transported away from the cells in the blood.

The word equation for respiration is:

glucose + oxygen → carbon dioxide + water + energy

The energy released is used in a human body in many ways:

The table compares the processes of respiration in cells with burning a carbon compound as fuel.

Respiration in cells	Burning a carbon compound as fuel
Uses food containing carbon, e.g. glucose	Uses fuel containing carbon
Uses oxygen	Uses oxygen
Produces carbon dioxide and water as wastes	Produces carbon dioxide and water as wastes
Releases energy, some as heat, some locked up	Releases energy, most as heat, some as light

Exercise 1

1 Write down three similarities between respiration in cells and the burning of glucose.

2 Write down one difference between respiration in cells and the burning of glucose.

Tactics

The process of respiration can be compared to burning.

RED ALERT Students often think that respiration only takes place with animals. It takes place with plants too. RED A

Respiration in plants

Respiration also takes place in a similar way.

The apparatus in the diagram can be used to show that respiration in a plant produces carbon dioxide and water.

Air is drawn through the apparatus by the pump. The air first bubbles through potassium hydroxide solution, where any carbon dioxide is removed. It then passes through limewater which turns cloudy when carbon dioxide is passed through it. As all the carbon dioxide has been removed, the limewater in this flask is unchanged.

The air then passes through the large jar containing the plant and through the second flask containing limewater. In a couple of minutes the limewater turns milky showing that carbon dioxide has come from the plant.

At the end of the experiment there are droplets of colourless liquid on the inside of the large jar. If this is tested with cobalt chloride paper this paper turns from blue to pink showing the presence of water.

Exercise 2

1 Write a word equation for the respiration process in a plant.

2 How would the results be different if a small animal was in the large jar instead of the plant?

Tactics

Don't forget that limewater is used to test for carbon dioxide.

Lungs

What is the role of the lungs?

The diagram shows the human respiratory system. The lungs provide a means of getting oxygen into the bloodstream and removing the waste carbon dioxide. The process taking place is called gaseous exchange.

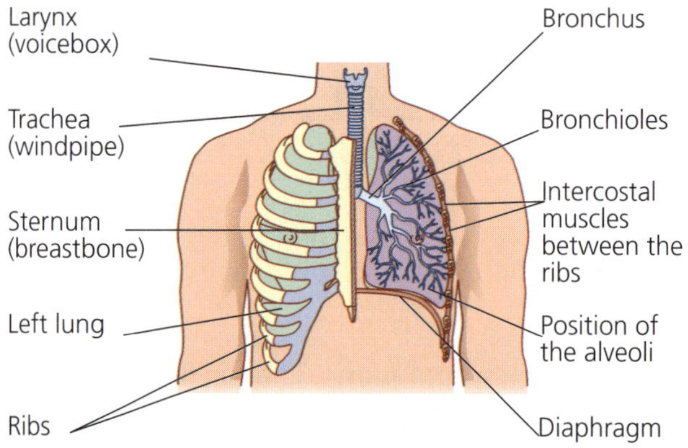

Air is drawn into the lungs by the process of breathing. This is a mechanical process of inhaling and exhaling air. When you breathe in:

- the rib cage moves upwards and outwards
- the diaphragm moves downwards
- there is now more space inside your chest (called the thorax)
- there is less pressure inside the thorax than outside
- this causes air to be pushed into your lungs.

Exercise 1

1 Describe what happens when you breathe out.

2 How does air get into the lungs from the mouth?

Tactics

If you know the changes when you breathe in, the exact opposite will give you what happens when you breathe out.

Gaseous exchange in the lungs

When the air is in the lungs gaseous exchange can take place.

The lung tissue consists of millions of tiny air sacs (called alveoli) and blood vessels. This brings the air and blood in close contact so exchange can take place. The exchange happens easily because:

- each alveolus has very thin walls so oxygen and carbon dioxide can diffuse through
- the surface of each alveolus is moist
- there is a good blood supply through the blood vessels
- the alveoli have a very large surface area. The total surface of all the alveoli in a human being is about the area of a tennis court.

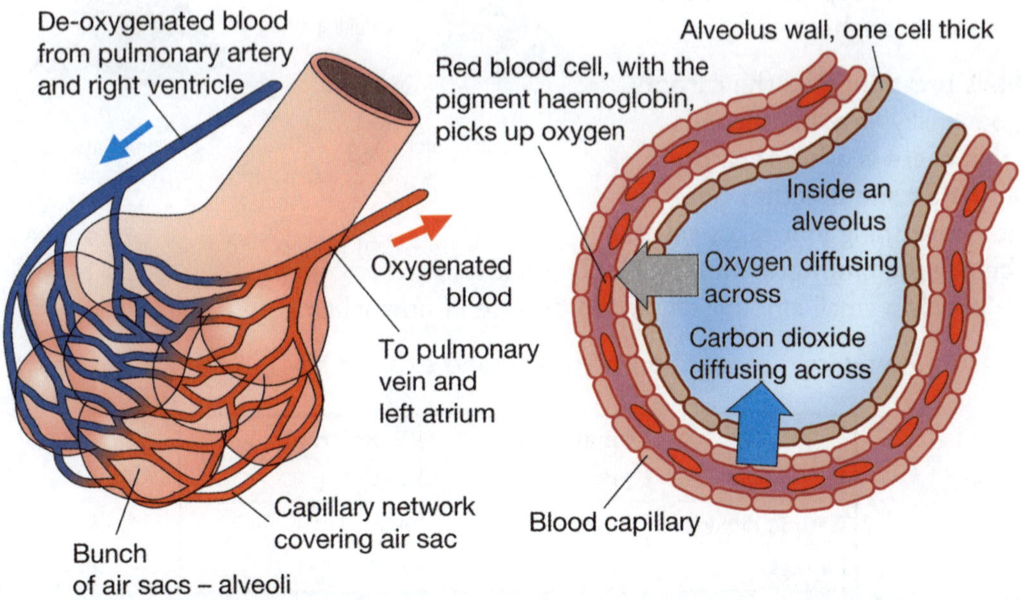

Exercise 2

1 The diagram shows an alveolus from a healthy person and a person suffering from the lung disease emphysema.

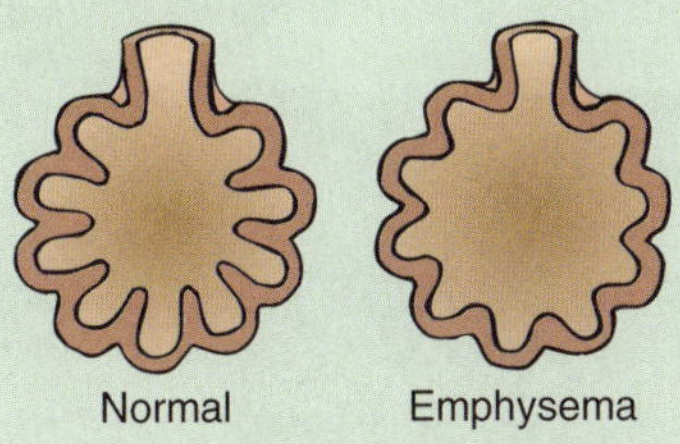

Explain why people suffering from emphysema find it difficult to breathe.

2 Why is it important that oxygen gets into the blood from the lungs?

Tactics

You will often be asked why gaseous exchange in the lungs is efficient. Learn the four bullet points.

Here is an example of surface area being used in an explanation. It is a very important idea.

Inhaled and exhaled air

The air we breathe out (called exhaled air) is different in composition from the air we breathe in (called inhaled air).

The diagram shows Sam breathing air out and in. She is doing it in such a way that the air passes through limewater. Limewater turns cloudy when carbon dioxide passes through it.

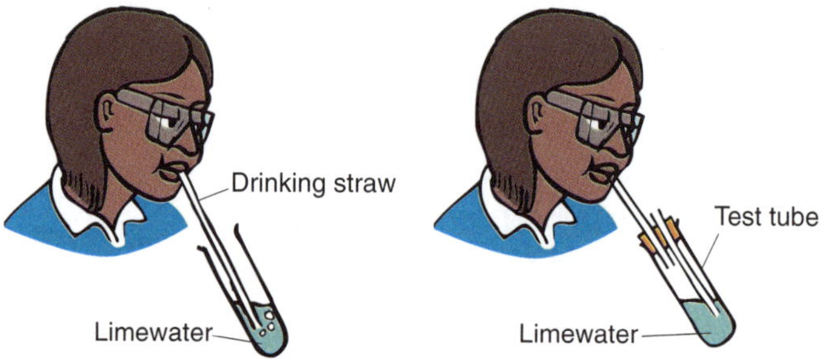

When she is breathing out, the carbon dioxide goes milky in a few seconds showing that there is a lot of carbon dioxide in the air she breathes out. When she is breathing in it takes several minutes before the limewater turns milky. This shows that there is only a small amount of carbon dioxide in normal air.

The table gives the typical composition of inhaled and exhaled air.

	Inhaled air	**Exhaled air**
Oxygen	21%	17%
Carbon dioxide	0.04%	4%
Nitrogen	79%	79%

Exercise 1

1 How do the percentages of oxygen and carbon dioxide change between inhaling and exhaling air?

2 A person is having breathing difficulties. What treatment can be given to improve breathing?

3 A magazine article states that the percentage of oxygen in air in the year 1700 was 38%. Suggest why this might have reduced.

4 Give two other differences between the air we breathe in and the air we breathe out.

Tactics

Remember that exhaled air contains more carbon dioxide than inhaled air.

Experiment comparing inhaled and exhaled air

This experiment links up what you know about burning with what you know about inhaled and exhaled air.

Sam set up the apparatus in the diagram and breathed out through the tube and collected a beaker full of exhaled air.

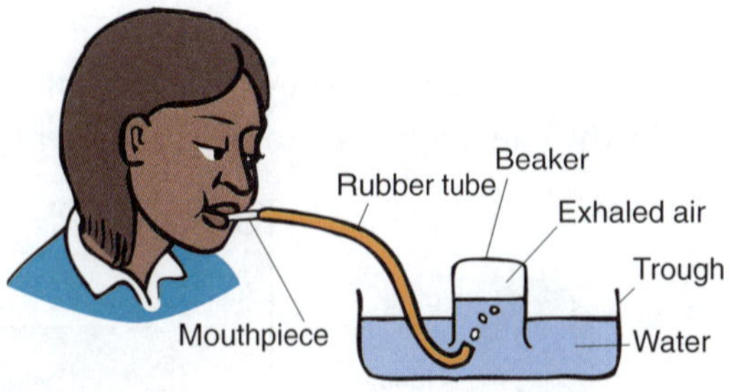

She then lit two small candles and covered them with beakers full of exhaled air and normal air.

She found that the candle covered by the beaker of exhaled air went out after 10 seconds.

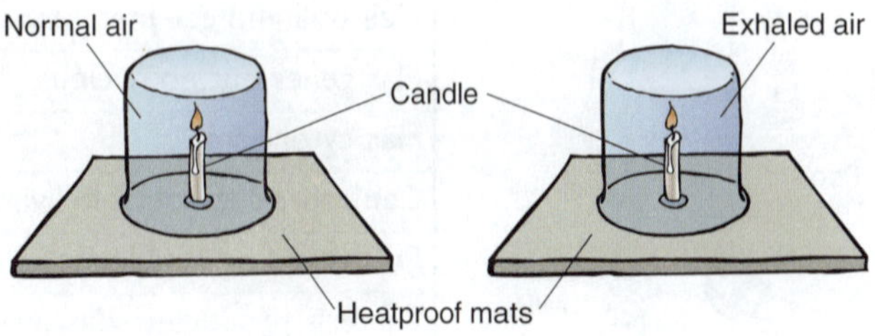

The candle covered by the beaker of normal air went out after 24 seconds.

It is important that Sam used a beaker of the same size each time to make sure it is a fair test.

She might also try each experiment three times and calculate an average time. The average times should be more reliable.

Exercise 2

1 In which beaker did the candle burn for longer?

2 Which gas in the air is used up when the candle burns?

3 What can you conclude from Sam's experiment?

Tactics

A frequent mistake students make is to think that all the oxygen has been removed from the air we breathe out.

RED This investigation requires you to link work on respiration to work from another part of your studies on burning. RED

Bacteria and viruses

Ill health can be caused by a variety of micro-organisms, including bacteria and viruses entering the body. The diagram shows places where they can enter the body.

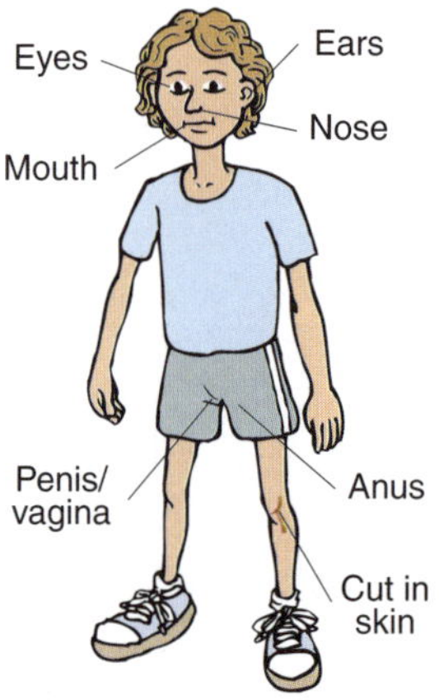

Bacterium	Virus

Cell wall and cell membrane	Protein coat
Has genes but no nucleus	Has genes but no nucleus
Has cytoplasm	No cytoplasm
Can reproduce outside living cells	Can only reproduce inside living cells
Destroyed by antibiotics	Not destroyed by antibiotics
Bacteria produce toxins (poisons)	Viruses damage the cells in which they reproduce

The table above summarises some of the similarities and some of the differences between a bacterium and a virus.

Bacteria multiply very quickly by repeatedly dividing into two. Viruses cannot reproduce themselves. They can only reproduce inside other cells. This is summarised in the diagram.

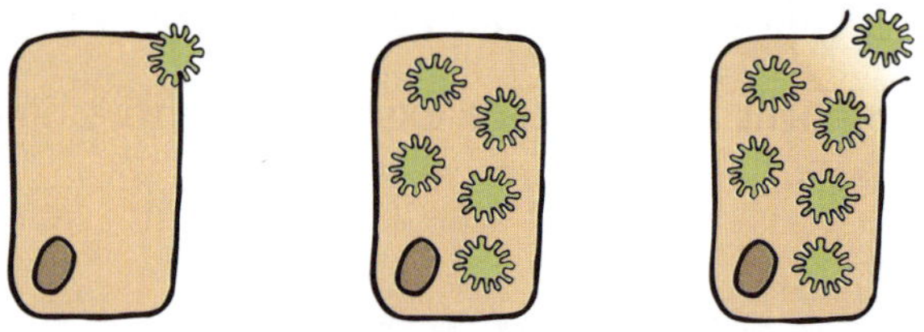

The virus attacks a cell... it enters the cell and new viruses are made inside the cell... then the cell bursts, releasing new viruses to infect more cells.

Exercise 1

1 If 100 bacteria get into your body and reproduce to double their number every 30 minutes, how many will there be in 3 hours?

2 Which two features are in a bacterial cell and a human cell?

3 If you visit the doctor and the doctor diagnoses a virus, you do not get a prescription for antibiotics. Why is this?

4 Why is it important to take the full course of antibiotics when they are prescribed?

Tactics

Make sure you are clear about the differences between a bacterium and a virus.

How the body prevents micro-organisms entering

- The skin acts as a barrier.
- The breathing organs produce sticky mucus to trap microbes.
- Blood platelets produce clots to seal cuts.

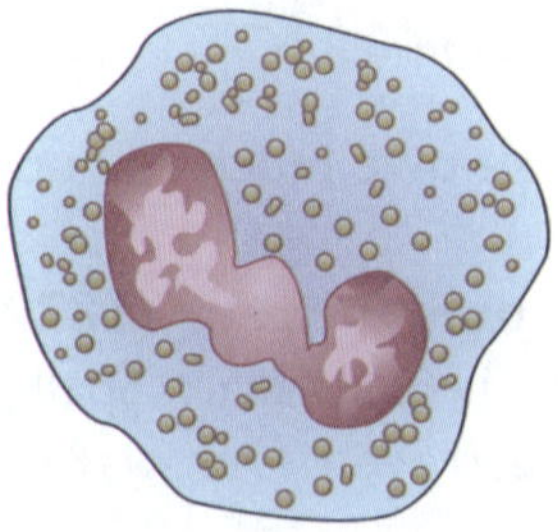

White blood cells have a defensive role.

- They engulf and destroy microbes.
- They produce antibodies that destroy microbes.
- They produce antitoxins that counteract the toxins produced by microbes.

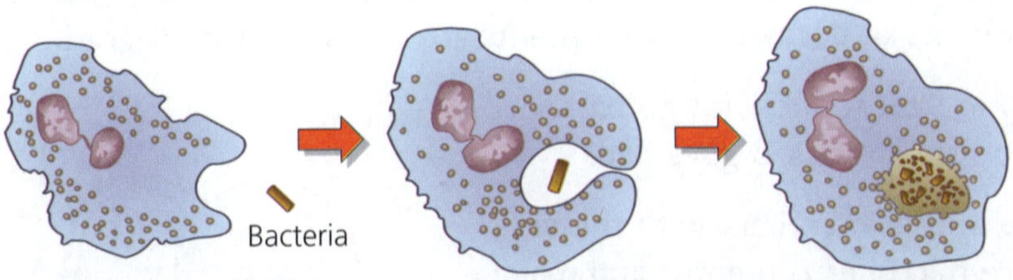

Once we have had a particular disease, the body knows how to produce antibodies and so the white blood cells can produce them quickly before the disease takes hold. We are then said to be immune to that microbe.

Antibiotics were discovered by accident in 1928. Sir Alexander Fleming noticed that staphylococcus (a strain of bacteria) in contact with a mould disappeared. He rightly concluded that there was an antibacterial substance in the mould. This was later found to be penicillin. Fleming did not succeed in making penicillin. That was 15 years later by HW Florrey and EB Chain. The ease with which penicillin can be destroyed is one reason why it was difficult to make. Since then the use of penicillin and other antibiotics has saved millions of lives.

Exercise 2

1 Milk is pasteurised before being sold. What is this process and why is it done?

2 Once a person has had a bacterial disease, they are unlikely to suffer from the same disease in the future. If they do, it is less likely to be serious. Suggest why.

Tactics

You will know that people handling food have to take precautions to prevent infections being transferred.

RED ALERT Many important substances were discovered by accident – penicillin is one of these. RED ALER

Understanding the role of micro-organisms in disease

We now know that a healthy diet and regular exercise are important in maintaining good health.

We owe much to Louis Pasteur for our understanding of what causes ill health.

Louis Pasteur (1822–1895)

In 1765, Lazzaro Spallanzani showed that food would not go bad if the microbes in it were destroyed. One way of killing the microbes in soup was to boil it.

Louis Pasteur was a French scientist who studied microbes and proved they were responsible for the process of decay. His experiments are shown in the diagram.

The soup in flask A does not go bad.
The same soup in flask B goes bad.

The soup in B is in contact with the air. From here microbes can enter and make the soup go bad.

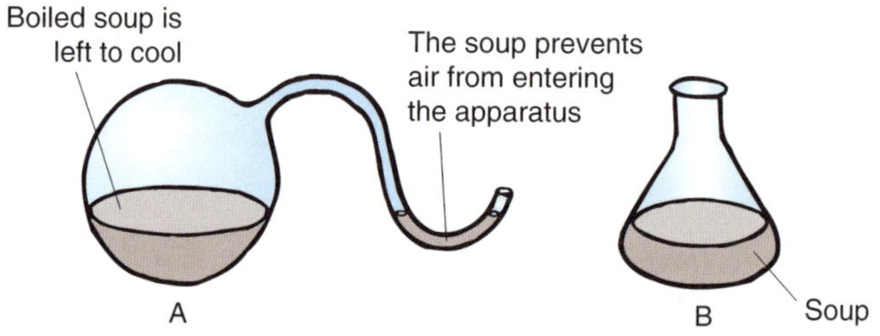

Pasteur was able to isolate the bacteria that caused diseases such as cattle anthrax and chicken cholera.

Pasteur also carried out vaccinations to prevent illnesses developing. Vaccination was already known for diseases such as smallpox. Pasteur used vaccines for anthrax and rabies.

Vaccination involves injecting a weakened form of the microbe into the bloodstream. Because the microbes are weakened, the patient does not become ill. The white blood cells produce antibodies to fight the disease. This gives the person immunity.

Exercise 3

1 How can you explain why the soup in A does not go bad but the soup in B does?

2 Parents are encouraged to have their children vaccinated with the MMR vaccine. This protects against three diseases. Can you find out what the three diseases are? (*Hint: MMR gives the first letters of the three diseases.*)

RED ALERT You may read or hear about advantages and disadvantages of vaccination. RED

Recovering from the flu

Sally has a bout of influenza or 'flu'. There are different types of flu. Some are caused by bacteria and others are caused by viruses.

The graphs show how Sally's temperature and the number of viruses and antibodies change in the three weeks following infection.

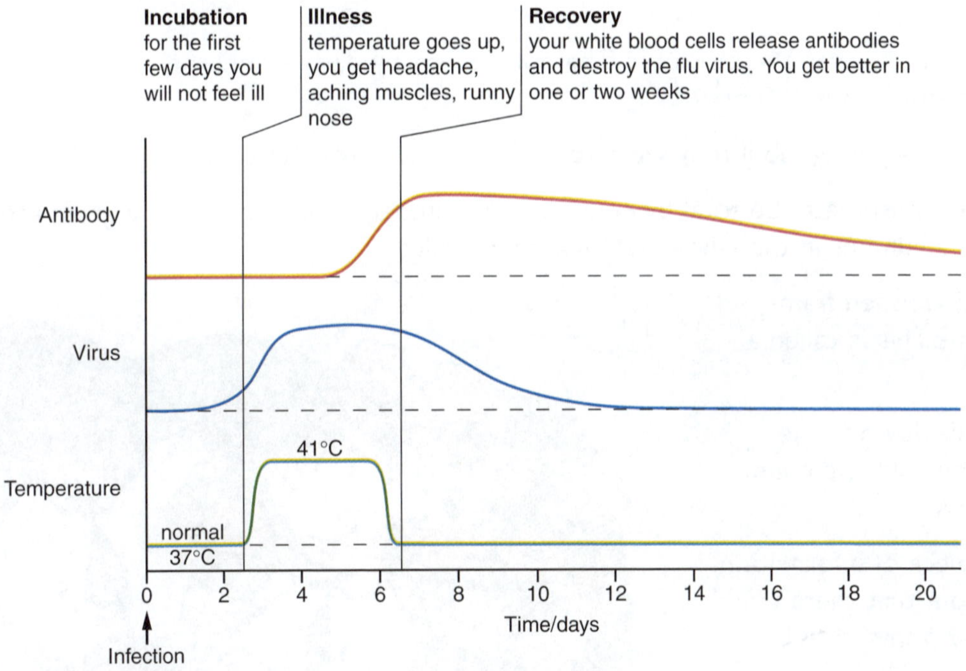

Looking at the graph you will notice that the viruses start to increase. After a couple of days the symptoms start to show and the temperature rises. Sally, in addition to the high temperature, has a headache, aching muscles and a runny nose.

The white blood cells in the body start to produce antibodies which fight the infection. The number of viruses reduces and in a couple of weeks Sally has fully recovered.

Exercise 4

1 What was Sally's maximum temperature?

2 How long did it take for Sally to stop feeling ill?

3 Old people are offered a flu vaccination before winter.

Why are old people offered this and not everybody?

4 Why does this injection not give total protection?

Tactics

Remember antibiotics are not effective against flu because it is caused by a virus.

Carrying out a piece of fieldwork

Ann and Colin are given the task of finding out how many daisy plants there are in the school field. The school field is 100 m^2.

It would be a very long job if they were to try to count every daisy plant.

They decide to estimate the total by counting the number of daisy plants in a given area and work out the number in the whole field mathematically.

They have a wooden frame covering 1 m^2. This is called a quadrat.

They put this down in the middle of the field and count 7 daisy plants.

Using this piece of information, they work out that there could be 700 daisy plants in the whole field.

Exercise 1

1 Their teacher suggests that their results might not be very accurate. What should they do to get a more accurate estimate?

2 Why is it easier to estimate the number of plants than the number of spiders in the field?

Tactics

You should have opportunities to carry out this sort of survey. Remember to plan to collect enough data to make a conclusion.

Feeding relationships

The food web shows the relationships between organisms in a woodland tree.

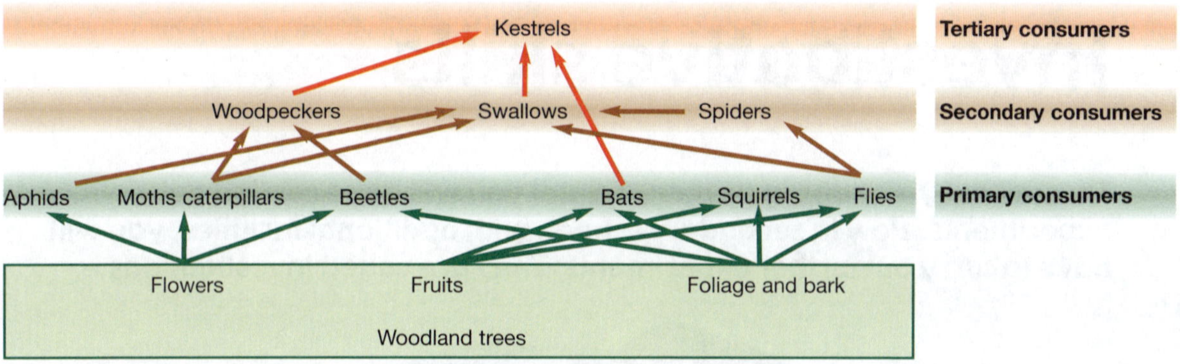

The pyramid of numbers for this food chain is shown in the diagram.

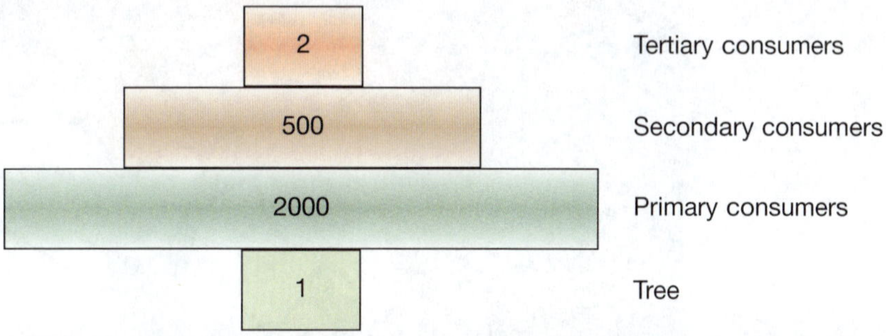

Exercise 1

1 Write down the food chain in the food web above that involves beetles.

2 How many separate food chains in the food web involve swallows?

3 Which primary consumer does not have a predator shown in the food web?

4 If the number of swallows were to drop dramatically, what effect would it have on the aphids and kestrels?

Tactics

Look back at what you did in Year 7 on habitats and feeding relationships.

RED The arrows in a food chain and a food web show the flow of energy along each chain. ALERT RED

2

Investigative skills

Throughout your time in primary school you will have carried out experiments. Now in secondary school, with additional facilities, you will have to carry out further experiments. They are called Investigations.

By the time you reach the end of Year 9 your teacher will make an assessment of your practical skills. Through Years 10 and 11 you will get further opportunities, and at the end of Year 11 some of your written work from these investigations may be sent off to a moderator who will compare the standards of your work with other students in other schools. It becomes part of your GCSE assessment. But that is a long way off.

The investigations cover four areas:

1. Planning

When given a problem to solve you have to develop a plan which uses your scientific knowledge. You might be able to use your knowledge to make a prediction. You will have to decide what apparatus to use and how many results to take.

2. Obtaining and presenting evidence

In your experiments you should take a large number of observations and measurements. These could include results taken from the computer. It is important to take them as accurately as possible. When you have taken these they should be recorded in a table if possible. Your teacher may help you to design a suitable table.

Time (s)	Temperature (°C)
0	100
30	94
60	88
90	82
120	78

Notice that these results are put in a logical order and not mixed. Because the unit of measurement is at the top of each column, it does not need to be repeated.

3. Considering evidence: including drawing graphs, carrying out calculations and drawing conclusions

In the Year 7 book there was a survival sheet on bar charts and in this book there is a survival sheet on line graphs. You have to look for patterns in the results. In the table above, as the time increases the temperature drops. You might be able to draw a conclusion from the results and this might either support or contradict your prediction made earlier. Again you might try to explain the results using your scientific knowledge.

4. Evaluating your experiment

This is the area many students find difficult. There are two things for you to do. You have to look at the results and see if any seem to be 'out of line'. We call these anomalous results. They are the ones that do not fit on the graph line you draw. If you have any of these try to explain why they are out of line.

The second thing you have to do is try to suggest improvements to your experiment. Often when you have done something, you see a better way of doing it next time around. It is not enough to write that repeating it will make it better. You may decide you needed to use other equipment or take different results.

The important thing is, as you develop your investigative skills, you enjoy what you are doing and think carefully about what you are doing.

Elements

You will already know about a large number of different materials.

> Materials are all made up from basic building materials called **elements**.

Sometimes a material is a single element, such as gold or sulphur.

Sometimes it is made up of two or more elements.

The picture shows a model made of Lego bricks. You know that this model is made up of a number of different types of brick. Using the same bricks, we could make a number of other models.

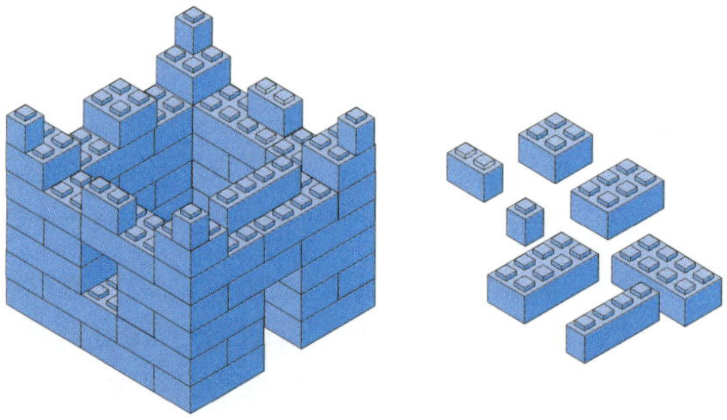

Polyester and wood are two materials with widely different properties and uses.

Both materials are made up of the same three elements – carbon, hydrogen and oxygen.

> Elements are made up of tiny particles called **atoms**.

The elements are put together in different ways in different models, just like the Lego bricks.

A piece of iron is made up of iron atoms and a piece of sulphur is made of sulphur atoms.

Exercise 1

1 Is each statement true or false?

A All materials are pure elements.

B Each element is made up of tiny particles called atoms.

C Water is made up of two elements, hydrogen and oxygen.

D Wood is an element.

2 Atoms are very, very small. Even a powerful microscope cannot show an atom. The most accurate balance cannot weigh a single atom.

People have suggested for over 2000 years that all materials are made up of atoms.

Why was it very difficult to convince people that atoms exist?

Elements and symbols

Scientists use shorthand to represent the elements. Each element is given a symbol.

The table gives the symbols of some common elements.

Element	Symbol	Element	Symbol
Aluminium	Al	Lithium	Li
Argon	Ar	Magnesium	Mg
Barium	Ba	Mercury	Hg
Bromine	Br	Neon	Ne
Calcium	Ca	Nitrogen	N
Carbon	C	Oxygen	O
Chlorine	Cl	Phosphorus	P
Copper	Cu	Potassium	K
Fluorine	F	Silicon	Si
Gold	Au	Silver	Ag
Helium	He	Sodium	Na
Hydrogen	H	Sulphur	S
Iodine	I	Tin	Sn
Iron	Fe	Zinc	Zn
Lead	Pb		

Exercise 2

1 Write down the names of the elements represented by the following symbols.

a N **b** S

c Ca **d** Zn

e Na **f** K

2 A bag of fertiliser has the letters NPK printed on it. Which three elements are present in the fertiliser?

3 Sulphuric acid can be represented by a formula H_2SO_4.

Which three elements are present in sulphuric acid?

Tactics

You should learn the names and symbols of these common elements. Notice that it is easy to guess the name of some elements from the symbol. S is the symbol for sulphur but it is not easy to guess the name of an element from a symbol such as Na.

D ALERT

The symbols are the same throughout the world. Scientists use these as an international language. It is important you learn to use this language.

ALERT

Putting elements into groups

Elements can also be grouped as solids, liquids and gases.

Room temperature is normally 20°C.

- An element with a melting point below 20°C is solid at room temperature.
- An element with a boiling point below 20°C is gas at room temperature.
- An element with a melting point below 20°C and a boiling point above 20°C is a liquid at room temperature.

Example

Chlorine has a melting point of -101°C and a boiling point of -35°C.

a What state will chlorine be in at room temperature?

Answer: A gas because the melting and boiling point are below 20°C.

b What state will chlorine be in at - 40°C?

Answer: A liquid because the boiling point is above - 40°C and the melting point is below.

Remember that the state of an element depends upon conditions. Bromine can be a solid at the North Pole, a liquid in England and a gas on the equator.

Exercise 1

1 The table gives the melting and boiling points of five elements. They are labelled A–E but these are not chemical symbols.

Is each element a solid, liquid or a gas at room temperature (20°C)?

Element	Melting point in °C	Boiling point in °C
A	–218	–183
B	1410	2360
C	–39	357
D	420	970
E	–7	58

2 Most elements are solid at room temperature. True or False?

Tactics

If you have the melting and boiling point you can work out the state of a substance. This can be used for all substances, not just elements.

RED AL Classifying elements as metals or non-metals is not clear-cut. RED A

Metals and non-metals

Elements can be grouped in various ways.

Most of the known elements are metals. There are fewer non-metals. In the table on the previous page the elements in the left-hand part of the table are metals and the elements in the right-hand part of the table are non-metals.

The table below gives information about some elements.

Element	Symbol	State at 20°C	Appearance electricity	Conductor of not	Magnetic or
Iron	Fe	Solid	Shiny grey	Conductor	Magnetic
Sulphur	S	Solid	Dull yellow	Non-conductor	Not magnetic
Bromine	Br	Liquid	Dull red	Non-conductor	Not magnetic
Copper	Cu	Solid	Shiny brown	Conductor	Not magnetic
Nickel	Ni	Solid	Shiny grey	Conductor	Magnetic
Selenium	Se	Solid	Shiny grey	Semi-conductor	Not magnetic

Looking at the data in the table, iron, copper and nickel are metals. They are shiny and metallic in appearance and they conduct electricity. Sulphur and bromine are non-metals.

Selenium is difficult to classify. It looks metallic but does not conduct electricity like a metal. Unlike metals it breaks easily. Elements between metals and non-metals are called metalloids.

Metals burn in air or oxygen to form oxides that are neutral or alkaline. Non-metals burn to form acidic oxides.

Exercise 2

1 Which of the elements A, B, C, D and E are metals and which are non-metals? (These are not chemical symbols)

Element	Melting point in °C	Appearance	Conductor of electricity	pH of oxide
A	114	Dull	No	4
B	327	Dull	Yes	7
C	3730	Dull	Yes	5
D	1063	Shiny	Yes	7
E	–39	Shiny	No	7

2 Metals often end -ium. For example: aluminium, sodium. Can you think of a non-metal ending in -ium?

Tactics

Remember the important physical properties of metals – high density, good conductors of electricity and heat.

RT There are some elements, e.g. selenium and germanium, with properties between metal and non-metal. RED ALERT

Patterns in elements

The Periodic Table

You have probably seen a chart in books or on the wall of your school laboratory showing the names and symbols of all the elements. This is called the Periodic Table.

From the position of an element you can predict whether an element is a solid, liquid or gas, a metal or non-metal.

The table shows part of the Periodic Table.

			Hydrogen **H**				Helium **He**
Lithium **Li**	Beryllium **Be**	Boron **B**	Carbon **C**	Nitrogen **N**	Oxygen **O**	Fluorine **F**	Neon **Ne**
Sodium **Na**	Magnesium **Mg**	Aluminium **Al**	Silicon **Si**	Phosphorus **P**	Sulphur **S**	Chlorine **Cl**	Argon **Ar**
Potassium **K**	Calcium **Ca**	Gallium **Ga**	Germanium **Ge**	Arsenic **As**	Selenium **Se**	Bromine **Br**	Krypton **Kr**

In this table, elements that are solids at room temperature are printed in black, elements that are liquids are printed in blue and elements that are gases are printed in red.

Exercise 1

1 Which element in the table above is a liquid at room temperature?

2 Write down the symbols of the elements that are gases at room temperature.

3 Which of these statements are true and which are false?

A More elements are solids than liquids and gases.

B The gases are towards the right and the top of this table.

C All elements with single letter symbols are gases at room temperature.

Tactics

Remember you never need to learn the Periodic Table.

RED ALERT **Get used to using the Periodic Table. It can help you.** RED ALERT R

Metals and non-metals

Look back at the table on the opposite page. You will notice a bold line printed on the table. It looks like steps going downward.

It separates metals on the left-hand side of the line from non-metals on the right-hand side.

The table might mislead you into thinking that there are more non-metals than metals. Remember that this is only part of the Periodic Table. Overall there are far more metals than non-metals.

When the Periodic Table was first drawn up in 1869 many of the elements that we know today had not been discovered. This left gaps in the table and these gaps helped scientists predict the properties of the missing elements.

The elements gallium and germanium were two elements not known in 1869. Gaps were left and the properties of these missing elements were predicted. Scientists started to look for them. Gallium was discovered in 1875 and germanium was discovered in 1886. The properties of these elements when found were close to the predicted properties.

In the modern Periodic Table there are over 100 elements. About 70 of these elements are metals. Ninety-five of the elements occur in the world around us. The remainder are made synthetically in particle accelerators.

Three of these synthetically produced elements are Berkelium (Bk), Californium (Cf), and Americium (Am). Most of these elements have been made at the University of Berkeley, California, USA.

Exercise 2

1 For each of the following elements, write down the symbol, the state at room temperature and whether it is a metal or a non-metal.

- **a** Calcium
- **b** Krypton
- **c** Boron
- **d** Carbon
- **e** Sulphur
- **f** Phosphorus
- **g** Lithium

Tactics

If you come across an element you have not met before, look at a Periodic Table. You should be able to work out whether it is a solid, liquid or gas and whether a metal or a non-metal.

Mixtures

What is a pure substance?

A pure substance is a single substance, element or compound.

It contains no impurities.

A pure substance melts at a fixed temperature. A mixed substance melts at a lower temperature than the individual substances that make up the mixture.

> Many everyday substances are not pure elements or compounds but are mixtures.

Some common mixtures are:

Air
A mixture of gases containing about 80% nitrogen and 20% oxygen with small quantities of other gases. Its composition can be varied.

Air can be separated by fractional distillation. This involves cooling air until it is liquid (about –200°C) and allowing it to warm up. Different gases boil off at different temperatures.

Sea water
Sea water consists of water with dissolved solids. There is a wide range of dissolved solids including sodium chloride (salt). The water can be removed by distillation.

Exercise 1

1 Solder is an alloy made up of tin (melting point 232°C) and lead (melting point 327°C). It is used to join metals together.

   a Is the melting point of solder
      A above 327°C?
      B between 327°C and 232°C?
      C below 232°C?

   b When soldering, the solder is melted and when it solidifies, the metals are joined together. Why is solder better than pure tin or pure lead?

2 Look at the picture.

   It gives one reason why air is a mixture of different gases in a city compared with the countryside. What is this reason?

RED ALERT The method used to separate a mixture depends upon the properties of the different components of the mixture.

Petroleum

Petroleum is a complex mixture of compounds of carbon and hydrogen. Since the compounds have similar boiling points, they are difficult to separate. Industry separates petroleum into different fractions, each with their own range of boiling points and different uses. For example, petrol is a low boiling point and very flammable fraction used for fuel in car engines.

Metal alloys

Mixtures of metals e.g. with better properties than pure metals.

Differences between pure substances and mixtures

The table gives the differences between a pure substance (element or compound) and a mixture.

Pure substance	Mixture
Contains a single element or elements joined in fixed proportions.	Contains elements or compounds in proportions that are not fixed.
Difficult or impossible to separate elements in a compound.	Elements can be separated.
Properties of a compound are different from elements combined together.	Properties of the mixture are the same as the properties of the things making it up.
Energy is often given out when a compound is formed.	No energy change when a mixture is formed.
Melts and boils at a fixed temperature.	Melts at a lower temperature than the pure substance and over a range of temperatures. Boils at a higher temperature than the pure substance.

Exercise 2

1 A solid acid is heated until it melts. It is then left to cool and the temperature taken at intervals. The graph shows the results.

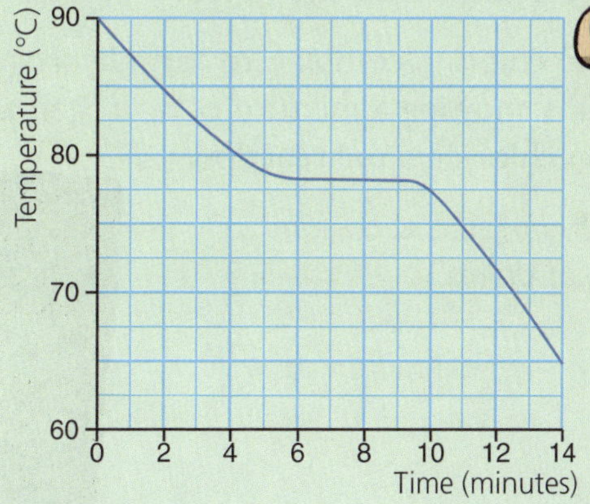

a What is the melting point of the acid?

b How would this melting point have been different if the acid was impure?

2 The composition of air varies from place to place but the composition of water is fixed. What does that tell you about air and water?

Compounds

Elements combining to form compounds

Certain mixtures of elements combine together to form compounds.

A chemical reaction where elements combine to form a compound is called synthesis.

The reaction can be represented by a word equation:

hydrogen + oxygen → water

Example

A chemical reaction takes place when a lighted splint is put into a mixture of hydrogen and oxygen in a test tube.

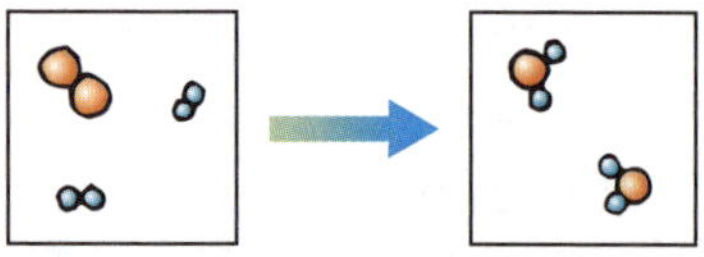

Hydrogen and oxygen are colourless gases. A mixture of hydrogen and oxygen explodes to form water (hydrogen oxide). The hydrogen and oxygen atoms join together to form liquid water.

The diagram shows what is happening when water is formed.

Iron sulphide is a compound formed when the elements iron and sulphur combine. The diagram shows what is happening when this reaction takes place.

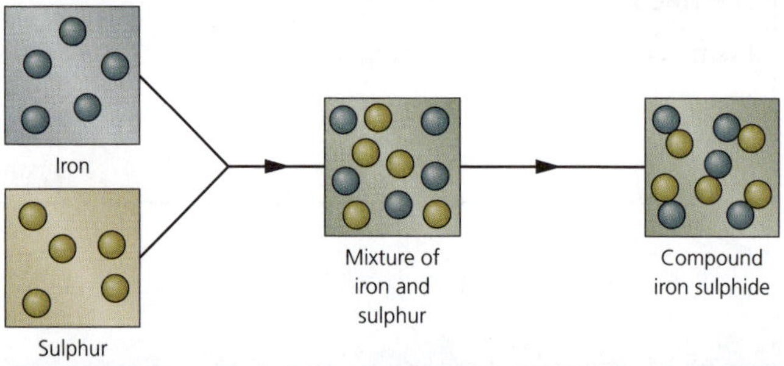

Exercise 1

1 Write a word equation for the reaction of iron and sulphur.

2 Hydrogen and chlorine combine to form hydrogen chloride. Draw diagrams showing a mixture of hydrogen and chlorine and hydrogen chloride after reaction.

(HINT: Both hydrogen and chlorine exist as pairs of atoms.)

Tactics

Remember when the reaction between iron and sulphur takes place one iron atom joins with one sulphur atom.

RED ALERT Many students fail to realise that atoms combine in fixed numbers when a reaction takes place. **RED**

Properties of compounds

The properties of a compound are different from the properties of the elements that make it up.

Hydrogen and oxygen are gases but water is a liquid.

The mixture of iron and sulphur can be separated using a magnet. Iron and sulphur cannot be separated from the compound iron sulphide.

In the same way that each element has a symbol, each compound has a formula.

The formula of water is written as H_2O. This shows that two atoms of hydrogen combine with one atom of hydrogen.

The formula of iron sulphide is written as FeS. This shows that one atom of iron combines with one atom of sulphur.

The table gives the names and formulae of some common compounds. It also gives the numbers of atoms of the different elements present in the formula.

Name	Formula	Number of atoms of different elements present
Sodium chloride	NaCl	1 atom of sodium and 1 atom of chlorine
Magnesium oxide	MgO	1 atom of magnesium and 1 atom of oxygen
Calcium carbonate	$CaCO_3$	1 atom of calcium, 1 atom of carbon and three atoms of oxygen
Copper sulphate	$CuSO_4$	1 atom of copper, 1 atom of sulphur and four atoms of oxygen
Sodium nitrate	$NaNO_3$	1 sodium atom, 1 atom of nitrogen and three atoms of oxygen

Exercise 2

1 The chemical sodium hydrogencarbonate has a formula $NaHCO_3$.

  a How many different elements are there in sodium hydrogencarbonate?

  b How many atoms are there of each element?

  c What is the total number of atoms in the formula?

2 Potassium permanganate has a formula $KMnO_4$.

  a How many different elements are there in potassium permanganate?

  b How many atoms are there of each element?

  c What is the total number of atoms in the formula?

Tactics

There are rules for working out the formula of a compound, but at this stage you do not need to learn the rules. Just try and remember them as you meet them.

It is important as you study science to learn the formulae of simple compounds.

Weathering

Weathering is the process that breaks down exposed rocks by the action of rain, frost, wind and other elements of weather.

The effects of weathering can be seen in old buildings or old gravestones. Some rocks are broken down more easily than others.

Weathering can take place in two main ways.

Mechanical weathering

This is sometimes called physical weathering.

During the day rocks heat up and expand. At night they cool and this cooling causes stresses within the rock. When this happens over and over again it breaks down the rock.

If there are cracks in the rock, water gets into the cracks. When water freezes, ice forms and expands. This breaks down the rocks.

This is sometimes called 'freeze-thaw'.

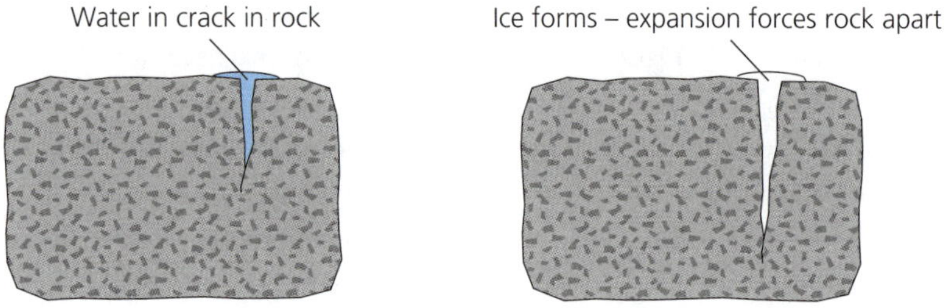

Exercise 1

1 In a desert, there is little water. There are big changes in temperature – it is cold at night and very hot during the day. Also there are strong winds that blow sand around. Suggest two ways rocks can be broken down.

Tactics

Remember if a piece of glass is heated and then put into cold water it cracks. Rocks can be affected by rapid changes in temperature.

RED ALERT Weathering of rocks is the way rocks are broken down and this leads to the formation of new rocks. **RED**

Chemical weathering

This is the breaking down of rocks by chemical reactions.

Limestone is a form of calcium carbonate. It is broken down by rainwater. Rainwater contains dissolved carbon dioxide. This forms carbonic acid. Carbonic acid attacks the limestone, forming calcium hydrogencarbonate. This is soluble in water.

This weathering is speeded up when other acids are present in the atmosphere from acid rain.

Soil

Soil is produced when rocks are broken down into small pieces by weathering.

The sizes of the pieces (called grain size) vary in different soils.

A sandy soil drains well because it has large grains which have big spaces between them.

A clay soil soon becomes waterlogged because the spaces are small and they soon fill up with water.

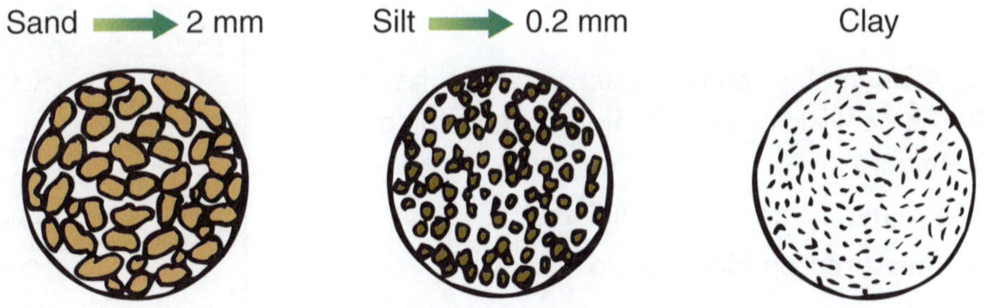

Magnified 100 times

Exercise 2

1 The breaking down of calcium carbonate can be summarised by word equations.

Finish the word equations

water + carbon dioxide → ________________

calcium carbonate + carbonic acid → ________________________

2 Acid rain occurs when sulphuric acid is formed in the atmosphere. Why does chemical breakdown of limestone take place faster with sulphuric acid than with carbonic acid?

Tactics

Rocks are also broken down by erosion. You will learn about this later.

Rock

What is a rock?

A rock is a solid part of the Earth's crust. Some rocks are almost pure substances but most are mixtures of chemicals called minerals.

The properties of a rock will depend upon:

- the type of minerals
- the concentration of minerals in the rock
- how the minerals are held together.

Rocks can be classified as sedimentary rocks, metamorphic rocks and igneous rocks.

Identifying the minerals in rocks.
Scientists who study rocks are called geologists. They use tests to identify minerals in rocks.

1 Colour.

2 Streak test. A mineral is scratched across an unglazed ceramic tile. The colour of the streak can be used to identify the mineral.

3 Lustre. Is the mineral shiny, glassy, dull etc?

4 Hardness is measured on Moh's scale.

5 Density.

6 Testing with acid. When a dilute acid is added to a carbonate, mineral fizzing will be seen.

Moh's scale	Mineral
1	Talc
2	Gypsum
3	Calcite
4	Fluorite
5	Apatite
6	Feldspar
7	Quartz
8	Topaz
9	Corundum
10	Diamond

Exercise 1

1 If a mineral can be scratched with a fingernail it has a hardness of about 2.

A 2p coin has a hardness of about 3.5 and a steel penknife about 6.

a Name a mineral that will be scratched with a fingernail.
b Name a mineral that will be scratched with a 2p coin but not with a fingernail.
c Name a mineral that will be scratched with a penknife but not with a 2p coin.
d Name a mineral that is not scratched by a fingernail, a 2p coin or a penknife.

2 Which gas is produced when an acid is added to a carbonate rock?

Sedimentary rocks

When existing rocks are weathered, small bits of existing rocks are broken off. These bits are washed along in rivers and then, when the speed of water slows, they settle as sediment. This is then compressed by other rocks and the grains cemented together. This process can take millions of years.

New rocks are deposited on existing rocks and so, the older rocks are, the lower they are in the Earth's crust.

The diagram shows layers of rock in a cliff face. After they are formed these layers can tilt and fold.

> Sedimentary rocks are not crystalline but are made up of grains. Sedimentary rocks may contain fossils.

When tiny grains of sand are deposited the rock formed is called sandstone. When even tinier grains are cemented together mudstone and shale may be formed.

Limestone is a sedimentary rock formed from the shells of millions of tiny sea creatures in water millions of years ago. When they died they sank to the bottom of the sea and were buried and squashed.

Conglomerate is a sedimentary rock formed from large pebbles cemented together.

Exercise 2

1 Write down the names of five sedimentary rocks.

2 The fragments that break off existing rocks have sharp edges but the grains of a sedimentary rock are smooth. How does this happen?

Tactics

Try and look at some rock samples. If you cannot get rock samples look at photographs.

Metamorphic rocks

When clay is baked in an oven a chemical change takes place. A similar process takes place in the Earth. High temperatures and high pressures turn sedimentary rocks into metamorphic rocks. These rocks may be non-crystalline or contain tiny crystals.

Both limestone and marble are made of the same chemical. They are both calcium carbonate in the form of calcite. Limestone (sedimentary rock) is made of tiny grains, and marble (metamorphic rock) is made of crystals. The change takes place when the rock is heated to a high temperature or compressed to a high pressure or both.

Another metamorphic rock is slate. This is made when the sedimentary rock called mudstone is compressed to a high pressure.

> Fossils are found in sedimentary rocks and sometimes in metamorphic rocks. Where they exist in metamorphic rocks they are often distorted.

Although sedimentary rocks are changed into metamorphic rocks, it is possible for all rocks to be changed or metamorphosed. The metamorphic rock slate can change further with even higher temperatures and pressures. It can form other metamorphic rocks – schist and gneiss (pronounced nice).

Metamorphic rocks are usually found within mountain ranges. It is here that great temperature and pressure changes occurred. The oldest rock in Europe is gneiss that forms the Scottish islands of Lewis and Harris.

Exercise 3

1. Write down the names of two metamorphic rocks.
2. What conditions are needed to turn sedimentary rocks into metamorphic rocks?
3. How do limestone and marble look different?
4. Why do limestone and marble both fizz with dilute acid?

Tactics

Remember metamorphic rocks require high temperatures and pressures to form.

Igneous rocks

Igneous rocks are formed when the hot magma inside the Earth is cooled and crystallises. The size of the crystals depends on the rate of cooling. If the cooling is rapid, small crystals are formed. Slow cooling produces larger crystals.

Granite and basalt are two igneous rocks.

Granite typically consists of the minerals quartz, feldspar and mica. It is usually pink or grey in colour with large crystals. These large crystals are formed when the magma crystallises slowly within the Earth.

Basalt is usually dark grey but can be black, brown or green in colour. It has small crystals as the crystallisation of the magma takes place rapidly on the Earth's surface.

Intrusion

The diagram shows a section through the Earth. The Magma is pushing close to the surface. Metamorphic rocks are formed close to the intrusion.

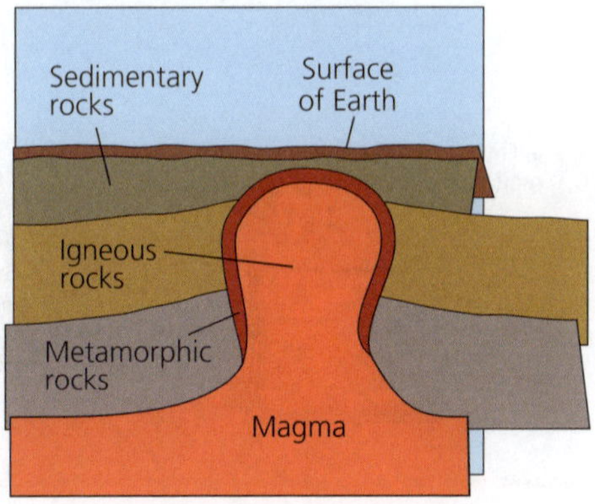

Exercise 4

1 Suggest why fossils are not found in igneous rocks.

2 Although granite crystallises within the Earth, it can be found on the surface of the Earth. How does the igneous rock get to the surface?

3 basalt granite limestone
marble sandstone

Which rocks in the list are igneous?

Tactics

Make sure you understand the three types of rock. You need this understanding before you study the rock cycle.

Recycling

Recycling glass bottles

The diagram shows the path that glass bottles take from starting out as a new bottle to being recycled as a new bottle again.

There are six steps in the process.

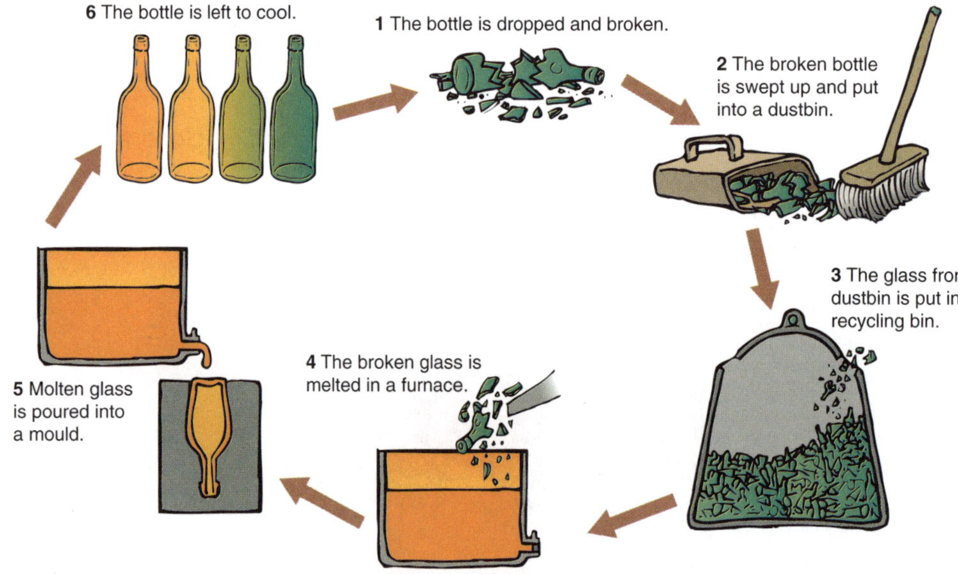

A path that finishes up back where it started is called a cycle.

Exercise 1

1 Glass milk bottles should not be recycled in this way. What should happen to glass milk bottles?

2 The materials used to make glass are not expensive. What is the economic benefit of recycling glass bottles?

3 Why does different coloured glass have to be put into different containers at the recycling centre?

Tactics

If you understand this cycle you will understand the rock cycle.

RED ALERT You will meet many other cycles in science – nitrogen cycle, carbon cycle etc. RED A

Rock cycle

In a similar way to the way bottles are recycled, inside the Earth, existing rocks can be taken back into the magma and new rocks formed. This is summarised in the diagram.

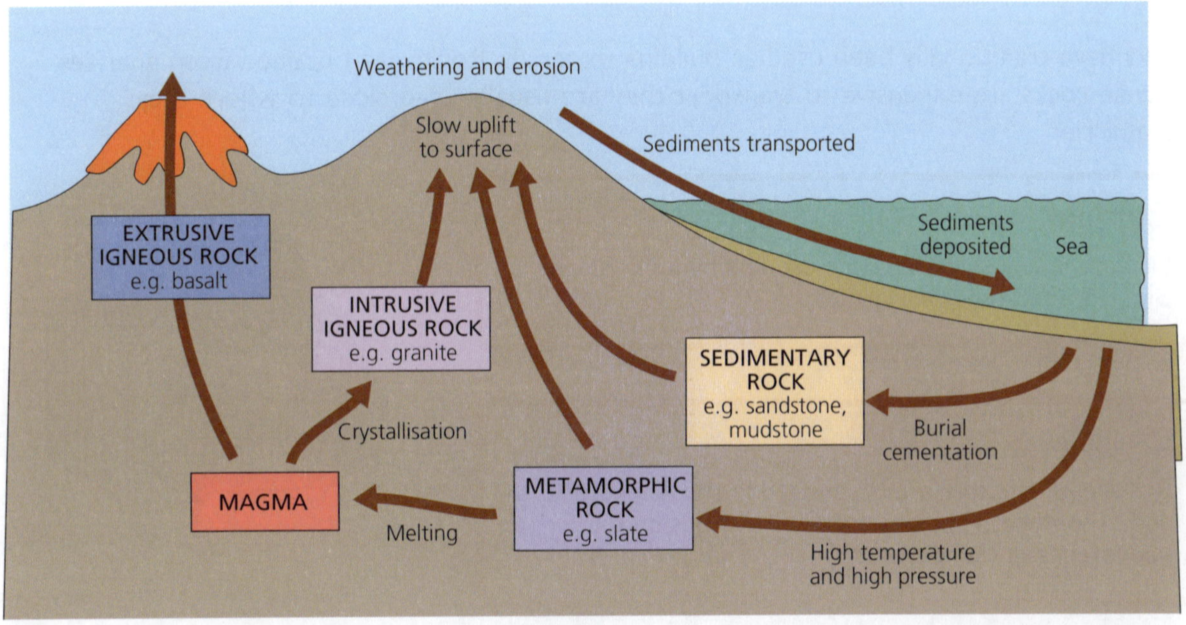

Rocks are being broken down and new rocks formed all the time. When magma crystallises, igneous rocks are produced. These are broken down by weathering and erosion to form sediments. Sediments are deposited and converted into sedimentary rocks. Sedimentary rocks can be converted into metamorphic rocks by high temperatures and high pressures. Rocks returning to the magma complete the cycle.

The rock cycle is driven by two energy processes. On the surface, processes are powered by the Sun's energy. Within the Earth, energy is provided by radioactive decay.

Exercise 2

1 Which processes are used when:

a sedimentary rocks are converted into metamorphic rocks?

b magma is converted into igneous rocks?

c sediments are converted into sedimentary rocks?

d igneous rocks are broken into sediments?

2 Six processes in the rock cycle are:

cooling deposition eruption melting

transport weathering and erosion.

Put these six processes in the correct order starting with weathering and erosion.

Uses of rocks

Rocks have traditionally been used as building materials. Rocks are obtained from quarries. Because rocks are expensive to transport they are usually used close to where they are quarried.

Example

Limestone and sandstone are used as building blocks. Slate is used for roofing tiles.

Example

Granite and marble are much harder than limestone and sandstone. They are used for statues and headstones in churchyards.

In a modern house cheaper alternatives are used.

Traditional material	New material
Sandstone or limestone blocks	Bricks
Slate for roofing tiles	Ceramic roofing tiles

Exercise 1

1 Apart from cost, what other benefits do bricks have over limestone blocks?

2 What other modern materials are used in building a house?

Tactics

Look around your environment for other uses of rocks.

Cement and concrete

Cement is a very useful material produced by heating limestone powder with clay. When water is added to cement, a chemical reaction takes place, which causes the cement to harden.

Usually cement is mixed with water, sand and gravel to produce concrete. Concrete is a very useful building material. It is poured into moulds to produce concrete railway sleepers, beams, lamp-posts etc. However, concrete is not a strong material unless it is re-inforced.

In the diagram you will see that a vertical force will cause the beam to bend and break.

Re-inforcing the concrete with steel rods transfers the force sideways and makes the beam stronger.

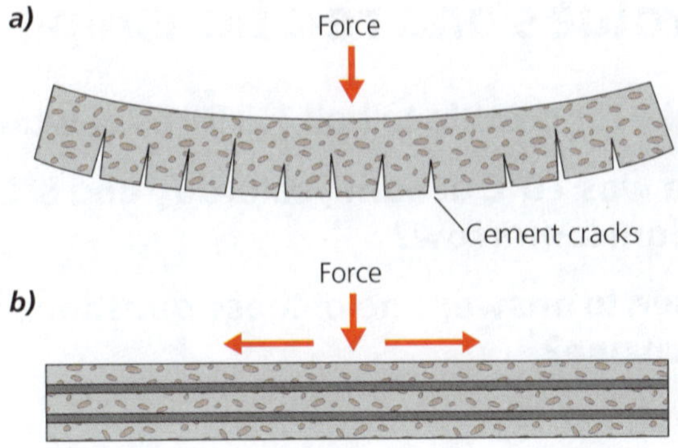

Exercise 2

1 Why is it important to keep a bag of cement dry?

2 When cement hardens, calcium carbonate and calcium silicate are formed.

Which elements are present in calcium carbonate and calcium silicate?

Tactics

Look around for examples of concrete used as a building material.

3

Drawing and using graphs

Variables, values and relationships

How long will it take for a kettle to boil 1.3 litres of water?

If the temperature was 10°C at 6am yesterday and 8°C at 6am today, what will it be at 6am tomorrow?

A graph can be used to answer one of these questions but not the other. Do you know which one?

Collecting the data

Before you can draw a graph to show how the time taken to boil depends on the volume of water, you need to collect some data.

Here is some sample data:

Volume of water (l)	0.50	0.85	1.10	1.55	1.90	2.20
Time taken for kettle to boil (s)	35	60	80	120	155	190

The grid

A graph is drawn on a **grid** – a set of equally-spaced horizontal and vertical lines. The grid has two **axes**:

- each axis is a scale of numbers that represents one of the variables
- the horizontal axis is used to represent the input variable
- the vertical axis is used to represent the outcome variable.

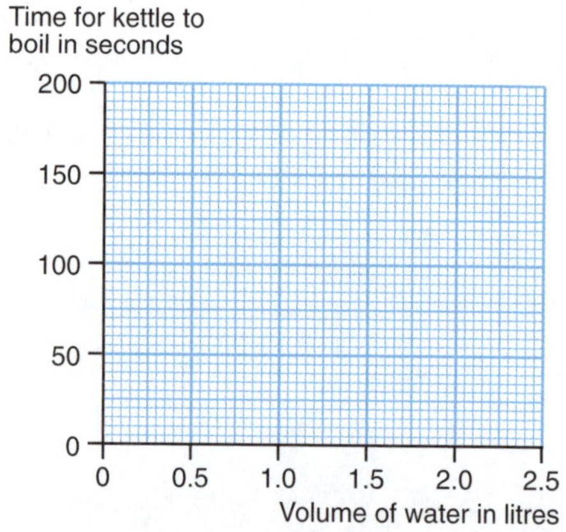

A suitable grid for drawing a graph of the sample data is shown on the previous page.

Plotting the points

Before you begin to plot the points, make sure that you understand the scales used on each axis.

Each pair of values of input and outcome variable is plotted on the graph using a cross. You will probably find it easier to plot each point as a vertical cross (+) rather than a ×, but either may be used.

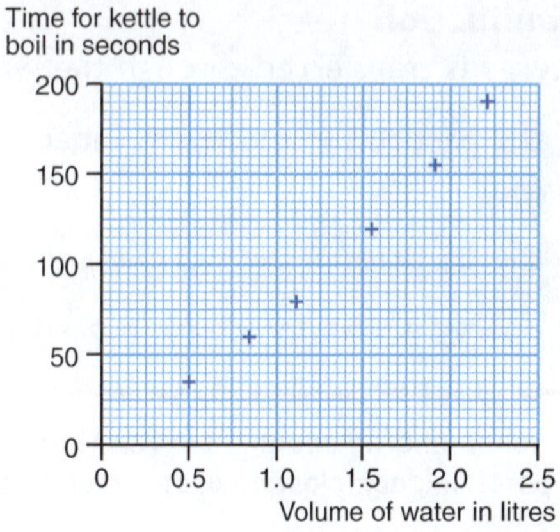

To plot the first point:

- using a pencil, move it over the horizontal axis until you come to the vertical line that represents 0.5 litres
- move the pencil over this line until you reach the horizontal line that represents 35 seconds
- mark a cross where these gridlines cross.

What shape is the curve?

Most graphs that you draw in science show the relationship between two variables that vary continuously rather than in 'jumps'. The line that is drawn on a graph to show this relationship is called a curve, no matter whether it is actually curved or straight.

To decide on the best line to draw:

- hold a ruler against the points and decide whether the pattern is better shown by a straight line or by a smooth curve
- remember that experimental measurements are often not precise, so the curve does not have to go through all of or any of the points
- position the ruler, or practise drawing a free-hand curve so that the points are equally scattered above and below the curve
- when you are satisfied, put pencil to paper!

Moving energy around

Moving energy around

If you leave a hot drink and an ice cube in the kitchen, the drink cools down but the ice cube warms up!

Objects that are warmer than their surroundings lose energy; those that are cooler gain energy.

There are a number of ways in which energy moves from warm objects to cooler ones.

Conduction

Energy is transferred through the walls of the mug by conduction. In conduction:

- the particles in the warm, inner part of the wall have more energy than those in the cool outer part
- the particles in the warmer part vibrate with more energy than those in the cooler part
- energy is transferred from particle to particle through these vibrations.

Solids and liquids are better thermal conductors than gases are. This is because their particles are closer together and can pass on the energy more readily.

Metals are the best conductors because electrons can move through metals, taking energy with them to all parts of the metal.

Exercise 1

1 Explain why an ice cube melts when left out in the kitchen.

2 Explain why energy flows from the outside air into the inside of a refrigerator.

3 Describe how energy is transferred through a solid by conduction.

4 Explain why gases are poor conductors of heat (thermal energy).

5 Why are metals better conductors of heat (thermal energy) than non-metals?

Tactics

Metals are good conductors of heat (thermal energy). Non-metals are poor conductors.

RED ALERT Do not use the term 'heat' to describe radiant energy. Heat is energy due to the movement of particles. RE

Convection currents

Energy that flows through the wall of the mug is carried away by convection currents in the surrounding air:

- air near the outside of the wall becomes heated
- the warmed air expands and becomes less dense
- the warm, less dense air rises and is replaced by cooler air from the surroundings.

Convection currents are due to changes in density caused by heating and cooling.

As the diagram shows, convection also takes place at the surface of the liquid.

Evaporation and radiation

Energy is lost from the surface of a hot liquid by evaporation. When a liquid evaporates:

- the more energetic particles near the surface leave the liquid, becoming vapour
- this reduces the average energy of the particles remaining in the liquid
- the result of this is that the liquid loses energy and its temperature falls.

All objects emit energy as electromagnetic radiation. Everything radiates energy, but the hotter the object the more energy it radiates.

For most objects, this energy is infra-red radiation. Radiant energy causes cooling when it is emitted and heating when it is absorbed. Very hot objects can also radiate energy as light and other forms of electromagnetic radiation.

Exercise 2

1 Describe how the air that surrounds a hot object can remove energy from it.

2 What is the cause of convection currents?

3 Explain why several layers of paper provides good insulation for take-away food.

4 Give two reasons why aluminium foil is a good insulator for hot food.

5 Explain why outdoor swimming pools are often covered with a polythene sheet at night.

Tactics

A common error when explaining convection current is to state that 'heat rises'. Heat is not a substance, so it cannot move. In convection currents, warm or cold liquid or gas rises or falls.

Heat and temperature

Which is hotter, a bath full of hot water or the filament of a lamp that is giving out light? The answer is the lamp filament; its temperature is around 2000°C, whereas that of the bath is about 50°C. The diagram shows some typical temperatures measured on the Celsius scale.

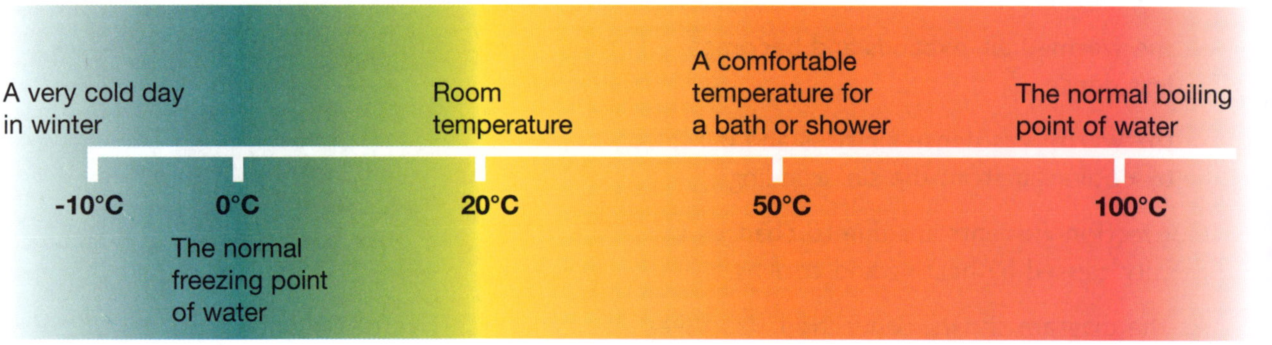

Although the bath water is cooler than the lamp filament, it takes more energy from the gas or electricity mains to heat it up from cold. This is because:

- it takes more energy to heat 1 kg of water by each degree Celsius than it does to heat 1 kg of lamp filament by the same amount
- there is much more material to be heated – it takes several kg of water to fill a bath but only a fraction of a kg of tungsten to make a lamp filament.

Exercise 3

1 On the Celsius scale, what temperature is:

a the normal boiling point of water?

b room temperature?

c a comfortable temperature for a bath or shower?

2 Explain why more energy is needed to heat a full tank of cold water to 50°C than to boil a kettle full of cold water.

3 On bonfire night, the sparks from a sparkler are very hot. Explain why they do not burn objects that they land on.

Tactics

Temperature is a measure of hotness. It does not show the amount of energy needed for an object to become hot.

RED ALERT Air is a good insulator if it is not allowed to form convection currents. **RED**

Insulation

The purpose of insulation is to reduce the energy transfer between an object and its surroundings.

Most forms of insulation use air as the insulator. This is effective because air is very poor at conducting energy in the form of heat. Air is very good at forming convection currents, so it needs to be trapped so that it cannot move.

Air is trapped between layers of clothing and pockets of air are trapped in foam insulation. This prevents energy transfer from taking place through convection currents and minimises energy transfer by conduction.

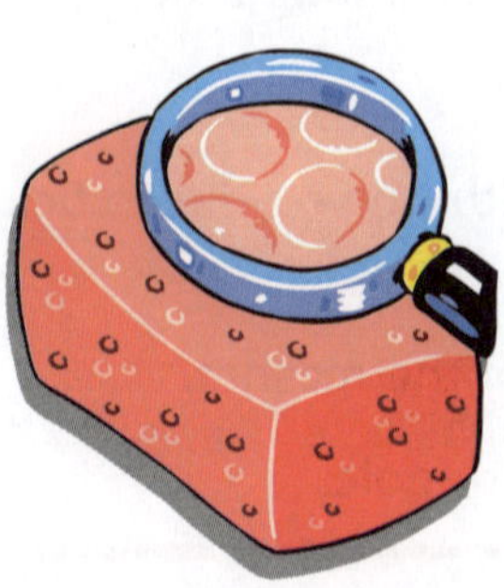

Two other methods of minimising the energy transfer between hot and cold objects are:

- if the object is liquid or contains a liquid, covering it reduces the energy loss through evaporation. This is very effective in keeping hot drinks hot.
- wrapping an object in aluminium foil reduces the energy loss through infra-red radiation. Foil reflects radiant energy.

Exercise 4

1 Explain why trapped air is a good insulator but air that is free to move is a poor insulator.

2 What is the insulator in a foam pack used as a container for a take-away burger?

3 What type of energy loss does aluminium foil reduce?

4 Explain why two thin layers of clothing provide better insulation than one thicker layer.

5 A modern house has two walls with air in the 'cavity' between them. Explain how filling the cavity with mineral wool insulates the house.

Tactics

Insulation is used to keep things cool as well as to keep things hot.

Magnetism

Magnets and electromagnets

Magnets attract iron, steel and nickel but they do not affect copper, brass, chrome, magnesium or zinc. This property makes them useful for sorting ferrous (iron-based) metals from non-ferrous ones.

Iron is easy to magnetise but quickly loses its magnetism.

Steel is harder to magnetize but it keeps its magnetism for a long time.

Magnets have been used for centuries to navigate.

- A magnet that is free to turn round always points with one pole (see below) pointing towards magnetic north.
- This is called the north-seeking pole or north pole of the magnet.
- The opposite pole is called the south-seeking or south pole.

Magnets can attract and repel other magnets. The strongest parts of a magnet are called the poles. Bar magnets have poles at the ends but slab magnets have them along the sides.

The north-seeking pole of a magnet is attracted to the Earth's north pole, so they must have opposite magnetism.

> Opposite poles attract and similar poles repel.

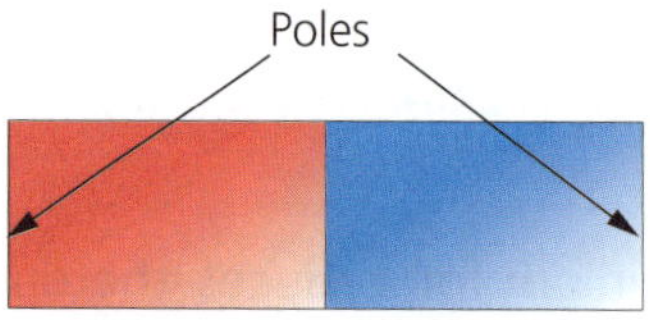

Bar magnet

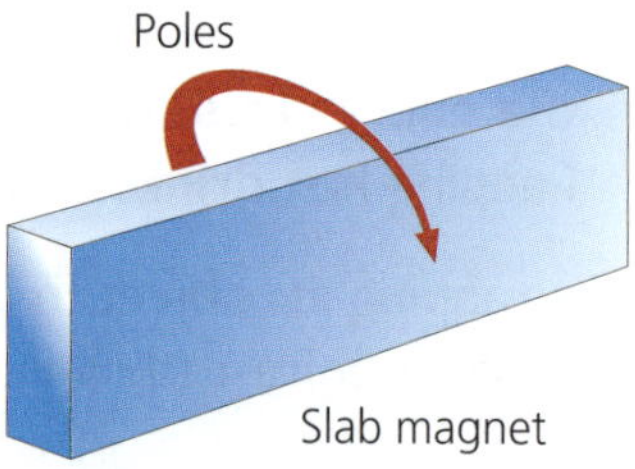

Slab magnet

Exercise 1

1 Which of these materials are attracted to a magnet?

brass copper iron plastic steel zinc

2 Explain why steel is better than iron for making permanent magnets.

3 Write out the rule that describes which magnetic poles attract each other and which poles repel each other.

4 Describe how a magnet can be used to tell the difference between brass drawing pins and iron drawing pins that have been painted the colour of brass.

5 You are given a magnet and a piece of steel that may or may not be a magnet. How can you tell whether the piece of steel is a magnet?

Tactics

Remember that when two magnets attract or repel each other, they experience the same size force in opposite directions.

RED ALERT

Opposite magnetic poles attract and similar poles repel.

RED

Magnetic fields

Compasses use small magnets pivoted on needles to enable them to turn round so that the poles point towards magnetic north and south. However, if a compass is placed near a magnetic material such as iron, it will point towards that instead.

A compass can be used to investigate the attractive and repulsive forces around a magnet. By looking at the direction of the force on the north-seeking pole of the compass, a set of straight lines can be drawn showing the force pattern all around the magnet.

When these lines are joined up they make a pattern.

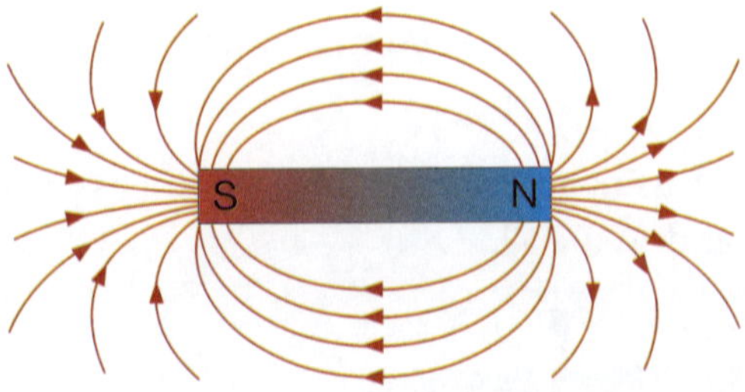

This is called a magnetic field pattern, because it shows the pattern of the forces in the magnetic field, the region round the magnet where it pushes and pulls magnetic objects. Magnetic field patterns are always drawn to show the direction of the force on the north-seeking pole of another magnet.

> Iron filings act like small compasses. They give a quick way of investigating a magnetic field, but they do not show its direction.

Exercise 2

1. Which end of a compass needle normally points towards the Earth's north pole?
2. What is a magnetic field?
3. Explain why the arrows on the magnetic field pattern of a bar magnet point away from the north-seeking pole and towards the south-seeking pole.
4. Explain why iron filings do not show the direction of a magnetic field.
5. Explain why a magnetic compass cannot be used to steer a ship that is made of steel.

Tactics

Remember that the direction of a magnetic field is always away from the north-seeking pole towards the south-seeking pole of a magnet.

Electromagnetism

Electromagnets are all around us; they are used:

- in motors to turn the washing machine drum and the lawn mower blades
- to make a loudspeaker cone vibrate
- to 'write' information in magnetic form onto audio and video tapes and computer discs.

All electric currents have their own magnetic field; this means there are magnetic forces around them.

Careful observation using iron filings and a compass shows these field patterns for the current in a straight wire and in a coil.

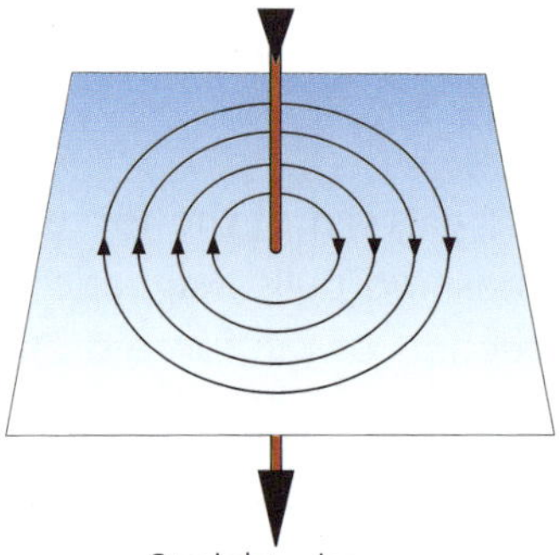

Straight wire

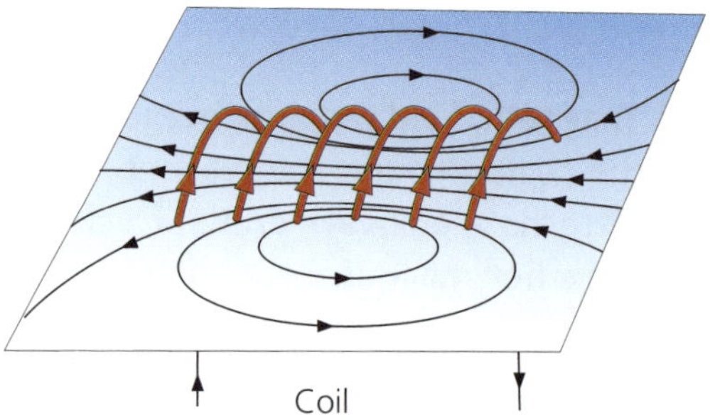

Coil

Electromagnetic forces can be made much bigger by wrapping a coil of wire around an iron core. When a current passes in the wire, the iron becomes strongly magnetised. This makes a useful electromagnet because it can be switched on and off and its strength can be varied by changing the current passing in the coil.

Exercise 1

1 Give three uses of electromagnets.

2 Which end of the coil behaves like the north-seeking pole of a magnet?

3 Describe how the direction of the magnetic field differs on the inside and outside of the coil.

4 An electromagnet is made by winding a coil of wire on a cardboard roll.

State three ways in which the strength of the electromagnet can be changed.

5 Explain why an electromagnet is more useful than a fixed magnet for some applications.

Tactics

The pattern of the magnetic field on the outside of a coil of wire is similar to that of a bar magnet.

RED ALERT Make sure that you are familiar with the different ways of changing the strength of an electromagnet. RED

Using electromagnetism

A useful electromagnet is made using a coil of wire on an iron core. This can cause movement when the magnet is switched on and off. Motors, bells and relays all use the movement caused by forces due to electromagnetism.

A relay is a switch operated by switching an electromagnet on and off. It may seem strange to use a switch to operate a switch, but using a relay does have advantages in certain situations.

The diagram shows a relay being used to switch a mains lamp.

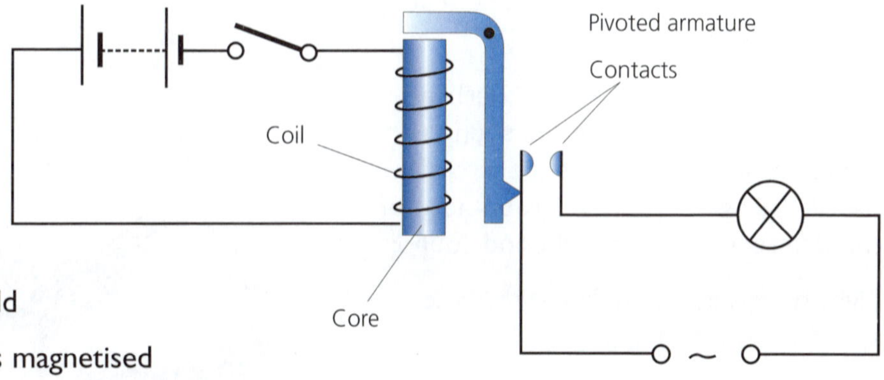

When the relay is switched on:

- current passes in the relay coil, creating a magnetic field
- the iron core becomes magnetised
- the armature is attracted to the core
- the switch contacts are pressed together and the light comes on.

A relay:

- can operate from a low voltage source and be used to switch devices that work from a higher voltage
- only needs a small current to operate it.

The electrical circuits in cars carry large currents that need thick wires. Relays are used so that thin wires can be used for the switches that the driver operates.

Exercise 2

1 State three devices that use electromagnetism to produce movement.

2 Describe how the relay contacts become pressed together when a current passes in the coil.

3 Explain why relays are used in cars to switch on high-current devices.

4 Some outside lights switch on automatically at dusk. The sensing circuit operates from a low voltage supply. Explain why a relay is used to switch the lamp.

Tactics

Iron is used for the relay coil because it is easily magnetised and demagnetised.

How light travels

Sharp shadows are formed when light from a small source such as a torch passes around an object that is opaque, i.e. one that does not let light go through it.

These shadows provide evidence that light travels in straight lines.

If a low-flying aircraft passes overhead, when you look at where the sound is coming from you see that the aircraft has already gone past. This is because of the different speeds of light and sound.

Light travels at one million times the speed of sound in air.

Because of the very fast speed of light, there is normally no noticeable time delay between an event happening and us seeing it.

Exceptions to this occur when the distances are vast, for example when looking at stars. Observations of our Sun see what happened eight and a half minutes ago. Light from the second nearest star to us takes more than four years to get here, so when you are star-gazing you are looking back in time!

Exercise 1

1 What is an opaque object?

2 What do sharp shadows show about the way in which light travels?

3 Explain why there is sometimes a time delay between seeing an event and hearing the sound from it.

4 How long does it take for light from the nearest star to reach the Earth?

Tactics

Always use a ruler for drawing the straight-line path of light on diagrams in tests and examinations.

RED ALERT Questions about the difference between luminous and non-luminous objects are common in Key Stage 3 tests. RED

Seeing

We see with our eyes, but we also need a brain to be able to see things!

- Eyes are sensors that send messages to the brain in the form of electrical signals along the optic nerve.
- When the brain interprets the signals from the eyes, it assumes that the light travelled to the eyes in a straight line.
- This enables the brain to work out where things are.
- The brain needs light from both eyes to be able to pinpoint the position of objects accurately, as the diagram shows.

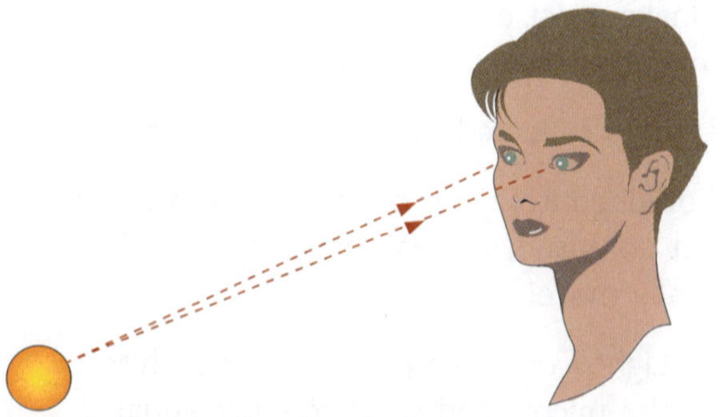

Television and computer screens are luminous; they give out light that our eyes detect. Lamps and the Sun also give out light, as do fires and candles.

We use light sources such as the Sun and artificial lighting so that we can see other things. Most surfaces scatter light, that is, they reflect it in all directions, so that some light enters your eyes even when you move to a different position.

Exercise 2

1 In vision, what job is done by
   a the eyes?
   b the brain?
2 Why does vision need two eyes, rather than just one?
3 What is meant by a *luminous* object?
4 Explain how you are able to see this book.

Tactics

Remember, most objects are seen by the light that they reflect into the eyes.

Mirrors

Unlike most everyday things, mirrors do not reflect light in all directions but they do reflect it in a regular and predictable way.

Light is reflected from a mirror at the same angle as it hits it.

Looking into a mirror causes the brain to get confused; it 'sees' things that aren't really there!

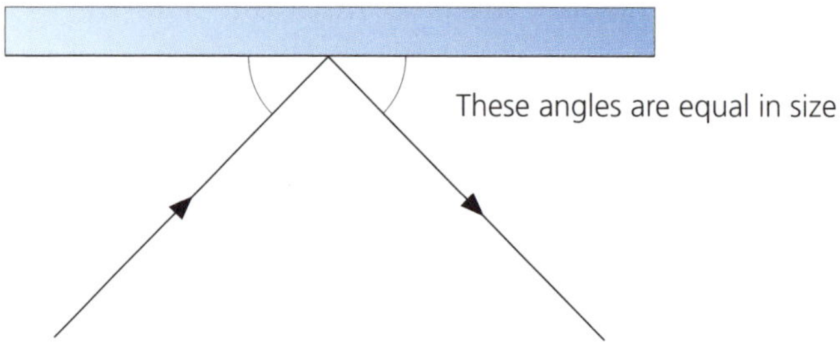

- Light from each part of the face hits the mirror and is reflected at equal angles. The reflected light is detected by the eyes.
- The brain then 'sees' the face, and works out where it is, assuming that the light has travelled in straight lines.
- In this case it gets things wrong; it 'sees' a face behind the mirror.

What you see is called a virtual image.

The word 'image' just means 'likeness', and in all respects the image is a likeness of the real thing; it is the same way up and the same size and colour. The image is called virtual because, unlike the image that you see on a television or cinema screen, it is not really there.

Exercise 1

1 A beam of light meets a mirror surface at an angle of 32°.

  a What is the angle between the reflected light and the mirror surface?

  b Calculate the size of the angle between the beam arriving at the surface and the beam leaving the surface.

2 What does the brain assume about the way in which light travels?

3 When you look at your image in a mirror, whereabouts is the image?

4 Explain why the image in a mirror is described as virtual.

Tactics

When using a drawing to show the reflection of light from a mirror, always use arrows to show the direction in which the light is travelling before and after being reflected.

RED ALERT The angle between a mirror and the incoming light is the same as the angle between the mirror and the reflected light.

Finding the image

Using the rule about the way in which light is reflected from a mirror, you can construct images. If you do this you will see that:

- the image in a mirror is always formed straight behind the mirror
- the image is the same distance behind the mirror as the object is in front of it.

Mirrors are used in periscopes to turn light round corners. Light hitting a mirror at an angle of 45° is reflected at the same angle and so is turned through 90°.

The diagram shows how two mirrors are arranged inside a periscope. You can make a periscope quite easily using two small mirror tiles and the cardboard tube from the inside of a roll of kitchen foil.

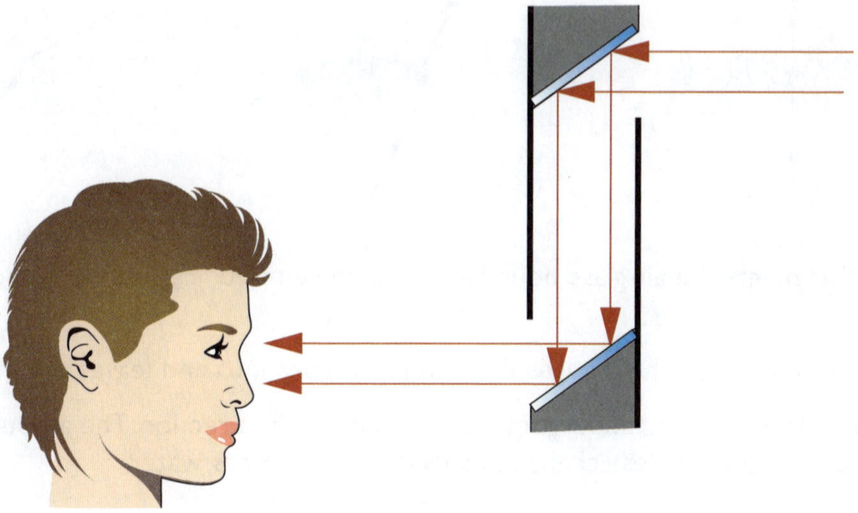

Exercise 2

1 A man stands 1.5 m from a mirror.

a What is the distance between the man's image and the mirror?

b What is the distance between the man and his image?

2 The diagram shows a lamp in front of a mirror.

Which letter A, B, C or D shows the position of the image of the lamp?

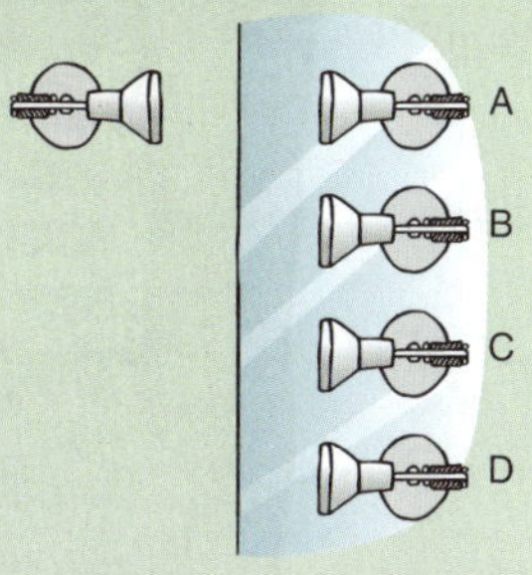

3 Explain why light is turned through 90° when the angle between the incoming light and the mirror is 45°.

Tactics

A common misconception is that the image in a mirror is 'laterally inverted' or turned round sideways. This is wrong. When you look into a mirror, you see the image of the left side of your face on your left.

Changing speed

Have you ever noticed how the water in a swimming pool never looks as deep as it says it is? This is another example of your eye-brain system being fooled when light does not travel in straight lines. A change in the speed at which light travels can also cause a change in direction.

As light enters water or any other dense transparent material, it slows down.

The change in the speed of light as it enters water or glass is called refraction. The diagrams show the effect of the change in speed when light passes through a sheet of glass.

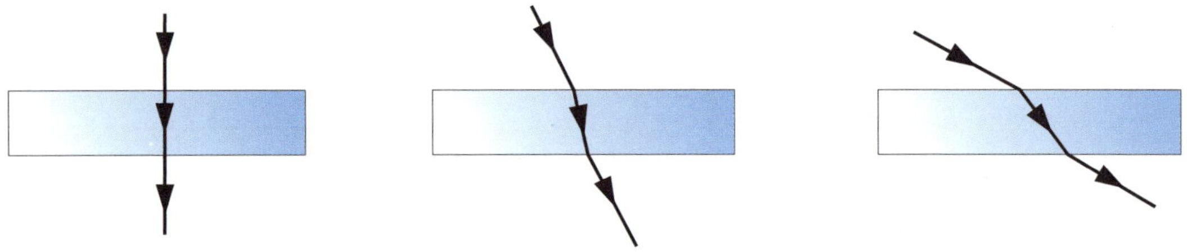

- The light that meets the air-glass boundary at an angle of 90° carries on without a change in direction.
- At any other angle the light changes direction as it goes into and leaves the glass block.

Light travelling through water undergoes a similar change in direction. The amount of change is slightly less because there is less change in speed as light enters water.

Exercise 1

1 What happens to the speed of light when it travels:

a from air into glass?

b from glass into air?

2 If light does not change direction as it passes from air into glass, what is the angle between the direction of the light and the surface of the glass?

3 In which of these materials does light have the smallest speed?
air glass water

4 Describe what happens when light waves are refracted.

Tactics

The greater the angle at which light meets an air-glass boundary, the greater the change in direction.

RED ALERT

When light crosses a boundary, some light is always reflected back.

RED

More images

Why does the swimming pool look to be shallower than it really is? The answer is because of the change in direction that occurs when light leaves the water and speeds up as it enters the air.

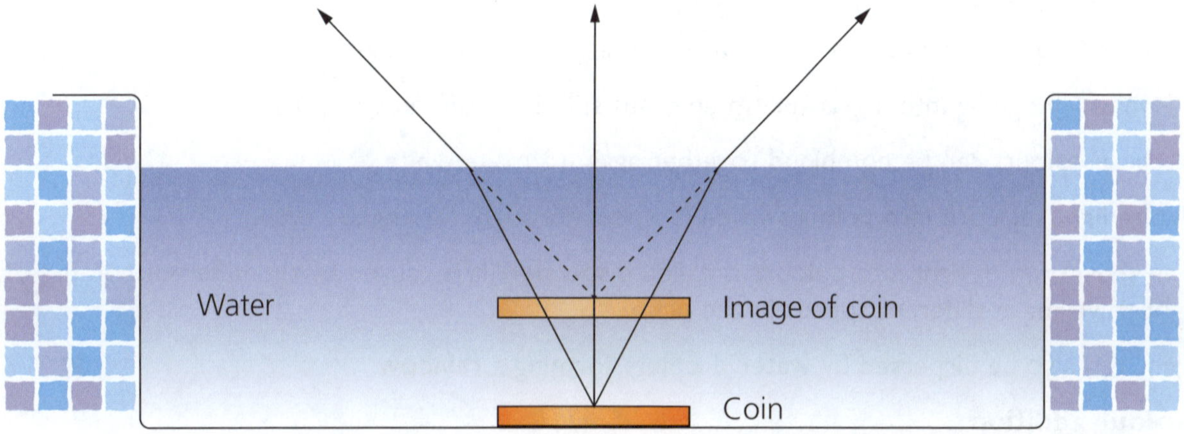

The dotted lines in the diagram show where the light appears to have come from, assuming that it has travelled in straight lines. This is another example of a virtual image. As with a mirror, the virtual image is just like the original object, except that it is not really there.

Exercise 2

1 What effect causes a swimming pool to look shallower than it really is?

2 When a person looks at a lamp through a block of glass the lamp looks nearer than it really is.

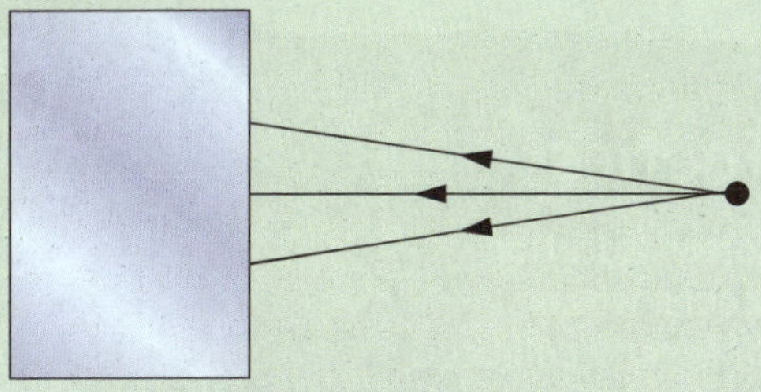

a Draw on the diagram to show where the lamp looks to be.

b What have you assumed about the way in which light travels?

Tactics

Remember that refraction is the change in speed of light as it crosses a boundary. The change in speed may also cause a change in direction of the light.

Colour

Manufacturers of paint make different colours and shades by starting with a white paint and then adding dyes to it.

Coloured objects do not add colour to white light; they take it away:

- white light going into a glass prism emerges split into different colours
- these colours can be combined together again to make white.

White light separate into colours when it passes through a triangular prism.

The separation of light into colours is called dispersion. It is caused by the different colours of light travelling at different speeds in the prism.

Light can also be dispersed by water droplets, forming a rainbow.

Colour addition

When you watch television you are seeing the effects of combining colours together. A television screen can glow with three different colours: red, green and blue.

These are called the primary colours of light because all other colours can be made by combining these three colours.

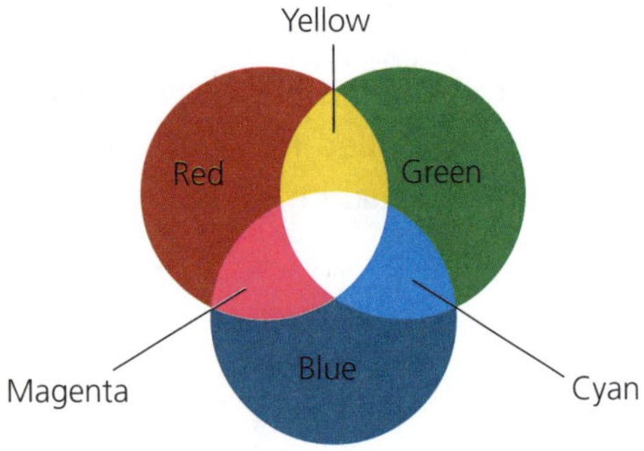

The diagram shows how the three secondary colours, yellow, magenta and cyan (turquoise) are each produced by adding together the light from two primary colours.

The area in the middle, where all three primary coloured lights add together, is white.

Exercise 1

1 When white light passes through a triangular glass prism, it splits into colours.

a What name is given to this effect?

b What causes this effect?

2 What are the three primary colours of light?

3 What are the three secondary colours?

4 Which primary colours of light are combined to produce:

a cyan? **b** magenta?

c yellow?

Tactics

Colour addition occurs when different coloured lights shine onto a white screen.

RED ALERT **Colours are added together on a television screen and a computer monitor.** RED ALER

Colour subtraction

Televisions and computer screens can reproduce any colour by adding the three primary colours together in varying proportions. The colour that a non-luminous object appears depends on the colours that it absorbs.

Coloured objects and colour filters absorb or take colours out of the light that falls on them.

- primary colours take out everything except their own colour
- each secondary colour removes just one primary colour; the colour removed is the one that isn't used when mixing the secondary colour from red, blue and green light.

To work out what colour different objects look under coloured lights:

- start with the primary colours present in the light
- take away the colours that the object absorbs
- you are left with the colours that are reflected.

As you can see, it's just a simple subtraction sum.

For example, a magenta-coloured light shines onto a yellow T-shirt. What colour does the shirt look to be?

Sometimes an object takes away all the colours in the light; when this happens it appears black.

Exercise 2

1 What effect do colour filters have on light?

2 Which primary colours of light can pass through a yellow filter?

3 What colour does a magenta-coloured book cover appear to be when viewed in:

 a red light?

 b blue light?

 c cyan light?

4 What colour light would make the magenta book cover appear to be black?

Tactics

It is important to remember that an object that appears black does not reflect any light.

ED **Colour subtraction operates when viewing non-luminous objects.** ALERT RED ALERT

Sound production

Sound and hearing

To make a sound, something has to vibrate in a to-and-fro motion.

Example

Televisions, radios and hi-fi all use loudspeakers to reproduce sound. A loudspeaker consists of a paper cone driven backwards and forwards by an electromagnet.

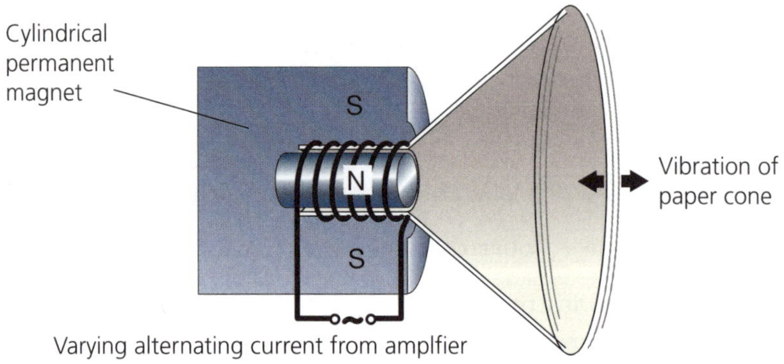

Example

Some musical instruments have strings that vibrate when they are hit or plucked; others have columns of air that vibrate when they are blown.

Travelling sound

Sound can travel through anything that has particles to transmit the vibrations. It travels very fast in solids, where the particles are close together, slower in liquids and slowest of all in gases.

Sound cannot travel in a vacuum – it needs a material to transmit the sound by vibration of its particles.

Exercise 1

1. What has to happen to cause a sound?
2. How does a loudspeaker cause a sound to travel through the air?
3. State two ways in which musical instruments cause sound.
4. Explain why sound cannot travel in a vacuum.
5. In which type of materials does sound travel with the greatest speed?

Tactics

It is important to remember that sound can only be transmitted by the vibration of particles.

RED ALERT All sounds are caused by vibrating objects. **RED**

You may have seen a demonstration of a bell ringing inside a glass jar. Sound from the bell travels through the air and the glass and then through the air again to the ear. When air is removed from the jar, the sound cannot be heard.

Hearing

In an ear:

- sound causes vibrations of the ear drum in the outer ear
- the ossicles are three bones in the middle ear that transfer this energy to the inner ear
- in the inner ear nerve endings are stimulated by the vibration and send messages along the auditory nerve to the brain.

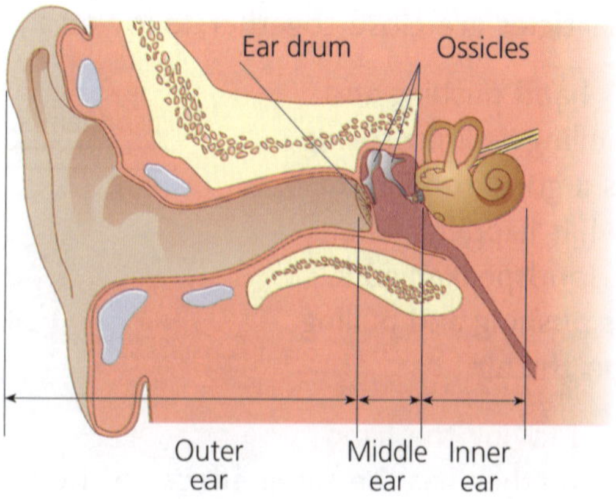

Not everybody can hear the same sounds:

- The ears of a normal young person detect sounds with a frequency (see p. 69) ranging from about 20 Hz to about 20 000 Hz.
- As you get older, the range of frequencies that you can hear is reduced.
- A middle-aged person may not be able to hear sounds with a frequency greater than 15 000 Hz although the hearing at low frequencies is less likely to be affected.

People who work in noisy environments should wear ear defenders to protect their ears from damage. Sudden exposure to a loud sound such as an explosion can cause immediate damage by breaking the ear drum or the ossicles.

Exercise 2

1 Which part of the ear detects sound?

2 Describe how sound waves travel through the ear.

3 How does the information from a sound wave travel from the ear to the brain?

4 What is the frequency of the highest pitched sound that a human ear can detect?

5 Describe how the hearing of a middle-aged person differs from that of a young person.

Tactics

Sound waves that have a frequency above the range of human hearing are called ultrasound.

Different sounds

As a wave moves along a slinky spring, each part of the spring vibrates. The particles in air vibrate in a similar way when they transmit sound. Each wave consists of a squash, where the particles are close together, followed by a stretch, where the particles are further apart.

A hand pushing and pulling a slinky spring is a good model of what happens when a loudspeaker cone is pushing and pulling on the air.

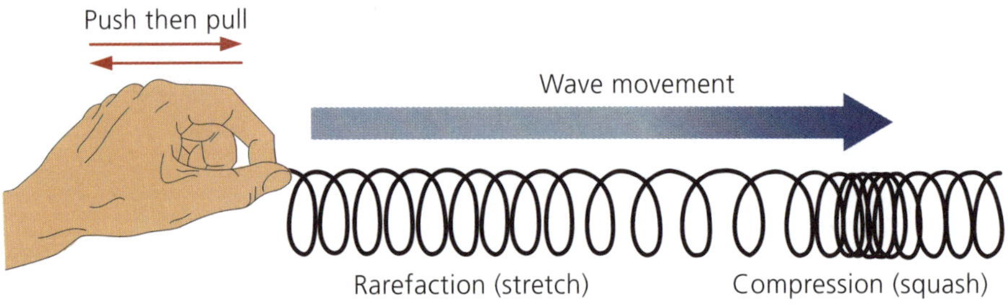

- Moving the hand further has the same effect on the spring as turning up the volume control has on the air particles.
- The particles move further and you hear a louder sound.
- When you push further you are increasing the amplitude of the vibration.

The amplitude of the vibration is the greatest distance that each part of the spring moves from its rest position.

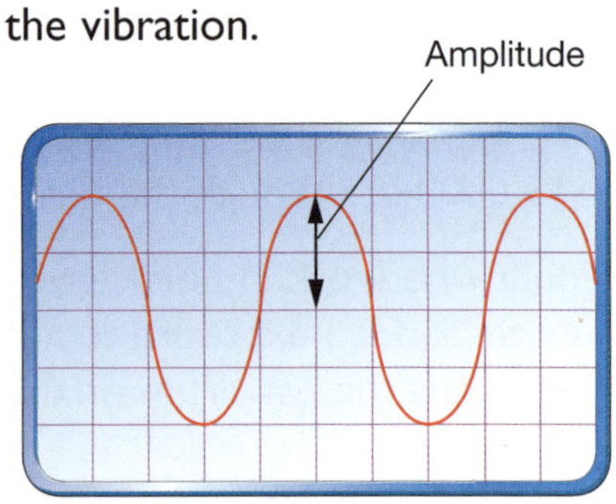

A microphone and an oscilloscope can be used to plot a graph that shows the movement of air particles when a sound wave passes. The upwards and downwards movement of the oscilloscope trace represents the forwards and backwards movement of an air particle.

Exercise 1

1 How do air particles transmit sound?

2 How many squashes and stretches make up one sound wave?

3 Describe the relationship between the loudness of a sound and the amplitude of vibration of the air particles.

4 A girl is listening to a CD on a hi-fi system. She turns the volume control down. Explain how this affects the movement of the air particles.

5 What is the difference between the movement of an oscilloscope trace and the movement of air particles that it represents?

Tactics

Unlike light and radio waves, sound is transmitted by vibrating particles.

RED ALERT Remember the relationships between loudness and amplitude, pitch and frequency. **RED**

Higher and louder

The trace on an oscilloscope screen shows the number of sound waves that are detected in a certain time. Adjusting the oscilloscope settings can change this time. A 'crest' and a 'trough' represent one complete wave. The trace shown in the diagram on the previous page shows two and a half waves.

The diagram on the right shows the trace when a note of higher pitch is played.

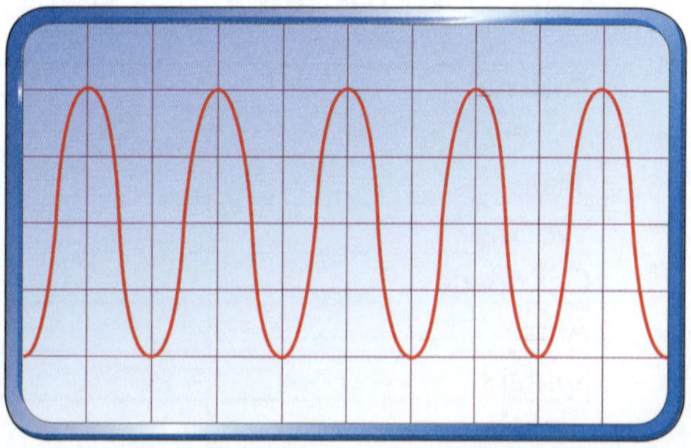

There are now more waves in the same time; the frequency (the number of waves per second) has increased.

Frequency is measured in hertz (Hz).
1 Hz = 1 wave per second.

These measurements using an oscilloscope display show that:

- increasing the amplitude of a sound wave makes it sound louder
- increasing the frequency of a sound wave gives it a higher pitch.

Sound waves that have a frequency too high for humans to detect are called ultrasound. Bats emit pulses of ultrasound and detect the reflections from fixed and moving objects. This is how they 'see' to navigate and find their prey.

Cats and dogs can also detect ultrasound; humans cannot hear a dog whistle but dogs can!

Ultrasound is also used in hospitals for producing images of body organs. It is safer than using X-rays as the ultrasound does not damage cells or tissue.

Exercise 2

1 What is meant by the frequency of a wave?

2 A sound wave has a frequency of 250 Hz. How many waves of the sound pass into an eardrum in 5 s?

3 Describe the relationship between the frequency of a sound wave and its pitch.

4 The oscilloscope trace shown above shows the number of waves of a sound that happen in 1/20 s (0.05 s).

a How many waves are shown on the screen?

b Calculate the frequency of the wave.

Tactics

Always give the correct unit, Hz, when writing down a frequency.

1 The table shows animals collected in two sites:

Site A

A damp shaded area of the garden.

Site B

A dry open pasture with a shaded position.

Animal	**Number of animals found at location**	
	A	**B**
Snails	55	1
Worms	20	5
Centipedes	5	1
Ants	40	25
Spiders	20	15
Beetles	20	10
Aphids	20	40

a Which animal occurred in larger numbers at site B than at site A?

____ [1]

b Finish the pie chart showing the distribution of animals at site A.

Each segment is 20°.

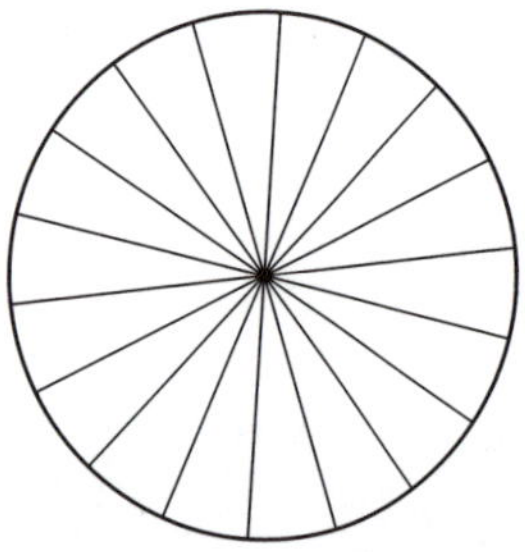

[2]

c Which animal is likely to be a secondary consumer? Give a reason for your answer.

____

____ [2]

d Suggest two reasons why there are more snails at site A than at site B.

____

____ [2]

2 The diagram shows an experiment with germinating peas, and peas that were boiled in water.

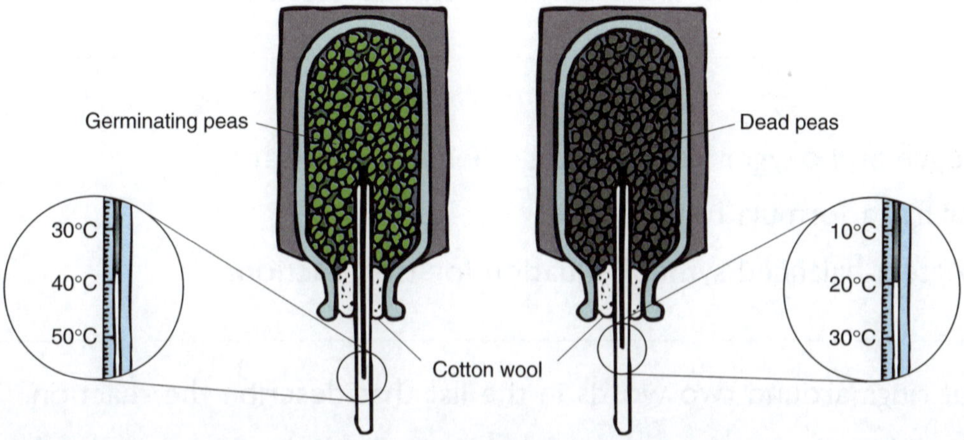

a Explain what this experiment shows.

____

____

____

____ [3]

b Write a word equation for the change taking place.

____ [2]

3 The table gives information about five elements A–E. (These are not the chemical symbols).

Element	Melting point (°C)	Boiling point (°C)	pH value of oxide	Electrical conductivity
A	–39	357	7	Good
B	3730	4830	5	Good
C	444	732	4	Poor
D	98	890	13	Good
E	44	280	2	Poor

a Which element is a liquid at room temperature? Explain your choice.

Element ______________

Explanation ____

____ [2]

b Which elements are non-metals? Explain your choice.

Elements ____________

Explanation ____

____ [2]

4 Hydrogen and oxygen combine together to form water.

Water has a formula H_2O.

a Write a balanced symbol equation for the reaction.

____ [3]

b Put rings around two words in the list that describe the reaction.

combustion **decomposition** **endothermic** **synthesis** [1]

5 The diagram shows the surfaces of two rocks A and B.

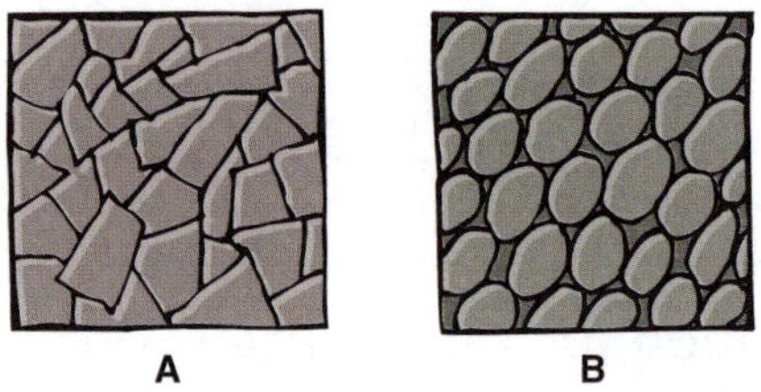

a Describe the shape of the grains that make up rock A.

____ [1]

b Suggest how the grains in rock B became rounded in shape.

____

____ [2]

c Why is rock B able to soak up more water than rock A?

____ [1]

6 This saucepan is used on a gas ring to cook some vegetables.

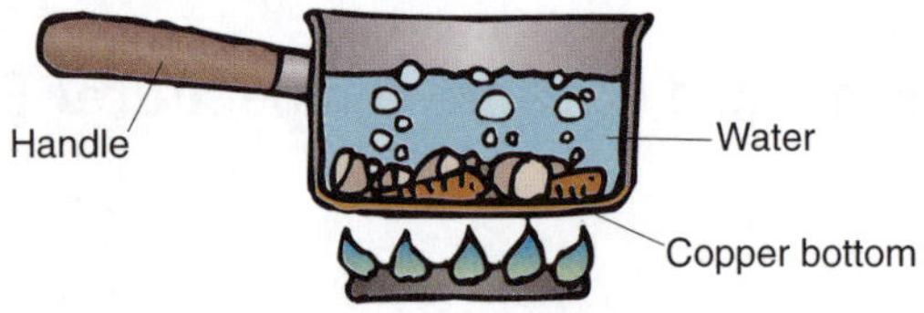

a Explain why copper is a suitable material for the bottom of the saucepan.

____ [1]

b Name a suitable material for the handle and explain why this is a suitable material.

____ [2]

c Explain how water at the top of the saucepan becomes heated.

____ [2]

d The saucepan is fitted with a lid. Explain why less energy is now needed from the gas flame to keep the water boiling.

____ [2]

7 The diagram shows what happens to light when it meets the glass in a window.

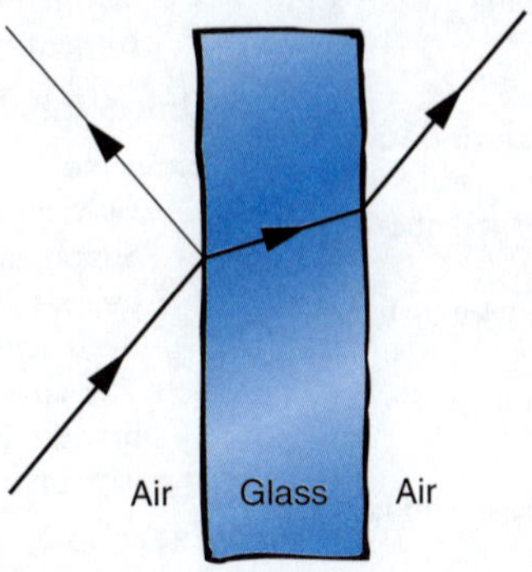

a What two things happen to the light when it meets the boundary going from air to glass?

____

____ [2]

b Underline three of the following properties of the light shown in the diagram that change as it enters the glass.

colour **direction** **frequency** **speed** **wavelength** [3]

Answers to exercises

Unit 1 A balanced diet (page 6)

Exercise 1

1 Proteins, carbohydrates, fats, vitamins, minerals, fibre and water.
2 Proteins and amino acids (made from proteins) cannot be stored in the body so regular supplies are needed.
3 To provide them with the energy needed to finish the race.
4 A balanced diet is eating just the right balance of food, minerals, vitamins, fibre and water to keep healthy.
5 Vegetables, wholegrain cereals, wholemeal bread.

Exercise 2

1 If you eat a healthy diet this will provide all the vitamins needed as vitamins are only required in small amounts.
2 Vitamins A and D.
3 Margarine is eaten instead of butter. If vitamins are not added people might not take in enough of these vitamins. Adding them ensures this.

Unit 2 Mineral salts (page 8)

Exercise 1

1 At this stage bones and teeth are developing and so a lot of calcium is needed.
2 Milk and cheese.
3 It hardens tooth enamel, which reduces tooth decay. Adding fluoride to tap water means all people have to drink it and some people might be concerned about its effects.
4 To help the body to produce more haemoglobin. Each red blood cell has iron in it.
5 Iodine is added to table salt in small quantities.

Exercise 2

A Starch **B** Protein **C** Starch, sugar and fat.

Unit 3 Digestion (page 10)

Exercise 1

1 Mouth, oesophagus, stomach, duodenum, small intestine, large intestine, rectum, anus.
2 Teeth, liver, pancreas.

Exercise 2

1 In the mouth.
2 Carbohydrates – carbohydrase; proteins – protease; fats – lipase.
3 In the stomach the mixture is acidic and in the small intestine the mixture is alkaline.
4 Small intestine.
5 The carbohydrate is broken down by carbohydrase into glucose. This is a sugar and tastes sweet.

Exercise 3

1 Plants do not digest food. They produce their own food by photosynthesis.
2.

Large food molecule	Enzyme	Small molecule produced
Carbohydrate	Carbohydrase	Glucose
Protein	Protease	Amino acids
Fat	Lipase	Glycerol and fatty acids

Exercise 4

1 Villi
2 The ileum is long and has a large surface area.
3 Any three from: glucose, amino acids, fatty acids and glycerol.

Unit 4 Respiration in cells and plants (page 14)

Exercise 1

1 Uses oxygen; Produces carbon dioxide and water; Releases energy.
2 Burning releases some energy as light (a flame) but respiration does not.

Exercise 2

1 Glucose + oxygen → carbon dioxide + water + energy.
2. The second sample of limewater would go cloudy faster.

Unit 5 Lungs (page 16)

Exercise 1

1 The rib cage moves downwards and inwards.
The diaphragm moves upwards.
There is now less space inside the thorax.
There is more pressure inside the thorax.
This causes air to be pushes out of the lungs.
2. Through the trachea and bronchus.

Exercise 2

1 When a person suffers from emphysema the alveoli break down so they have a smaller surface area. As a result gas exchange cannot take place as well.
2 Oxygen is needed in the bloodstream to provide the oxygen needed by the cells for respiration.

Unit 6 Inhaled and exhaled air (page 18)

Exercise 1

1 Oxygen decreases, carbon dioxide increases.
2 Supply of oxygen.
3 Increased population, more combustion of fossil fuels, destruction of green plants.
4 The air we breathe out is warmer than the air we breathe in. The air we breathe out contains more water vapour than the air we breathe in.

Exercise 2

1 The beaker filled with normal air.
2 Oxygen
3 There is less oxygen in exhaled air than normal air.

Unit 7 Bacteria and viruses (page 20)

Exercise 1

1 6400
2 Cytoplasm and cell membrane.
3 Antibiotics have no effect on viruses.
4 If you do not take the full course some bacteria may remain and these can multiply.

Exercise 2

1 Milk is heated to a high temperature for a short period and then cooled. This kills bacteria.
2 White blood cells produced antibodies to destroy the bacteria. Some of these remain, so if infection occurs again the body is quick to respond.

Exercise 3

1 Microbes which cause the soup to go bad are in the air. They are destroyed by boiling. They cannot re-enter the soup in A so the soup does not go bad. They can enter the soup in B and so it goes bad.
2 Measles, mumps and rubella (German measles).

Exercise 4

1 41°C
2 A week.
3 Old people may become seriously ill from some of the side-effects of the flu. This leads to many additional deaths each year.
4 The flu injection only protects against some strains of flu. They could catch a strain for which there is no protection.

Unit 8 Carrying out a piece of fieldwork (page 24)

Exercise 1

1 An estimate on the number in the whole field based upon 1 quadrat will be inaccurate. They should do it a number of times trying to choose positions that ensure more accurate numbers. Perhaps they should do it 10 times in 10 very different positions around the field and use the average.

2 Plants stay in one position but spiders will move about. Spiders are also smaller and more difficult to see.

Unit 9 Feeding relationships (page 25)

Exercise 1

1 Foliage and bark→beetles→woodpeckers→kestrels

2 Four

3 Squirrel

4 If there are no swallows the number of aphids would increase. The number of kestrels is likely to decrease.

Unit 10 Elements (page 28)

Exercise 1

1 **A** False; **B** true; **C** true; **D** false.

2 Because they could not be seen and there was no experimental evidence.

Exercise 2

1 **a** Nitrogen; **b** sulphur; **c** calcium; **d** zinc; **e** sodium; **f** potassium.

2 Nitrogen, phosphorus, potassium.

3 Hydrogen, sulphur and oxygen.

Unit 11 Putting elements into groups (page 30)

Exercise 1

1 **A** Gas; **B** solid; **C** liquid; **D** solid; **E** liquid.

2 True

Exercise 2

1 Metals: B, D and E; non-metals: A and C.

2 Helium

Unit 12 Patterns in elements (page 32)

Exercise 1

1 Bromine

2 H, He, N, O, F, Ne, Cl, Ar, Kr

3 **A** True; **B** true; **C** false.

Exercise 2

1	**a**	Ca	solid	metal
	b	Kr	gas	non-metal
	c	B	solid	non-metal
	d	C	solid	non-metal
	e	S	solid	non-metal
	f	P	solid	non-metal
	g	Li	solid	metal

Unit 13 Mixtures (page 34)

Exercise 1

1 **a** C below 232°C (lower than either of the metals)
b It melts more easily when the tip of the soldering iron touches it.

2 Exhaust gases from vehicles.

Exercise 2

1 **a** 78°C
b Lower than 78°C and over a range of temperatures.

2 Air is a mixture (its composition is not fixed). Water is a compound (its composition is fixed).

Unit 14 Compounds (page 36)

Exercise 1

1 Iron + sulphur → iron sulphide.

2

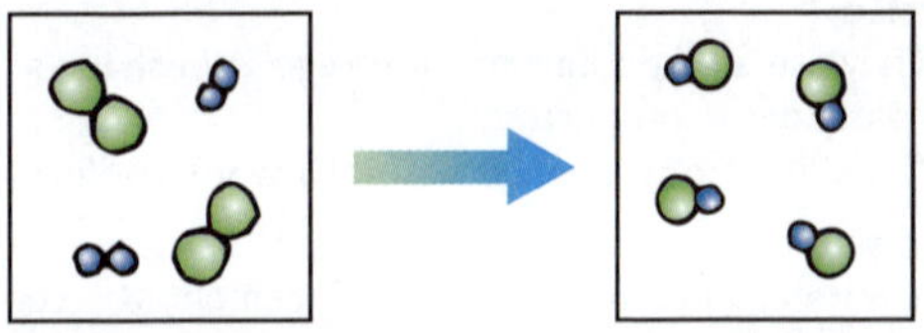

Exercise 2

1 **a** 4: sodium, hydrogen, carbon and oxygen
b Sodium 1, hydrogen 1, carbon 1, oxygen 3.
c 6

2 **a** 3: potassium, manganese and oxygen.
b Potassium 1, manganese 1, oxygen 4.
c 6

Unit 15 Weathering (page 38)

Exercise 1

1 The repeated heating and cooling of rocks can break them down. Also the wind picks up the sand and hurls it against exposed rocks breaking them down.

Exercise 2

1 Water + carbon dioxide → carbonic acid.
Calcium carbonate + carbonic acid → calcium hydrogencarbonate.

2 Carbonic acid is a weak acid but sulphuric acid is a strong acid.

Unit 16 Rock (page 40)

Exercise 1

1 **a** Talc **b** calcite **c** fluorite or apatite.
d Quartz, topaz, corundum or diamond.

2 Carbon dioxide

Exercise 2

1 Sandstone, mudstone, shale, limestone and conglomerate.

2 As the pieces travel along the river they rub against each other and the rough edges are removed.

Exercise 3

1 Marble and slate.

2 High temperatures and high pressures.

3 You will see tiny crystals in marble and grains in limestone.

4 They are both the same chemical – calcium carbonate.

Exercise 4

1 Igneous rocks are new rocks formed when magma crystallises so fossils cannot exist.

2 The other rocks above the granite have worn away.

3 Basalt and granite.

Unit 17 Recycling (page 44)

Exercise 1

1 Glass milk bottles are collected, washed and reused.

2 The energy required to produce a bottle is high. Recycling saves energy.

3 Coloured glass contains impurities. Mixing colourless and coloured glass will produce only coloured glass.

Exercise 2

1 **a** High temperature and high pressure.
b Cooling and crystallising.
c Transported, settles, compressed (or compacted), cemented.
d Weathering and erosion.

2 Weathering and erosion, transport, deposition, melting, eruption, cooling.

Unit 18 Uses of rocks (page 46)

Exercise 1

1 They are all the same size, are regular in shape and consistent in properties.

2 Glass, steel, plastic (PVC and polythene), roofing felt.

Exercise 2

1 If water comes into contact with cement, the cement starts to harden.

2 Calcium carbonate – calcium, carbon and oxygen. Calcium silicate – calcium, silicon and oxygen.

Unit 19 Moving energy around (page 50)

Exercise 1

1 It heats up as it gains energy from the surrounding, warmer air.

2 The air on the outside is warmer than the inside of the refrigerator.

3 Energy is passed on through the vibrations of particles from more energetic particles to less energetic ones.

4 The particles are widespread so contact between particles is rare.

5 Energy is transferred by electrons that are free to move through the metal.

Exercise 2

1 Air that has been warmed rises and is replaced by cooler air that in turn becomes warmed.

2 Changes in density.

3 Air is trapped between the layers so that it cannot form convection currents.

4 It prevents evaporation.
It reflects radiant energy back onto the food.

5 It prevents energy loss by evaporation and convection currents.

Exercise 3

1 **a** 100°C **b** 20°C **c** 50°C

2 There is a lot more water to be heated in the tank than in the kettle.

3 Each 'spark' is a tiny piece of red-hot iron. It only loses a small amount of energy as it cools down.

Exercise 4

1 Air is a poor conductor but if it is free to move it removes energy by forming convection currents.

2 Trapped air pockets.

3 Radiant energy.

4 Two thin layers of clothing trap a layer of air between them.

5 It stops energy transfer by convection currents in the cavity.

Unit 20 Magnetism (page 54)

Exercise 1

1 Iron and steel.

2 Steel keeps its magnetism but iron quickly loses it.

3 Opposite poles attract and similar poles repel.

4 The iron drawing pins are picked up by the magnet but the brass ones are not.

5 Hold each end of the steel in turn next to the same pole of the magnet: if both ends of the steel are attracted it is not a magnet.
If one end of the steel is attracted and one end is repelled it is a magnet.

Exercise 2

1 North-seeking pole or north pole.

2 The region around a magnet where it exerts magnetic forces.

3 The arrows show the direction of the force on the north-seeking pole of a compass; this is repelled from the north-seeking pole and attracted to the south-seeking pole of the magnet.

4 Iron filings are not permanent magnets so they do not have fixed poles.

5 The compass will point to the steel of the ship rather than to the magnetic north.

Unit 21 Electromagnets (page 56)

Exercise 1

1 Electric motors, loudspeakers and magnetic recording heads.

2 The left hand end in the diagram.

3 Inside the coil the direction of the magnetic field is from the south-seeking pole to the north-seeking pole.
Outside the coil the direction of the magnetic field is from the north-seeking pole to the south-seeking pole.

4 Using more turns of wire.
Winding the coil on an iron core.
Increasing the current in the coil.

5 It can be switched on and off and its strength can be changed.

Exercise 2

1 Any three from: motor, bell, relay, loudspeaker.

2 The core becomes magnetised, the top of the armature is attracted to the core as the armature moves, it presses the switch contacts together.

3 The relays operate from small currents so only thin wires are needed for the switches.

4 The relay coil is operated by the low voltage sensing circuit.
The relay contacts can be used to switch the mains voltage lamp.

Unit 22 How light travels (page 58)

Exercise 1

1 One that light cannot pass through.

2 It travels in straight lines.

3 Light travels much faster than sound, so it takes less time to reach an observer.

4 Eight and a half minutes.

Exercise 2

1 **a** The eyes detect light.
b The brain puts together information from the eyes to 'see' a picture.

2 To judge distance.

3 One that gives out its own light.

4 Light from the surroundings lands on the book.
Some of this light is scattered.
The eyes detect light that has been reflected by the book.

Unit 23 Mirrors (page 60)

Exercise 1

1 **a** 32° **b** 116°

2 That it travels in straight lines.

3 Straight behind the mirror, the same distance behind as you are in front.

4 It is not really there.

Exercise 2

1 **a** 1.5 m **b** 3.0 m

2 A

3 The angle between the reflected light and the mirror is 45°, so the angle between the incoming light and the reflected light is $180° - (45° + 45°) = 90°$.

Unit 24 Changing speed (page 62)

Exercise 1

1 **a** It decreases. **b** It increases.

2 90°

3 Glass
4 Their speed and wavelength both decrease.

Exercise 2

1 The change in direction of light as it passes through the water surface.
2 **a** The light leaving the block should be traced back using straight lines, the position of the image is where these lines cross.
  b That it travels in straight lines.

Unit 25 Colour (page 64)

Exercise 1

1 **a** Dispersion
  b The different colours of light travel at different speeds in the glass.
2 Red, green and blue.
3 Yellow, magenta and cyan.
4 **a** Blue and green **b** Blue and red **c** Red and green.

Exercise 2

1 They absorb some colours and allow others to pass through.
2 Red and green.
3 **a** Red **b** Blue **c** Blue
4 Green

Unit 26 Sound production (page 66)

Exercise 1

1 An object has to vibrate.
2 Moving backwards and forwards.
3 Vibrating strings and vibrating air columns.
4 There are no particles to transmit the vibrations.
5 Solids

Exercise 2

1 The ear drum.
2 Vibrations of the ear drum are transmitted through the ossicles to the inner ear.
3 Signals along the auditory nerve.
4 20 000 Hz
5 The young person can hear high frequency sounds that the middle-aged person cannot detect.

Unit 27 Different sounds (page 68)

Exercise 1

1 Vibrations
2 One squash and one stretch.
3 The greater the amplitude, the louder the sound.
4 The air particles vibrate with a smaller amplitude.
5 The trace moves up and down to represent forwards and backwards motion of the air particles.

Exercise 2

1 The number of waves per second.
2 1250
3 The greater the frequency, the higher the pitch.
4 **a** 5 **b** 100 Hz

Answers to Year 8 Test Paper

1 **a** Aphids 1
  b

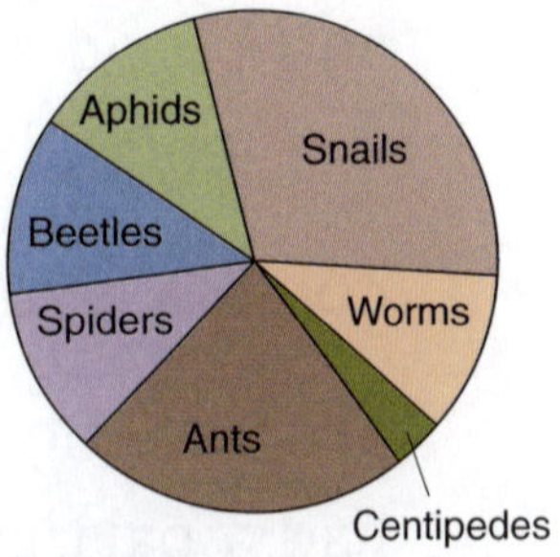

2

  c Centipedes 1
  There are fewer centipedes so they are likely to be higher up the food chain. 1
  d Dampness so they do not dry out 1
  lack of light. 1
2 **a** There is a temperature rise with germinating peas but not with dead peas. 1
  The temperature rises with germinating peas because respiration is taking place. 1
  There is no respiration with dead peas. 1
  b Glucose + oxygen → carbon dioxide + water + energy. 2
  (One mark for left-hand side and one mark for the right-hand side).
3 **a** A 1
  Room temperature between melting point and boiling point. 1
  b A and D 1
  pH values of oxide neutral or alkaline. 1
4 **a** $2H_2 + O_2 \rightarrow 2H_2O$ 3
  (One mark for formulae on left-hand side, one for formulae on right-hand side and one mark for balancing).
  b Combustion, synthesis. (both required) 1
5 **a** Interlocking crystals. 1
  b Pieces of rock rub together (1) as they travel along the river (1). 2
  c Water can fit into the spaces between grains. 1
6 **a** Copper is a good conductor of heat. 1
  b Plastic or wood (1) because it is a poor conductor/good insulator (1). 2
  c By a convection current (1); the warmed water from the bottom of the saucepan rises and the cold water at the top sinks to become heated (1). 2
  d The lid reduces the energy lost by evaporation (1) and by convection currents in the air above the saucepan (1). 2
7 **a** Some is reflected (1) and some passes into the glass (1); other valid answers: slows down (1), changes wavelength (1). 2
  b Direction, speed and wavelength (1 each correct). 3

Total: 36 marks

Alveoli are millions of tiny air sacs in the tissue of the lung. The lung also contains blood vessels, so that the air and blood are in close contact and exchange of oxygen and carbon dioxide gases can take place.

Antibiotics contain a substance that kills bacteria.

Antibodies protect the body from certain diseases. Once we have had a particular disease, the body knows how to produce antibodies to it which the white blood cells can produce quickly before the disease can take hold if it comes into contact with the body again. We are then said to be immune to that microbe.

Atoms are tiny particles that make up all elements.

Bacteria are a kind of micro-organism that can cause ill health. Bacteria multiply very quickly by repeatedly dividing into two.

Compound is formed when a chemical reaction takes place as certain mixtures of elements combine together.

Diet is what you eat. The word is often used wrongly when people only associate the word with slimming and losing weight.

Digestion the breaking down of large insoluble food molecules into small molecules that the body can then absorb and use.

Digestive system is a long tube, called the gut, several metres long, starting at the mouth and finishing at the anus. At different places along the journey food is treated in different ways to break it down and absorb it.

Elements are the basic building materials that make up all other materials.

Periodic Table is a chart showing the names and symbols of all the elements.

Peristalsis is the movement of food along the gut. Muscles of the gut contract and relax in a special way to squeeze food along.

Pure substance is a single substance, element or compound which contains no other substances.

Respiration is the process that takes place in all cells to produce energy from glucose and oxygen.

Synthesis is a chemical reaction where elements combine to form a compound.

Thermal energy means heat.

Vaccination involves injecting a weakened form of a microbe (micro-organism) into the bloodstream. The white blood cells produce antibodies to fight the disease. This gives the person immunity.

Virus is a kind of micro-organism that can cause ill health. Viruses cannot reproduce themselves. They can only reproduce inside other cells.

Weathering is the process that breaks down exposed rocks by the action of rain, frost, wind and other types of weather.

INDEX

Absorption 13
Air 18–19, 34
Alveoli 17, 78
Antibiotics 21
Antibodies 21–23
Atoms 28
Bacteria 20–23
Building materials 46–47
Cement and concrete 47
Colour 64–65
Compounds 36–37
Conduction 50
Convection 51
Cooling 50–53
Diet 6–8, 78
Digestion and digestive system 10–13, 78
Disease 20–23
Ears 67
Ecology 24–25
Electromagnetism 56–57
Elements 28–33
Energy movement 50–53
Evaporation 51
Feeding relationships 25
Fieldwork 24
Flu 23
Food 6–13
Fossils 42
Gaseous exchange 17
Gases 30, 32
Geological changes 38–47
Glass recycling 44
Graphs, drawing and using 48–49
Hearing 66–67
Heating 50–53
Igneous rocks 43
Images 60–61, 63
Inhaled and exhaled air 18–19
Insulation 53
Intrusion 43
Investigative skills 26–27
Jargon buster 78–79
Light 58–65
Liquids 30, 32
Lungs 16–17
Magnetism 54–57
Materials 28–37
Metals 31–33, 35
Metamorphic rocks 42
Microbes and disease 20–23
Mineral salts 8
Minerals in rocks 40
Mirrors 60–61
Mixtures 34–35
Non-metals 31–33
Pasteur, Louis 22
Periodic Table 32–33
Peristalsis 12
Plant respiration 15
Pure substances 34–35
Quadrats 24
Radiation 51
Recycling 44–45
Reflection 60–61
Refraction 62–63
Research 4–5
Respiration 14–19
Rock cycle 45
Rocks 40–43, 45–47
Sedimentary rocks 41
Seeing 59
Soil 39
Solids 30, 32
Sound and hearing 66–69
Speed of light 62–63
Symbols, elements 29
Synthesis 36
Temperature 52
Test paper 70–77
Vaccinations 22
Viruses 20–23
Vitamins 7
Waves, sound 68–69
Weathering 38–39

A Lot o Genuine and A Wheen o Rogues

True stories of Catrine lives as told by the people who were there.

Compiled by Richard Stenlake

First published in the United Kingdom, 2011,
by Stenlake Publishing Ltd.
54-58 Mill Square,
Catrine, KA5 6RD

Telephone: 01290 551122
www.stenlake.co.uk

ISBN 9781840335347

www.catrine.org.uk

It has been my pleasure to compile this book. The only problem has been making the difficult choices of what to leave out as a book twice this size or more could easily have been filled. The oral history transcriptions have been taken from Catrine Community Trust's Catrine Memories Project which has been wholly financed by the Heritage Lottery Fund. Interviews were conducted, recorded, transcribed and edited during 2009-2010. The interviews were conducted by Gillian Davies-Nippel and Graham Hendry and were transcribed by Graham Hendry, James Kleboe and Linda Pirrie. For the purposes of this book I have had to abridge the interviews or just select extracts. The ellipses (three dots) indicate that material has been omitted between these quotes. The full interviews will be available in due course in audio form on the community trust's web site. To this material I have added material from other earlier sources to tell the first part of the Catrine story namely George Dempster's account of his visit to Arkwright's mill in Cromford which set forth the chain of events which led ultimately to the building of Catrine the mill town, letters written to and from Claud Alexander between 1772 when he first went to India and 1801 when he sold his share in Catrine, letters from David Dale to Claud while Catrine is under construction and in its first years of operation, and the recollections of the engineer William Fairbairn about the work he did at Catrine in the 1820s written down in his memoirs and in his treatise on *Mills and Millwork*. Although we cannot bring the dead back to life they can still speak to us all these years on through their written accounts and through their letters.

It is hoped that the Catrine Memories Project will continue for years to come. Today's junk is tomorrow's treasure. So it is with oral history. We all have it, it's part of every one of us who has lived in or worked in Catrine. Don't throw it away! Your memories are precious. Please write them down or ask the Trust if you can be interviewed and recorded. If you know anything more about any of the subjects in this book we'd also be delighted to hear from you. We welcome volunteers to help with interviewing, transcribing and other jobs associated with the project.

Richard Stenlake January 2011

PART ONE

Empire, Enlightenment and Improvement.

Birth of a Mill Town

Introduction

The road signs at the edge of Catrine read 'Historical Mill Town'. Besides being ungrammatical, this is something of an understatement, an underselling of Catrine's importance in history. Catrine was not any old mill town. At Catrine all the major themes of late eighteenth century Scottish history converge, with the world-renowned poet Robert Burns floating around too! The story of Catrine's origins as a mill town embraces all the vibrancy of the 1770s and 1780s, a period when Scotland pulsated with dynamism, when the spirit of the age was one of 'improvement', improvement of oneself, of others, of agriculture and of industry. For those at the helm these were exciting times, but for much of the populace the changes being wrought brought despair and misery. Five people are at the forefront of the story – George Dempster, David Dale, Richard Arkwright, Claud Alexander and Robert Burns. For this early period a reasonable amount of source material is available to tell their side of the story. In Part Two it is the voices of the workers that are heard.

A print of Catrine *circa* 1816. The original print of this would probably have been in colour but its whereabouts are unknown. Can you help?

George Dempster and Richard Arkwright

George Dempster

Richard Arkwright

Dempster is a fascinating character and is himself the subject of a huge tome *The Gentleman Usher The Life & Times of George Dempster 1732 -1818*. The book describes him as a 'Giant of a Man' – he was estate owner, passionate advocate of agricultural improvement, industrialist, member of parliament for 30 years, and a Director of the East India Company. He was always on the lookout for fresh ideas which could be transplanted to improve the Scottish economy (and occasionally his own pocket too) and so the circumstances of how he met the English cotton magnate, Richard Arkwright, on the journey back from parliament to his seat in Scotland in 1783, is thought to have been more deliberate than this account actually suggests:

To amuse my wife and myself, and to rest my horses I generally halted a few days at the differing watering places by the way; and in that year…being particularly captivated with the romantic scenery of Matlock, we staid a week or ten days there. In the course of a forenoon's ride, I discovered, in a romantic valley, a palace of a most enormous size, having, at least, a score of windows of a row, and five or six stories in height.

This 'palace' was Arkwright's cotton mill at Cromford. Dempster then called on the great man *to see the head from whence the mill had sprung*. Despite being a self-confessed workaholic (whose wife eventually left him as a result), Arkwright knew a networking opportunity when it presented itself (literally in this case) on his doorstep. The next time he was in London he looked up Dempster and offered to 'assist' him in setting up a cotton mill in Scotland. The following year, 1784, workaholic Arkwright found the time in the October to visit Scotland where he was given the freedom of the city of Glasgow. A visit to the Falls of Clyde near Lanark in the company of the banker and merchant David Dale took place the day after. Arkwright pronounced this the perfect site for cotton mills and he, Dempster and Dale together went into partnership. Work commenced on the mills at New Lanark in 1785. But being a partner in the biggest cotton works in Britain was not sufficient for Arkwright. This was just the foundation stone of a new cotton industry in Scotland that Arkwright hoped would come to rival that of Manchester and then ruin it. Arkwright had made a fortune from his patented water frame in the years from 1778 when it had been made available to other manufacturers under licence; they had to buy the machinery from him and pay an ongoing royalty per spindle, but by the time of Dempster's visit, enforcement had become difficult. Small manufacturers in isolated locations were simply stealing the technology and Arkwright pursued others in court, but with only a few years to run until his last patent was to expire in 1789 (and it was nullified in a 1785 court case) much of his income looked set to disappear. The matter had become heated, with threats to Arkwright's life should he step into Manchester. Scotland had little in the way of a cotton industry but plenty of available labour and water power. Arkwright's plan, and it was a big plan, was to populate Scotland with new large cotton mills, enriching himself further along the way and *take a razor to Manchester*. Enraged by the threat on his life and by years of attempts to break his patent, he sought revenge. Although he understood both the technical and business aspects of the industry intimately, he needed to cultivate the great, the good and the greedy to join him in this venture and so he toured Scotland encouraging men of power, money and influence to become mill owners and those he could not meet, like the Duke of Atholl, received an anonymous letter extolling the potential profits from spinning. To set the ball rolling, at New Lanark Dale, Dempster and Arkwright appear to have been equal partners in terms of capital invested. Arkwright also provided the technical know-how with engineers to design and construct the water supply system, designs for buildings and machinery, and training for key workers at his Cromford Mill in Derbyshire. Once New Lanark had been brought into operation and was profitable, Arkwright didn't need to be a partner at other mills as the potential riches of cotton spinning became more obvious, but he would still help (as he did at Catrine) with construction and machinery – and he would take a royalty from every spindle in the mill.

David Dale

Dale was born in 1739, the son of a grocer in Ayrshire's Stewarton. After an apprenticeship as a weaver and a period as a clerk, he set up on his own account in Glasgow as a linen merchant. His marriage to the daughter of one of the Royal Bank of Scotland's directors did his career no harm and in due course he became the Royal Bank's first agent in Glasgow, just at a time the West of Scotland was industrialising, funded by the profits from the transatlantic trades of slaves, sugar, tobacco and cotton. This was a heady financial environment with capital from the profits of these trades feeding a booming economy. The vastness of the profits possible in trade or industry allowed for fairly extravagant interest rates to be charged by lenders. For example a three month bill of exchange would cost the borrower 5% say. Such a bill would be payable three months from when written, a bit like a post-dated cheque, but the recipient instead of waiting three months for the cash could get paid immediately for it, although the bank took a further rake-off by discounting the full amount, the size of the discount depending on the risk of default. The margins being charged were sufficiently big to allow for the occasional default when a business went bust. Dale was in the right place at the right time. In the mid to late 1780s he made the transition from being a merchant and a banker to also being an industrialist, one of Scotland's foremost industrialists, for which he deserves greater recognition. At Catrine he was to become a partner with Claud Alexander.

Claud Alexander

Portrait of Claud Alexander, with his brother Boyd, attended by an Indian servant. Courtesy of Sotheby's.

Thanks to a wonderful set of letters in the National Archives of Scotland Claud Alexander's story can be told, at least in part. It begins in early 1772 with him travelling to India as a young writer (solicitor). By January 1774 he has already had his first promotion and has his life planned: *I am as well off at present as I ever could possibly expect, indeed a great deal better. For as things go just now, I don't dispair of scraping together a small pittance in the course of twenty or thirty years to enable me to spend my old days comfortably at home.* (GD 393-017)

In December that year his uncle writes to him about estates for sale in his native Renfrewshire: *Neither Fulwood nor Glandeston estates are sold yet more than Newton and are afraid more estates will be at market. So when you come home a rich Nabob, thinks there will be little fear of you finding an estate to purchase.* (GD 393-025) This has clearly not sunk in as in February 1775 Claud writes: *I don't know what possessed me of sending home money. It was a flight I took, I am ignorant how to employ it to any advantage. You must do the best you can, till I get more and think of some plan.* (GD 393-027) In a letter of February 1775, a common theme of Claud's letters, what a great time he is having, emerges: *my situation in this country is very agreeable. I eat well, and drink well and engage in no party.* (GD 393-040) In the meantime he is also in business on his own account investing in ships (cargoes) but despite dreadful losses remains upbeat. His letters are full of money and business matters, but his thoughts occasionally turn to women *much wanted here* as in this letter to his aunt in January 1778: *I am glad to hear that Miss Camille and Christy were gone to Edinburgh to pass a part of the winter and the spring. I hope they will not return single ladies. If they do, I shall say that the East Country gentlemen have no better taste than those in the West. I confess I have often found myself at a loss to decide which of the two I was most in love with.* (GD 393-057) and again in February 1779 in a letter to Mrs. Barclay: *Your niece Mrs. Clark is I am informed an excellent housewife, a great economist and fond mother, Good God what I have lost during my banishment. She told me she would have me and I have been sweating here saving my pay and batta expecting to get home before she took to herself a husband, and this is the way she has used me it is true I cannot boast of the fortune that Mr. Clark brings her but – Ah it does not signify twopence talking about it now.* (GD 393-080) He could perhaps console himself with the advancement to his fortune of his promotions. In May 1778 he was made Deputy Commissary General and then in the July became Commissary General. The appointment, based on merit, of a desk bound civilian outraged certain parties in the East India Company, which essentially was a military organisation, but Claud brazened it out and in a letter offers his viewpoint of the situation, that although they wanted a military man most of the previous occupants of the post have resigned it with pleasure and that the job entails the careful checking of accounts and requires a man with a mind for business, in his view *a man bred for business almost since his infancy is more likely to give satisfaction than a military man who has been bred to arms and a marching from camp to camp, of course used to a stirring life and must have contracted a dislike to accounts and a sedentary life.* (GD 393-092) By August 1780 thoughts were turning to coming home. David Anderson writes to Claud: *What a dark cloud begins to gather over this country! We must do everything in our power to secure a comfortable place to retire to. I am afraid of Renfrewshire – they say it rains there almost incessantly, and the people in the towns are greatly addicted to praying and drinking – neither of which do I excell or wish to excell in.* By January 1781 a plan has obviously formulated in Claud's mind, as Uncle Neilson writes to him: *...There is none of the lands you mention coming to market yett, but if they do, or any other in Renfrewshire, will remember your orders. There are a great many lands in Airshire at present to market, which I think preferable to this county* [Renfrewshire]. *But as yett knows of none with a good house upon them, which I suppose you would like. If any such cast up, as you seem to wish your money sunk that way, will if in health be a purchaser for you.* (GD 393-104) But love was not far from Claud's thoughts. In a long personal letter dated August 1781 McDonnell who is in Krishngar writes to Claud: *My dear friend Your letter of the 31st July gave me so much pleasure that I feel I must answer it immediately, but what shall I say first? You have given me a kind of history of your life and traced it to the consummation of all human wishes, vis. innate happiness. It was needless to tell me that however, for within the circle of my numerous acquaintances I cannot fix upon one who is so intrinsically happy, or who has so much reason to be as yourself. There is only one more thing which in my opinion can render you more so, and that is marrying a good-natured agreeable girl and becoming the father of a family. I know your cast of mind points*

Ballochmyle House prior to being remodelled in 1886.

this way as well as mine, but my dear friend it is a lottery in which we risk a great deal and the choice will require the utmost prudence to direct it. Your girls who want to get married never show their real tempers. It will require a long acquaintance with them before we are able to judge of the qualities of their hearts; for it is there and there only, we are to look for those comforts which we expect from the marriage state. I have no idea that there can be a greater hell (except a bad conscience) than finding the woman of your heart who you had married for her amiable qualities, turn out contrary to your expectations, and become a disturber of your domestick quiet instead of rendering home agreeable. I absolutely think such a thing would be the death of me… (GD 393-111)

This letter also offers an insight into how well Claud is thought of and maybe a hint of things to come: *…In short you have done an infinity of good and will do a great deal more. And nothing gives me so much pleasure as the hearing you so generally well-spoken of.* (GD 393-111)

By 1782 there was a definite plan in Claud's mind which he was approaching with military precision: *In my last I wrote to you particularly to know what estates in Renfrewshire and the neighbourhood were likely soon to be at market and requested that you and your brother-in-law – G.H. would give me your opinion of them, mentioning their situation, rents, taxes, produce, number of acres, probable value etc. etc. in short I wished to have every information that a man wanting to buy land would be desirous of knowing…I am told by a gentleman lately arrived here from Airshire that the half of that county was to be sold and it was not expected that the estates would fetch more than from 18 to 21 years purchase…I keep my health exceptionally well and very happy – I wish I may be as much so at home, there is certainly much more pleasure in expectation of what is to come, than in real possession…* (GD 393-113+114)

By 1782 Claud had resolved to come home and was attempting to buy an estate. The Ballamyl (Ballochmyle) estate was mentioned as being likely to be on the market soon, but Claud meantime was outbid for the Houston estate in his native Renfrewshire *...It is true that the money in Mr. Neilson's hands in November last would not have been sufficient to have paid for the Houston estate. But in a few months after the date of your letter I suppose that I would have money and good Bills* [of exchange] *under acceptance to the amount of £35,000...And besides this sum I have about £6,500 at Madras laying there for Navy or Army Bills, and about £6,000 more at Bencoolen...You will perhaps wonder where I got all this money. Be it known to you that from the 1st of August 1781 to 31st July 1783 I cleared, after paying all my expenses, one lack, fifteen thousand, one hundred and forty rupees. So that I found myself on the 31st July last, when I balanced my books, worth four lc, sixteen thousand, three hundred and forty two current rupees...If all my Remittances turn out good, I expect to arrive in England worth fifty thousand pounds...*(GD 393-133) He then turned down the Craigie estate for the reason it was too near to Ayr and he would be pestered with disagreeable visitors and gives us an insight into his frugal lifestyle and good husbandry *...Your brother-in-law and I had a good laugh when we came to that part of your letter wherein you tell me "That I must reserve at least £15,000, after purchasing an estate of a thousand a year, for the purpose of furnishing my house, purchasing carriages, horses etc. etc. and even to support the East Indian Stile of Life" Day observed, when I had got to the end of the paragraph, "he does not know you, Claud". Indeed my Friend, you do not if you think so, for in the first place I mean to have nothing Indian about me except my brown face, which I cannot help. No Sandie, I shall do as other lairds do, and show the world that we Company's servants are not all the people that they take us to be. Plain roast and boiled is good enough for me, with a little East India Madeira to wash it down. And in place of setting at the bottle, pouring punch into my guts and destroying my bowels, I would prefer walking out or retiring to the drawing room to drink tea or coffee and enjoy the agreeable conversation of the ladies. As for gambling and horse-racing, I know nothing about them, and am determined never to spend more than a thousand a year...It is owing to the extravagance of living in Scotland that so many estates are now at market. I was sorry to see in a late letter from Edinburgh to a friend of mine "that it was as common nowadays for a Scotch laird to break as it was for Crockery. The simile is not a very good one however I am afraid it is too true."* (GD 393-134+135) Although he'd been outbid on the Houston estate it turns out that the owner didn't want to sell it to him anyway on account of a love match with his first cousin which had gone sour. By the time of this letter from Claud to Barclay in September 1785 Ballochmyle had been bought for him instead *...Mr. Speirs has, to be sure, paid pretty well for the* [Houston] *estate but...I would have given more money for it. For I have a great pre-election for the Gryffe* [river in Renfrewshire] *and the neighbourhood to me was worth all the difference of price. Besides, I had a plan of making the town a place of great industry. However, notwithstanding all I have wrote, it is most probable I shall like Ballochmyle equally well...I see that I have paid a good deal for the house, which I am told is elegant, and the pleasure grounds are well laid out. Everybody writes me what a beautiful place I have got, but I should have been contented with a house half the size.* (GD 393-146+147)

The key sentence in the above is *I had a plan of making the town a place of great industry.* But for an eighteenth century lovers' tiff there would have been no Catrine as we know it today. But Ballochmyle it was! In December 1784 Claud had written about adding to the estate: *Should any farm near to the house of B-myle be in the market such as Kingencleugh, ...I would not like that they went past me...* (GD 393-168) The second part of the letter gives an insight into the form that his paternalistic approach to Catrine will take: *...I always act on the extremes I am either a warm friend or a great enemy according as those whom I take by the hand behave themselves, experience teacheth me that there is nothing better in this world for making a young man turn out well than by hanging out rewards and punishment to him.* (GD 393-169) Later in this letter Claud refers to a painting of himself and his brother Boyd: *By the same ship* [the Southampton] *I have sent my picture which I request you will get out of India House as soon as possible as it is a capital painting and I should be sorry if it got any damage; as it was painted by Zoffany a member of the Academy. I imagine it will be exempted by duties.* (GD 393-171) This painting (illustrated on page 6) was auctioned by Sotheby's on 8th December 2010 and sold for £769,250 including buyer's premium. As the final act of his preparations to coming home in July 1786 Claud wrote a new will (in case he was lost at sea).

Building Catrine

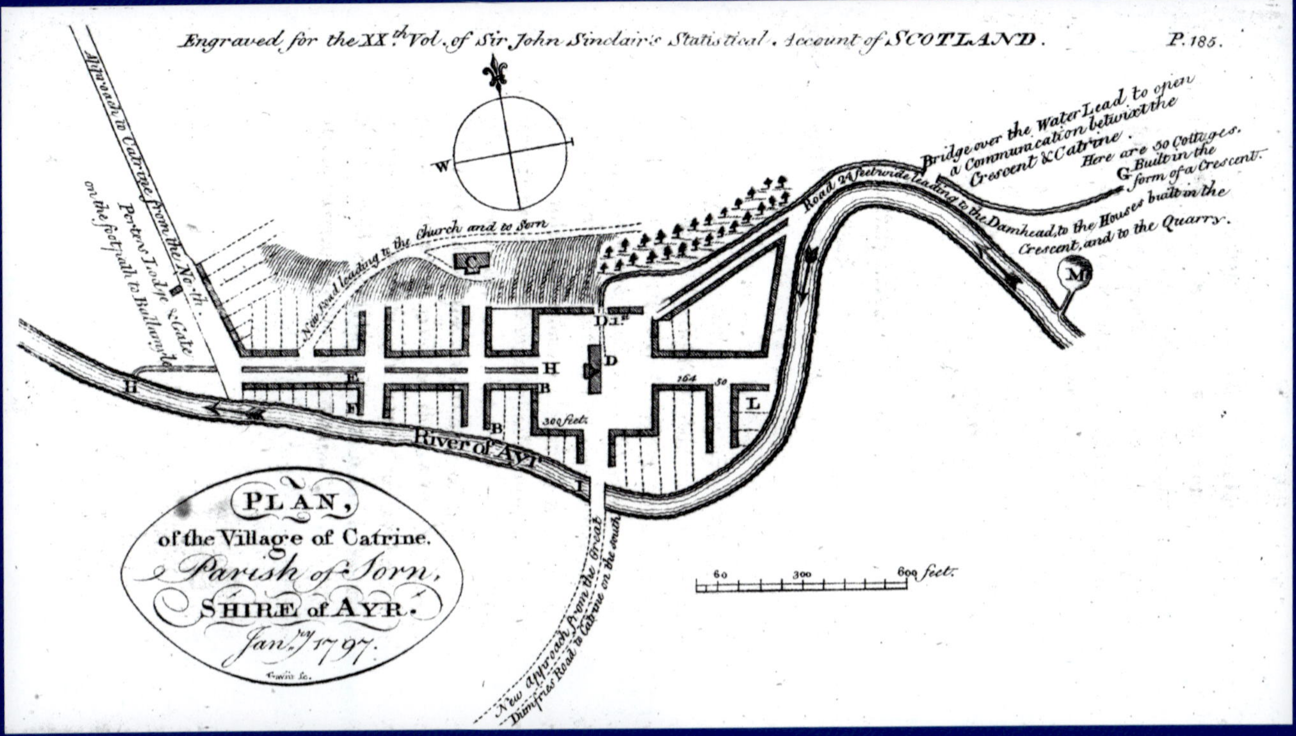

Claud didn't waste much time on his return home. By February 1787 he was in partnership with David Dale at Catrine to build a cotton works, and construction was underway soon after.

On 5th March 1787 Claud Alexander wrote to his neighbour, the renowned James Boswell, biographer of Dr. Johnson and laird of the Auchinleck estate. The letter gives us a rough date for when construction at Catrine began (spring 1787), the location of the corn mill, and also suggests that Alexander and Boswell were meeting socially:

…I should have written to you sooner, had not I expected to have had the pleasure of seeing you, to have made known to you a favourite scheme which I have had in my mind these two mon[ths] *past of erecting a Cotton Mill on Catrine Holm and to have requested your assistance, every thing I believe is now settled I now intend beginning as soon as the weather will permit altho' the mill is to be set down above your property yet as it will require more water than the present Corn Mill which is situated about two hundred yards below where the Cotton Mill is intended to be erected it will be necessary to have your consent best any objection should be made after the work is begun. I hope it will be of benefit to your tenants as well as to mine, we intend to weave the coarse cottons on the*

EXPLANATION.

A, The twiſt-mill, in the centre of a ſquare of 300 feet. The great wheel has a fall of $29\frac{1}{2}$ feet.

B to B, The jeanie factory; the carding and roving in which is performed by the water after it comes from the twiſt-mill; the lade from which is all arched.

C, The church.

DD, Is an aqueduct-bridge, which conveys the water from the hill to the top of the twiſt-mill wheel.

E, Is the corn-mill, and is alſo worked by the tail-water of the twiſt-mill.

F, Is a ſituation feued for a wauk or fulling mill.

From G to D 1ſt, Is the water brought from the dam to the aqueduct-bridge.

H to H, Is the tail-water from the twiſt-mill; it is arched until it paſſes through the ſquare, and then runs through the centre of the principal ſtreet, with bridges over it oppoſite to the three croſs ſtreets.

I, Is a propoſed bridge over the river Ayr, to communicate with the Dumfries road.

L, A brewery.

M, A fine free-ſtone quarry.

N. B. The proprietor of the village of Catrine does not feu to the river ſide, but has reſerved the ground along the river for a walk, 12 or 15 feet broad, for the health of the inhabitants, and which he is now facing with a ſtone and lime wall.

spot and to bring as many manufacturers there as possible. My partner David Dale is perhaps not unknown to you. You will oblige me by sending an answer to this as soon as may be convenient to you. I hope we shall have the pleasure of seeing you and Mrs. Boswell here next summer...

Boswell replied from London on 14th March with a messy letter full of scorings out: *I am favoured with your letter informing me of your scheme of erecting a Cotton Mill on Catrine Holm above my property, which will require more water than the present corn mill. I do not understand it enough to judge how I may be affected by it. But as I am desirous to comply with the wishes of a neighbour whose character I respect, I do not hesitate to assure you of my acquiescence in what you propose...*(Boswell Collection, Beinecke Rare Book and Manuscript Library, Yale University.)

Arkwright's technicians designed a state of the art water supply system consisting of a curved weir of a silt-clearing design, a reservoir, an open lade and a masonry aqueduct to take the water into the Twist Mill, which contained 5,420 spindles. With just the Twist Mill operating work could commence. Raw cotton came into the works in bales and it left as cotton twist or thread. This was either sold on or woven into cloth on handlooms by weavers in their own houses, hence Catrine's main street being named after St. Germain, the patron saint of weavers, although by a cruel 'twist' of fate the town was the first location in Scotland to have power looms installed, in 1806.

Catrine was an ideal site for a mill complex on account of a good fall of water – from weir to Twist Mill wheel was twenty-nine and a half feet. In 1790 a jeanie house (spinning mill) was added and there was still sufficient water power to work the carding and roving there after leaving the Twist Mill. This water went on to power the corn mill in Cornmill Street.

Claud's letter to Frank Redfearn of April 1791 tells of the maelstrom of activity he had been engulfed by since his return from India: *I am a most terrible fellow. You may abuse me as you please. I deserve every bad epithet that the language affords for neglecting thus scandously to reply to your most friendly letters. I can account for it in no way but the eternal hurry and confusion that I have ever been in almost since my arrival. But I have now got pretty well over it.* (GD 393-187) The letter continues with detail of not just the works but family also: *John Bayne, John Fergusson and Day McDowall passed some days with me at Ballamyle last harvest. The two former were quite confounded with the cotton mill – (I should rather say mills), as we built another last summer. McDowall had seen one before. You would be surprised to see our great water-wheel of 30 feet diameter turning a great number of lesser wheels which spin about 5,000 spindles at a time, and also prepare the cotton for spinning by carding and roving it. But for a more particular account of my operations here, I must refer you to James Colvin who has seen some part of them.*

I have got two fine boys, and I am now busy building an addition to my house as I found a nursery in a retired part of the house absolutely necessary. (GD 393-188)

There was no resident population so an entire company town was built around the works to accommodate the incoming workforce. These were Highlanders who had been evicted in the infamous Clearances and who faced the stark choice of starvation, forced emigration or employment in the new cotton mills. This may sound hard, indeed it was hard, but works like these had need of great numbers of women and children, able to slip under machines and with nimble fingers. Dempster was involved with the mills at Stanley, together with Arkwright and others, so was asked for plans of houses. Go to the village of Stanley today and it is like looking at Catrine in the mirror. Dale and Dempster were concerned about emigration from the Highlands – in providing this new employment they thought this was helping not just themselves, but the nation as a whole. When war broke out with France it was their patriotic duty also to prevent potential soldiers slinking off to America through lack of work.

Dale had a two-pronged approach to supplying himself with a workforce. He advertised in the papers in Argyll and the Highlands, and perhaps more controversially scoured the workhouses of Glasgow and Edinburgh for children, brought to his mills and indentured for seven years. In return he offered regular food, shelter, clothing and education and in comparison to other company towns Catrine was considered humane. Children were not employed at the works until they were nine years old and could attend school on the fifth floor of the mill. Workers hurt in the company's service were allowed medical assistance and full wages. Villagers were also able to lease tacks of land on which to grow potatoes. Despite all this, things did not go to plan for the partners, as this letter from Ballochmyle to Miss Touchet in India dated 16th April 1791 shows. Claud begins by bemoaning the lack of 'Indians' [meaning former colleagues returned from India like himself] locally but consoles himself …*Perhaps I should not be so much at home neither, were it not that Mrs. Alexander has nursed both our children, which has kept her much at home. And I have such a large family in my newly erected village to look after, that these and the management too of my estate keep me constantly employed. I have now got above a thousand souls in the village, altho' the mill is not yet compleated. You would wonder to see what a deal of carding, roving and spinning and reeling is going on there. Not less than a ton of yarn is spun and sent into market every week. I have just been finishing a house for a Sunday's school, and a subscription is now going about for a Church. We are getting on apace, you see.* (GD 393-190)
But then there is a discordant note, that all his 'improvements' have not been universally lauded:

But I am much blamed about these cotton works. They say it is not the employment of a gentleman to give bread to so many people. I beg your pardon, I meant to say that a cotton spinner is not the employment of a gentleman. But I am satisfied in my own mind that I am doing good. Therefore I do not mind what they say. (GD 393-190)

Above & opposite: These are the two faces of the famous "two-faced clock", two grandfather clocks housed side by side in a single case. The clock was made *circa* 1795 and used to be in the mill manager's office in the Old Mill.

Support for the subscription for the Chapel of Ease was only lukewarm and Claud ended up paying for most it not all of it himself. Worse than this some of the villagers chose to dissent and not bother with going to church. This was unheard of, although the poet Robert Burns, made to sit on the repentance stool in the kirk at Mauchline for his amorous adventures, had little time for its hypocrisy. The new villagers were also over-fond of whisky (something else they had in common with Burns), so Claud arranged for a brewery to be built (which stayed in business until it finally closed in 1928) to wean them off the water of life and onto ale.

A small, obviously incomplete, collection of letters in Glasgow's Mitchell Library from David Dale to Claud Alexander during the period February 1787 to August 1796 give a series of snapshots of the rise and fall of Catrine. The letters are a mixture of micro management and woe, with Dale passing on his knowledge of operations at New Lanark (where he seems to have been a regular visitor). Already a financial wizard, he became a hands-on industrialist in a trade that had to adapt quickly to technological developments.

Essentially these first years at Catrine went well. Profits flowed enabling the complex to be expanded and the workforce rose to about 1,600. But in 1789 the French Revolution took place. In Scotland the initial reaction was not one of horror, but enthusiasm that a despot had been overthrown in favour of a constitutional monarchy. By 1790 both sides of the argument were in print and being debated vigorously by the public at large. By 1792 Scotland was being torn apart as the argument raged with more emotion. When dogs barked at strangers the gentry were nervous. France was threatened with invasion by Austria and others. Robert Burns bought four confiscated carronades at a roup with the intention of sending them to France. In Ross-shire, roles were reversed as tenants evicted sheep. Demonstrations in the towns turned to riots, the military were increasingly involved and the government's nerves were on edge. By the beginning of 1793 the government was trying people for sedition but later that year war broke out with France and this crystallised feelings, so much so that by 1795 the songsmith Burns had changed his tune and churned out a forgettable and forgotten jingoistic piece entitled *Does Haughty Gaul Invasion Threat?* and joined the Dumfries Fencibles.

As soon as hostilities broke out there was a run on the banks as silver and gold were drained away to pay for the war. This had a devastating effect on first the banks, then the entire Scottish economy which had been building itself on a mountain of bills of exchange, financial derivative instruments, bits of paper intrinsically worthless bearing a promise to pay not now but later. Suddenly cash was king again. Loans were called in. On 23rd March 1793 the seeds of the problem were already apparent to Dale: *paper transactions are at present so precarious* he wrote. As the principal agent handling this form of finance in the West of Scotland he should have known!

Around this time £6,000 of the partners' money seems to have gone adrift in London. In May Dale reports *Dennistoun have stopd payments today* and then answers a question about how safe Royal Bank shares are to hold, that the owners do not have unlimited liability for losses. By June the problem of the £6,000 is still unresolved: *...No blame lies at our door with regard to the transfer of the £6,000 for we reap no benefit from its present situation.* And where is the money? *...We would be had to think that no part of the money is in Messrs Ingram possession whether this is the case or not I shall not pretend to say but the disappointment has very much discouraged me and I must fear that I will be obliged to discharge a number of work people as the weekly wages of Lanark and Catrine Mills is very considerable besides discharging a number of engagements I am under by bills* [of exchange] *for cotton wool – it is a great misfortune that your health does not permit you going to London as that would be the most efficient way of getting the affair settled...I wish it were in my power to go with you as I think I might perhaps get* [the truth] *out from person or another in London if I were on the spot but I can't get away even for an hour.*

Things got worse as Dale, unable to call in term loans, left his masters at the Royal Bank's head office financially embarrassed. He was accused of ruining them and the bank had to be bailed out by the government. Now he was vilified, but it had not been long since Dale had been the golden boy, with not too many questions being asked when the profits were flowing. Over 200 years later Sir Fred Goodwin found himself in an almost parallel position, and for many of the same underlying reasons, atop a house of cards built on paper profits. However, in the eighteenth century smaller banks could be let go of as Dale's letter of 1st November of 1793 observes: *I have but a moment before the post goes away to say that the Thomsons Bank will stop today desire the manager at Catrine to take some of their notes...this information may also be of some use to you.* By stop he means that the bank will cease trading, literally by shutting its doors, leaving holders of their notes with worthless paper. However, the banks were all in it together then every bit as much as they are now (as Western economies recently discovered to their cost when

Lehman Brothers was allowed to go bust and it caused a chain reaction through the banking system) and elaborate control systems were in place (or so they thought – aha this sounds familiar too) to stop banks over-reaching themselves. Banks employed note pickers and pushers. Banks pushed (into circulation) their own notes – a bank might lend to a business concern and make the advance with its own notes. The theory was that these notes were backed by assets, whether it be precious metal, land or property. A bank's note could be presented at its office and exchanged for gold or silver. Clearly there was a danger that banks could (and did) issue more notes than were backed by assets. The free market offered the check in the system. If a bank was suspected by its rivals of overissuing notes, its competitors employed note-pickers who went about picking up the rogue bank's notes by exchanging other notes for them. Having gathered up a large number these would then be presented at the bank's office for payment in silver or gold coin. If the bank could not meet its obligations it would simply shut its doors either permanently or temporarily. When a bank stopped (ceased trading) it might be closed for months before opening again. But when a bank went bust other banks still trading would honour its notes and exchange their notes for its. A cynic might observe that this was the exchange of one worthless bit of paper for another, but from the banks' point of view it was a question of ensuring that the public did not lose confidence in paper money as a whole. This theme also plays on over 200 years later!

This letter of 1st November ends with a partly indecipherable plea to *raise* [?] *money for carrying on the works*

In January 1794 Dale reports how bad trade is due to war pressures: *...Mr.* [??] *informs me that Mr. Arkwright and the great spinning houses have reduced their prices very low to make orders*

On 24th March 1794 Dale writes a wretched letter: *I have rec'd of the 22nd current to day it took a great deal of thought to bring myself to write to you on a subject that I knew must give you so much pain* [?] *you cannot have a greater aversion than I have to throwing the people out of employment but alas what can I do I believe there are few individuals in the nation that have made greater exertions than I have done to carry on the works in which I am engaged and I know you have as much as I am inclined to continue to do this to the utmost of my power and win* [?] *beyond my power I will try to carry on the works for another month...*

The dream was over. Dale's business empire was falling apart. Blantyre had already been sold to James Monteith. The other mills would go over the following years. On 27th August 1796 Dale writes to Claud: *Yesterday Mr. Allan Clark's brother* [?] *dined with me and we had a good deal of conversation about the Jenny House concern...they could not accept...taking the jenny house off your hands and mine...*

Catrine was up for sale! And in 1801 it was finally sold as a going concern to James Finlay & Company. As this letter dated 15th May 1801 from Claud to his brother Boyd indicates it was something of a relief... *I have never yet thanked you for your letter dated in March enclosing McLeans* [?] *acct. discharged, the fact is I rec'd it in Edi. where I was only in for six days having sold the mills to Kirkman Findlay & Co I was hurried back to deliver them over to the new Comps which was done on the 13th of last month that is to say they began spinning on their own account on that day but all my trouble began from that period & I have scarcely written to any person since then excepting to Mrs. A & to my friend David Dale – However as it is the last year's trouble I shall have with the Mills I do not begrudge it.*

JAMES FINLAY & Co LTD
BOMBAY & CALCUTTA.

Robert Burns

When it comes to Catrine, the man who has come to dominate Ayrshire's tourist industry today was something of a bit player. So much of his correspondence is lost, and the story of his loves and lyricism is more sexy (sometimes literally!) that the association between him and the Industrial Revolution exploding on his doorstep in the years 1786-7 at Catrine has completely slipped under the radar of his biographers. His 'bit of a lad' reputation antagonises women and his extensive use of the Scots language is problematic to the English who for the most part find it impenetrable, but he remains lauded by much of the former communist world who suffered bastardised and sanitised translations of his work but loved it anyway, and the Americans who think he 'invented' Hallowe'en. Amongst all this passion, some very interesting questions about Burns do not seem to have been asked, let alone answered.

We lack the smoking gun of a letter of Burns' feelings about the nascent mill town of Catrine, which would tie the strands of the historical themes together, but given the fraught relationship he had with the Alexanders it's doubtful if he could have brought himself to discuss it dispassionately.

This story begins with a major banking scandal of the eighteenth century, the demise of Douglas Heron & Co, otherwise and popularly known as the Ayr Bank. This bank's notes were underwritten by the estates of the landed gentry who were its shareholders. The bank quickly expanded, giving out cash advances (overdrafts) with too much haste. Some of these were employed usefully, but others were gambled on bills of exchange, a case of rogue traders dealing in derivatives. Instead of "fessing up" the compromised bank became complicit and used several dubious methods to keep afloat, such as raising bills of exchange on London agents working in cahoots with them (fraud), keeping the truth from the shareholders (deception) until in 1772 the inevitable happened and the bank imploded spectacularly. Shareholders not only lost all their investment but discovered to their horror that they had unlimited liability and had to make good all the bank's losses in the proportion to the number of shares they held (hence the importance of the question about Royal Bank shares answered in Dale's letter to Claud of March 1793). And so it was that the Whitefoords' estate of Ballamyl (Ballochmyle) was sold to Claud Alexander although Claud did not evict Sir John Whitefoord but allowed him to stay on in the house for a while. Burns had been a frequent visitor to Ballochmyle House and the Whitefoords' departure occasioned his writing in 1783 of *The Braes of Ballochmyle*, a mournful song of loss and farewell.

Besides talking to small rodents the ploughman poet also pursued (perhaps admired is a better word) the women of the parish with vigour (the "belles of Mauchline"). His sulking about the Whitefoords' departure evaporated when he caught sight of Claud Alexander's sister, Wilhelmina (whom in the summer of 1786 he immortalised in "The Lass o Ballochmyle") who qualified for his admiration on the usual basis, namely that she was female and had a pulse. Wilhelmina was walking on her own along the Ladies' Walk, a path that ran from Ballochmyle House to the Gorge but is now mostly densely overgrown. The bemused lady, in her early thirties and still unmarried, thought Burns was mocking her with the title of the song and failed to reply to the letter which he sent to her requesting her blessing for it to be published, which scholars suggest was mostly unnecessary as she wasn't actually named in it. Perhaps the letter to Wilhelmina was just an attempt to incite an invitation to the big house, but his letter was ignored and Burns was also ignored by Claud Alexander whose letters indicate his nature was that he had little time or inclination for social callers at his home. However, it is known that they met on at least one occasion. The following year, 1787, Burns presided over the 25th July meeting of St. James Lodge in Tarbolton when Claud and Professor Dugald Stewart of Edinburgh University were admitted as honorary members. Perhaps this rapprochement had come about from when in October 1786, Burns had been a guest at Nether Catrine House, Professor Stewart's country home. This could be seen from Ballochmyle (Claud Alexander used a telescope to survey his estate from an upstairs window) and sat about a mile away on the other side of the River Ayr beyond a fertile holm which nestled by some bends of the river. Despite its historic significance this building suffered a deeply inappropriate conversion not so many years ago.

The exact date work began on the construction of Catrine is not known, but in February 1787 a Mr. Abercrombie was tendering to supervise the work so it cannot have been much after. Tantalisingly Burns, who had spent most of his adult life pottering around in a rural area, would suddenly have found himself face to face with the Industrial Revolution if he had remained farming at Mossgiel at that time. However, although he had been considering emigrating to Jamaica, where he had intended to work as an overseer (of slaves) on a sugar plantation, on 31st July 1786 he had published the Kilmarnock Edition *Poems Chiefly in the Scottish Dialect* having carefully pre built a subscription list . His career as a celebrity poet took off and Burns headed off to Edinburgh for a year funded by the proceeds of the book. Rich and poor alike were fans of his work. George Dempster was a great admirer of it. The feeling was mutual. In *Epistle to James Smith* Burns wrote *a title, Dempster merits it.* At other times he described Dempster as *a true blue Scot* and in a nod to his views on 'improvement' approvingly described his *zeal-inspired tongue.* Alas, despite the links between Dempster and Claud Alexander, and the latter's intentions as an 'improver', Burns maintained his sulk. When he added notes to *The Lass o Ballochmyle* for the Glenriddell manuscript he wrote:

Well, Mr. Burns, and did the lady give you the desired permission? No! She was too fine a Lady to notice so plain a compliment. As to her great brothers, whom I have since met in life on more equal terms of respect [presumably this is a reference to meetings at the Lodge?] – *why should I quarrel their want of attention to me? When Fate swore their purses should be full, Nature was equally positive that their heads should be empty. 'Men of their fashion were surely incapable of being impolite?' Ye canna mak a silk-purse o a sow's lug.*

Pot, meet kettle! Claud Alexander loses the Houston estate in his beloved Renfrewshire as a result of a petty grudge arising from the vendor being jilted by his cousin. Burns makes a personal attack on just the kind of Scot he approves of elsewhere, because he feels he has been snubbed by the Alexanders. Perhaps he simply failed to understand Claud's personality as a man focused on devotion to work and family. Claud Alexander's letters show him to have been far from empty-headed, but instead, sober, dependable, responsible and careful with his money. There's no doubt that at the time of the snub Robert Burns had an interesting mind, but given what we know of Claud it's easy to see how Burns failed to get an invitation to his home. It is so very unfortunate that on account of his wounded feelings the viewpoint of an otherwise rational man about what was happening at Catrine with the birth of the mill town is lost to history.

So it went from the carding to the drawing and then moved up to the roving?

And the roving made it smaller again…and then it was put up to the spinning until it was like threads… Once the roving was done it was sent up to all the spinners.

The spinning was on three floors and the very top one was trainees?

Yes, they were all spinning. Once the spinning was done and the bobbins were all ready they were moved by carts across the street. Another sort of spinning took place to get it ready for the weaving. They made fine cotton and very fine, and then it went to the Bleach Works as large bales of fabric where they were made into sheets and some into towels. And even some bales were sent out for the army during the war and I know one or two people who put their name and address in the bales and got boyfriends and married them!

John Johnston (born 1923): *I had two or three different jobs in the mill. I worked the elevator for a while; I worked in the Carding Room; I pushed the stuff from the big mill to the Weaving Shed. …You used to go where you were put. The Carding Room dealt wi the raw cotton and it went through the machines. It was teased up and then it went in tae a roll…a beam. Then it was put onto the machines and it made the cotton into…a rope…just like a rope, and it coiled into these…beacons they called them or something like that. Then that went up through the mill, you see, to the different departments. You had the Carding Room, the spinning, the roving, the winding and it finished up at the top. Then it went from the top across the road to the new mills to the Weaving Shed. It was made into cloth there. Sheets, towels, blinds…anything! They made everything! …Oh, I liked the mill. I was quite happy there. When I started in the mill, I think it was eight shilling a week…and that went on till I was 16. It wisnae a great wage. The miners were making more money…it was a dangerous job down the mines! They were entitled to that, a better wage…*

How many people worked in the mill?

Well, it could vary. It's hard to tell…because there were flats. Say the Carding Room where I worked to begin with there was two boys, what we ca'ed boys then, and there were maybe two men and four or five women and of course we had the foreman. That's about that room. But when you went up to the next flat there could have been maybe fifty in it, and it could be the same right up to where I told you. I would reckon the old mill, there would be close to…nearly two hundred…it took five buses to take them home at night. There was an awfu work in Catrine at that time. Then you had, over at the Weaving Shed…that was hard work! Likes o ma wife, she was a weaver. She would maybe have four looms, three looms tae look after…they made their own pay in the Weaving Shed…like a bonus for how good the cloth was…I met her there in the mill.

…When I started it was from 8 o' clock in the morning till…6 at night. You had a half hour break for your meal at midday and then you worked until 11 o' clock on a Saturday. Five and a half days. Dinner was half an hour. Some went home. Some even went to Auchinleck because there was a special bus laid [on] *to run them o'er and run them back.*

…I remember a man getting his hand getting caught in a machine and he lost…two fingers or something…he must just have been putting the cotton in a wee bit too far…just the same as if he was turning…a washing wringer and if you went too near the end wi the cloth your hand would go in. I'm quite sure it was…Anthony Hennigan! But he survived and was back at his work…you got no time for being off ill. You had to be at work if you wanted to get money…holidays you didn't get a pay. The mills stopped for a fortnight…or a week, but you never got a pay, not when I worked in it…I don't think there was any holidays [at Christmas]*…everything went on. If there was a holiday at all it would be New Year holiday…in Scotland Christmas was just for children…it was just a weans' thing, ye ken, Christmas. There were nae great celebrations about Christmas that I remember, no. New Year, Hogmanay that was the night, it was great! …You had a bottle wi you and you first-footed. Maybe there wasn't much in the bottle but you first-footed. So you gave them your Ne'erday and they gave you your Ne'erday. You could be in five or six hooses before you were finished…open houses, open doors. It was open doors but it was maistly relations you went tae, ken, like maybe I would go tae ma aunties or cousins or something like that…if somebody came to your door, they would get in… Oh you got songs sung, aye, sure…I was never a good singer, no! I liked my own voice for singing, but not many else liked it! You got some good singers though. It was a good night…New Year, that would be the main holiday.*

CAPSTAN
P

Robert Dalziel (born 1946): *Of course,* [in] *the mill workers' time possibly…the men could be in the mines and the women would be in the mill cos they were predominantly female workforce in the mill, although the tenders and people* [like] *that were all male, and the foremen were mostly male… My mother was a weaver in the mill, she could be in charge of anything up to twelve looms at a time. In 1938 she was up at the Empire Exhibition in Bellahouston Glasgow doing weaving demonstrations for the company.* [Finlays] *had a big stall set up there: several looms were put up and they were demonstrating the weaving there… There were three or four of them chosen…it sounds silly but going from here to Glasgow in the 1930s was still quite a big thing, and to attend a big international exhibition was obviously quite a big thing so she remembered that very fondly. Her mother before her was my grandma Archibald. She was also a weaver in the mill, so was born in 1880s. You are now going back quite a long time to the mill history and her brother, my great uncle Robert, he was a foreman in the Lapping Room in the mill where they folded the cloth in great, huge, long lengths and could be anything up to 500 yards of cloth and to hold it up to the light to examine it for flaws, of course, and see there was no damaged sections. He had less happy memories. He was older and could remember the early 80s maybe 1870s and he talked of starting in the mill at the age of 13 or 14. The wet floor: because they kept the floor damp for the threads not to be broken when they were spinning… He was quite happy when the old mill was to be demolished although…many people felt shame when it was knocked down. Maybe people that could remember it from the earlier days had* [an] *ambivalent attitude. It had not always been happy memories, it was hard work and it was difficult work and the hours were long. He remembered twelve hour shifts…his father talked of fourteen hour shifts…people worked normally six days…my father for example was…for 20 odd years a labourer at Findlay the builders in Mauchline and he worked on Christmas Day…and he worked…all day on a Saturday and then fairly soon after he was out there in the 50s they got Saturday afternoon off and then shortly after that they – wonder of wonders – got holiday pay and they actually got paid the two weeks they had off on holiday.*

The mill bell controlled the world! …It didn't ring ridiculously early in the morning when I was a youngster. I think it was 8 o' clock that it rang and it rang at 6 o' clock at night… It controlled the life of the village, dominated the life of the village…"That's the mill bell! Back for teatime"! You certainly could hear it from a long way away.

THE GLASGOW HERALD
EMPIRE
EXHIBITION
SCOTLAND 1938

The Old Mill

Harry Houston (born 1939): *She* [his mother] *worked wi the looms and that and she stayed in Corn Mill Street, which was just next to the mill. She worked in there as a girl until she got married…it wasnae an easy job. It was a hard job for them. Her hands were always taped up and that sorta thing… She used to tell me aboot how there was a lot o dust below the looms and younger wans used to go in and clean a' this oot which…you had to watch what you were doing there as well…that's where the first time I realised they had a mill bank. She ta'en me to this one day and I always remember the big gates as we went in – they had roon buts and these big steps and we went up to this big office which was huge to me and there was an old guy brought this huge book oot, this ledger, …and that was the first time I had ever seen a five pound note.*

…When they worked they got paid, when they didnae work they didnae get paid, and that was basically it! …What they had to dae, they had a wee insurance thing. They used to have a penny insurance scheme, my mum and dad. They used to save up that way.

Ruth Sharp: *I was born in this house here* (below)*…It was the old school house where they educated the workers…this building here was the school…so I was born practically in the yard there! It's demolished now. That's where the big mill was. This was the corner of the yard…these are the trees at the entrance to the big gate that let them into the mill…there were four of them. In fact there was quite a lot of trouble about these trees, for they wanted to cut them down… They got away with one and there was three left! …They were in the middle of the traffic, you know…*

…I remember the old mill when I was wee. They used to have an archway in [finds a photo of the mill building] *…and there was a wee office at the side here. There were two old men that kept the…they looked after the place and let people in, you know. I remember they had a fight about a cushion! They both brought their own cushion to sit on. They were very old! I must have been about five then… They had a bank. Through the week you could put money in, into the Glasgow Savings Bank.*

Actually [during] *the First World War they had great business because their stores were full of cloth when the war broke and then all of that was sold to the government agencies…and with the Second World War, the same thing happened: they were piling it up because there was this trouble from India and Japan… It was after the Second World War they started to go down…*

…The weathervane from the old mill is up in Sorn, near Bridgend.

John Sharp: *Brigend. There's only one house left there. The old mill gates: the stone pillars are there. The weathervane's up on the house. How they got that I don't know…in thae days you'd just take it when it was getting knocked doon!*

Maureen Kiernan: *My mother would work in the old mill, the old, original building and that's* [why] *we stayed in Mill Street because my mother got a mill company house when she married. My daddy belonged to the miners' rows up there at Darnconner and a' that. He came to Catrine to live because my mother had got the company house. She worked in the roving, which was really, really hard work! Then she left, and when we went to the school they couldn't get rovers, it was such hard work. My mother went back to the roving…I would maybe go in to see my mother. I would be looking for thruppence! I'm serious! I would be looking for money for the pictures! …It was huge frames. She would maybe have four of these frames to watch. It would be putting the bobbins on and everything else. It was really, really hard work, dangerous work as well! If a bobbin fell, your machine didn't go off. It was the same in the Weaving Shed. The Weaving Shed wasn't attached to the big mill. The Weaving Shed would be on the side of the street that we stayed on…that would be the Weaving Shed at that time, and it was an awful noise! It was dirty, dirty, dirty, but that was the only employment for the women in Catrine…unless they went into service.*

Mill Street *circa* 1904 photographed from the gates of the Old Mill.

Mary McCluskie: *I left* [school] *at 14 because I had to, because we needed the money. I started in the mill and I got eight* [shillings] *and elevenpence…from 8 o' clock till 6 at night. I was a spinner. I was just a helper but when the war came in 39, a' the older girls that had, we cried them frames, machines, big machines, we were pushed forward although we hadn't been properly trained, because these* [girls] *were all called up for munitions…they went to Bowhouse. That's when they used to come home with yellow skin, you know, bright yellow! The stuff they working with…and they were given cream, but half of them couldnae be bothered putting in on and they were yellow as anything, but we just got used to them you know!*

We just had to get in at it and do what we could. It was hard work. When you went in you'd to wait to the power came on. That came from the voes, the reservoirs…when the power went you could put your machines on. I don't know if you know about spinning? Bobbins: do you know about bobbins? Well you had a row of them, about a hundred, with five sides of those to contend with. If one broke it went into a lap, you know…

Like a big ball?

Aye. Then you'd to stop your machine and get it all sorted out and everything. I mean, you were anxious to make money and you were trying to get on with it. It was a hard life. The other thing was most of us worked with our bare feet, because there was that much oil…you couldn't buy shoes…just all fell apart, stitching fell apart with the oil. …There were visitors came to see the mill and they used to look at us with our bare feet! Very little clothes: just a pinafore, you know. It was hot…there was waste – we called it fluff…floating about…we were all covered with the white. But when it came in at the beginning down in the Carding it was big bins of the pure cotton, and it went through machines and when it had went through the machines it was big, thick strands of cotton that come through…and then it went to the next one and that was [spun] *down and then when it came to us it was the actual thread. We actually made the thread that went over to the Weaving Shed across the road to be made into the cotton… It came into the Carding Room at the bottom and then it went through the machines and it came out like that* [uses hands to demonstrate thickness/thinness of thread] *and went to another one and it went through a bit thinner. And then the Spinning…your department, then you sent it off to the Weaving Shed…we sent it over in cans to the Weaving Shed and that was made into the cotton.*

How many people worked in the Spinning when you were there?

There would be about six of us on one end of it and six on the other, about twelve spinners on it and then we had our helpers – they brought the Roving up and it was bigger than that. You know what size a toilet roll is? Well you put one in your hand, one there and one there and you piled about five there and then four and then three, and that's how you carried them to us and they put them up the top of the frames for us to use, putting it in to make the thread. That was the helpers. That's what they were called, helpers.

…It was your own fault if you didn't have a pay…if you didn't attend to your frames, well, you weren't making a pay for the lap and then that's when you'd to bang it to the side for the helpers to come and help you to get it back started up again. Everything was hard work. I aye liked when it was Friday and didn't need to go back to Monday. I never liked it, never liked the mill, no! My sister went to the Bleach Works, but at that time they were on short-time so she was only working a week and off a week, so my mother says I couldn't go there. I'd to go to the mill…didn't like it…I wasn't there that long. That was 1938 and I got married in 1944. I only worked a year and gave it up.

…Round about Christmas we had what we called a party in the mill. We were allowed to stop the machines and have a wee party. One or two of us had to go out and get the fish suppers that we'd ordered and lemonade…things were rationed. We used to make cream cookies with plain cookies and you'd to take the cream off the top of the milk. You got cream on the top of the milk in those days, whipped it and whipped it to try and make it into cream and put on these cookies. We did a lot of things. You could make tattie scones cos tatties weren't rationed…we got powdered egg. That was a great thing: powdered egg… Ballochmyle was a military hospital…but the troops were stationed all through Catrine. There was a big lot of them: guards stationed up at the Works just before I left for [war service]. *There was a big contingent. They were drilled to the teeth! Then we had the Irish troops…they were not so well-trained, but they went into very heavy fighting too. A lot of them were killed. They were here for a month or two. We had two; one was billeted with us. Then, of course, we had all these children we had four children at a time from Glasgow…I was about 14 then. So we had quite a war…Catrine took children in…we had…Civil Defence. We'd to go into the mill and we were instructed with the stirrup pumps… The incendiary bombs, they said that was one of the worst things in the war because it caused an awful lot of fires and we'd this pail of water and this stirrup pump and we'd to pump away so if one fell we could get it quick.*

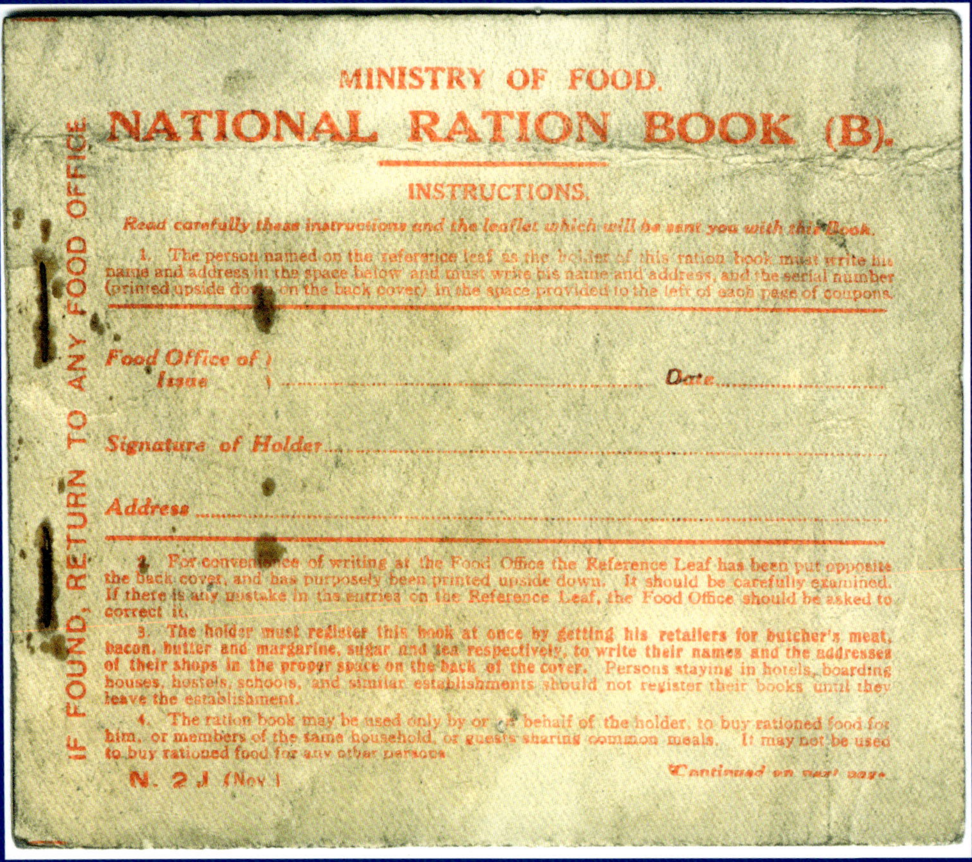

IF FOUND, RETURN TO ANY FOOD OFFICE

MINISTRY OF FOOD.

NATIONAL RATION BOOK (B).

INSTRUCTIONS.

Read carefully these instructions and the leaflet which will be sent you with this Book.

1. The person named on the reference leaf as the holder of this ration book must write his name and address in the space below and must write his name and address, and the serial number (printed upside down on the back cover) in the space provided to the left of each page of coupons.

Food Office of Issue .... *Date* ....

Signature of Holder ....

Address ....

2. For convenience of writing at the Food Office the Reference Leaf has been put opposite the back cover, and has purposely been printed upside down. It should be carefully examined. If there is any mistake in the entries on the Reference Leaf, the Food Office should be asked to correct it.

3. **The holder must register this book at once by getting his retailers for butcher's meat, bacon, butter and margarine, sugar and tea respectively, to write their names and the addresses of their shops in the proper space on the back of the cover.** Persons staying in hotels, boarding houses, hostels, schools, and similar establishments should not register their books until they leave the establishment.

4. The ration book may be used only by or on behalf of the holder, to buy rationed food for him, or members of the same household, or guests sharing common meals. It may not be used to buy rationed food for any other persons.

N. 2 J (Nov.)

Continued on next page.

DIG FOR VICTORY

Grow for Winter as well as Summer

DIG FOR VICTORY LEAFLET No. 1. New Series

Vegetables for you and your family every week of the year. Never a week without food from your garden or allotment. Not only fresh peas and lettuce in June—new potatoes in July, but all the health-giving vegetables in WINTER — when supplies are scarce - - - — SAVOYS, SPROUTS, KALE, SPROUTING BROCCOLI, ONIONS, LEEKS, CARROTS, PARSNIPS and BEET

Vegetables all the year round if you

DIG WELL AND CROP WISELY

Follow this Plan

ISSUED BY THE MINISTRY OF AGRICULTURE

The Old Mill Fire

In 1963 the Old Mill went on fire during the course of its demolition...

Jim Bunting: *...The buses had to go right round about the Square. It was quite difficult for them, quite tight for them to get round then obviously at the bank they turned up St. Germain Street... The old mill went on fire in 1964-65...it was lying empty...I worked in the lab at the hospital...at Ballochmyle...one of the chaps come in and he said, "That's the mill on fire down in Catrine", and I walked down to the top of Jacob's Ladder and you could see right down to the village and there it was blazing away. It was a wooden structure, everything was wooden and of course everything was saturated with oil over years from all the machines and everything... The likes of Fisher's building, George Fisher really thought he was going to lose his shop...the mill was only maybe 30, 40 yards away from his shop. The heat was so intense...you had all the houses they lived in round about the Square and the shops as well. There weren't far from it at all and it was quite touch and go whether they would go up as well. I think the firemen put their hoses on those houses rather than trying to put out the blaze on the mill...*

Evelyn Campbell: *Oh it blazed! You had the big Square, right, and see where the Royal Pub is just at the other corner there? ...We stayed just next door, that was where the shop was and we'd the hoose up the stair. Even the phones on oor side were a' doon...the flames was sky-high!*

Robert Dalziel: *Hildritch's was a sweet shop and grocers…Hillditch or maybe Hilldritch. They were in St. Germain Street just a few doors up from the Square. I can remember their roof going on fire the day the mill burned! We were quite lucky. When we came home we got a grandstand view of the mill fire beause I came home from school – I was in sixth year and we had to get off the bus at the bridge in Catrine. The fire was burning down the bottom of St. Germain Street, you could see the fire engines. So what we did was we went up Ayr Street and went up the steps behind the scout hut up to the Brae Tops and ran along…we were right above it and we could watch the fire burning. We had about three hours of entertainment watching it burn. It was a remarkable fire! I remember watching the firemen spraying the hoses on Hilldritch's roof because it was going on fire with the heat, and the cakes and things in Ferguson's the bakers window got completely ruined with the heat. They* [the fire brigade] *were spending almost as much time making sure that the fire obviously didn't spread to the houses in Mill Square rather than put the fire out because I think they realised they couldn't put the fire out in the actual big mill itself… They were spraying hoses on the houses and shops in the Square; particularly the roofs because they were obviously worried that the sparks would come over and catch. It was a huge fire! …Even standing at the top of the Brae Tops the flames alone were up at the top of your head, and you were about level, but obviously a fair distance away from it. You could feel the heat…it was quite spectacular…there used to be great rumours in the village, the truth of them nobody knows, about the fact that it may have been burned down deliberately, because it was an easy way to get it demolished, but nobody knows the truth of that… I'm not aware of anyone being hurt, no…the mill had been emptied and was being demolished… A friend of mine that was a technical teacher knew a chap who asked him to give a hand one night to move a big beam from the Catrine Mill because he was going to make a garage…* [he was going to] *cut enough planks of that beam to make a garage so it was a hell of a big beam…that's how he had got his garage, he got the old wood from Catrine Mill and that was before it burned.*

The Old Mill Fire

Mary McCluskie: *I was up in the Ballochmyle Quad...I was busy washing at the time, I didn't have a washing machine then. Somebody says, Mary, the big mill's on fire! I says, Is it? I thought it was just a wee fire. Mr. Cochran showed me he had taken a cine-film of it. I said, I never kent it was like that and I missed it, so I never saw it!*

Ruth Sharp: *...Thing was it was layered and layered with flats and the floors were full of oil with the machines, and it just went up* [in flames].

John Sharp: *You see, everythin was wood. It was only the outer-shell that was stone and it just collapsed on itself. They didnae try to put it oot. They hosed the roofs a' roon aboot the Square. They didnae try and put the fire oot: it was pointless. They just hosed a' the roofs and let it burn doon.*

Evelyn Campbell: *When the old mill was there we stayed in the Main Street...and when it got demolished when it had went on fire...where we stayed, the attic, it went on fire. I think it was the firemen made mair mess than what the fire did...with the hoses and the water.*

Robert Dalziel: *The stone that built the old mill could still be...found now lying in the Burnpark. It's actually now in the banking of one side of the burn in the Burnpark, the Burn o Need. It was dumped there because McKerrow was quite keen...the burn used to get into spate quite badly and it washed away quite a large section of the banking every odd time it was in spate. He got them to dump the old mill, basically, in his field and that's where most of the old stone is. So in a sense, it was quarried at one end of Catrine village and it found...its resting place at another end of the village! ...The folk that live in these houses could wander to the bottom of the garden, a wee kick at the banking, and see bits of the old sandstone that are still there. I remember seeing it being dumped, watching it being dumped, the trucks going into field.*

The Giant Wheels

Engineer Sir William Fairbairn's account of how he came to build the wheels of Catrine, written in March 1851

…In 1824 we had a visit from Mr. Buchanan of Catrine Bank, in Ayrshire, the partner of Kirkman Finlay… The object of his visit was to establish an entirely new arrangement of the water-power of the Catrine Cotton Works… I had been recommended to Mr. Buchanan as a person well able to devise, plan, and execute the work; and after several meetings and conversations, I was engaged to visit Ayrshire and spend a fortnight at Catrine Bank.

This was an important undertaking. The mills were extensive, and the water-wheels and steam-engines then at work were estimated at between 200 and 300 horse-power.

The Catrine Cotton Works are situated on the banks of the river Ayr, about fifteen miles from the town of that name. The mills were built by Mr. Alexander of Balochmyle, and were worked by him, I believe not very successfully… The machinery of the mills was driven by four water-wheels, erected by Mr. Lowe, of Nottingham. His work, heavy and clumsy as it was, had in a certain way answered the purpose, and as cotton-mills were then in their infancy he was the only person qualified from experience to undertake the construction of the gearing. Mr. Lowe was therefore in demand in every part of the kingdom where a cotton-factory had to be built.

The water-wheels at Catrine were ill-constructed, deficient in power, and constantly breaking down or out of repair. This was a grievous drawback at a time when trade was good, and to remedy the evil Mr. Buchanan erected two 40-horse-power steam engines, which for some years kept the works going, but at a considerable sacrifice arising from repeated failures in the water-wheels.

…It was not long before I discovered the evils under which the concern had laboured, and I did not hesitate to recommend a concentration of the whole of the motive power, and that instead of dividing a fall of forty-seven feet into two, the two falls should be united on two powerful wheels, each fifty feet in diameter, and 120, collectively 240 horse-power. This was computed to be equal to the entire resistance of the machinery in all the mills, and by a proper form of bucket, and a judicious application of the water, they were considered amply sufficient to turn the whole of the existing machinery without the aid of steam. In order, however, to provide for future contingencies and extension of the works, it was considered advisable to make provisions in the watercourses, tail run, and main gearing, for two more wheels of the same power and dimensions as those intended to be made, and thus to provide increased water-power in case of an increase of machinery… I set to work; and in the course of the week I had the whole laid down to a scale, and in less than a month from that date the order was given, and the work was in progress in Manchester.

The construction of the Catrine wheels, apart from the profits arising from the transaction as a matter of business, was one of the most interesting and gratifying circumstances I ever experienced in the whole of my professional career. My plans were approved, the prices proposed were accepted, and the works were completed in a manner highly satisfactory, not only to Mr. Buchanan and myself, but to every other person of the firm. The two first waterwheels were started in June 1827; they have never lost a day since that time, and they remain, even at the present day, probably the most perfect hydraulic machines of the kind in Europe.

Harry Houston: *I had an uncle, Hugh Clark, that worked in the Bleach Works and was a librarian. He was also the Fire Master at the Cotirn Fire Brigade, but their vehicle was based in a garage next to the Brewery Bar. It was him that tae'n me doon and showed me this…I couldnae believe the size o it! …I was only a wee boy. It was monstrous to me! I couldnae understand what it did even, but I knew when I saw it working and the power o it, it was really frightening as a kid. I thought, Im no goin near that! I actually was talking to a friend o mine who's a wee bit older and he was telling me that the houses just below where the wheel was, there was one hoose…Jim Ross…and in that house, just below it, there were a lot o shafts and what no and there was wan in there, and because he worked in the mill, he got in there and he greased this part o the machinery… I do know that there are still a lot of shafts in there which are all covered o'er.*

Maggie Bunting: *…I went in to see the big wheel and it was a really wonderful place. You walked up…the steps up the side and there was a pale and you could stand and watch down, and the big wheel was going round. There wasn't much water in it, but ohh, when you saw it dripping, it really was fascinating.*

Lara McPyke (*neé* Bunting): *I remember we had a neighbour who lived in Gordon Street years ago when we were growing up, and we used to go in and see her. Her dad was the mill wheel worker – Nelson. He operated the wheel and the story that sticks in my head, and the one she used to tell us, was what she remembers most about it was when there was sun there were windows in it and when there was sunshine the rainbows came off it. There were all these hundreds of wee rainbows coming of this big wheel! It must have looked amazing! As a wee girl that's what she remembered.*

The Big Mill Wheel of Catrine.
R.T.&S.Ltd London.

(Sir) William Fairbairn photographed probably in the 1860s or 1870s.

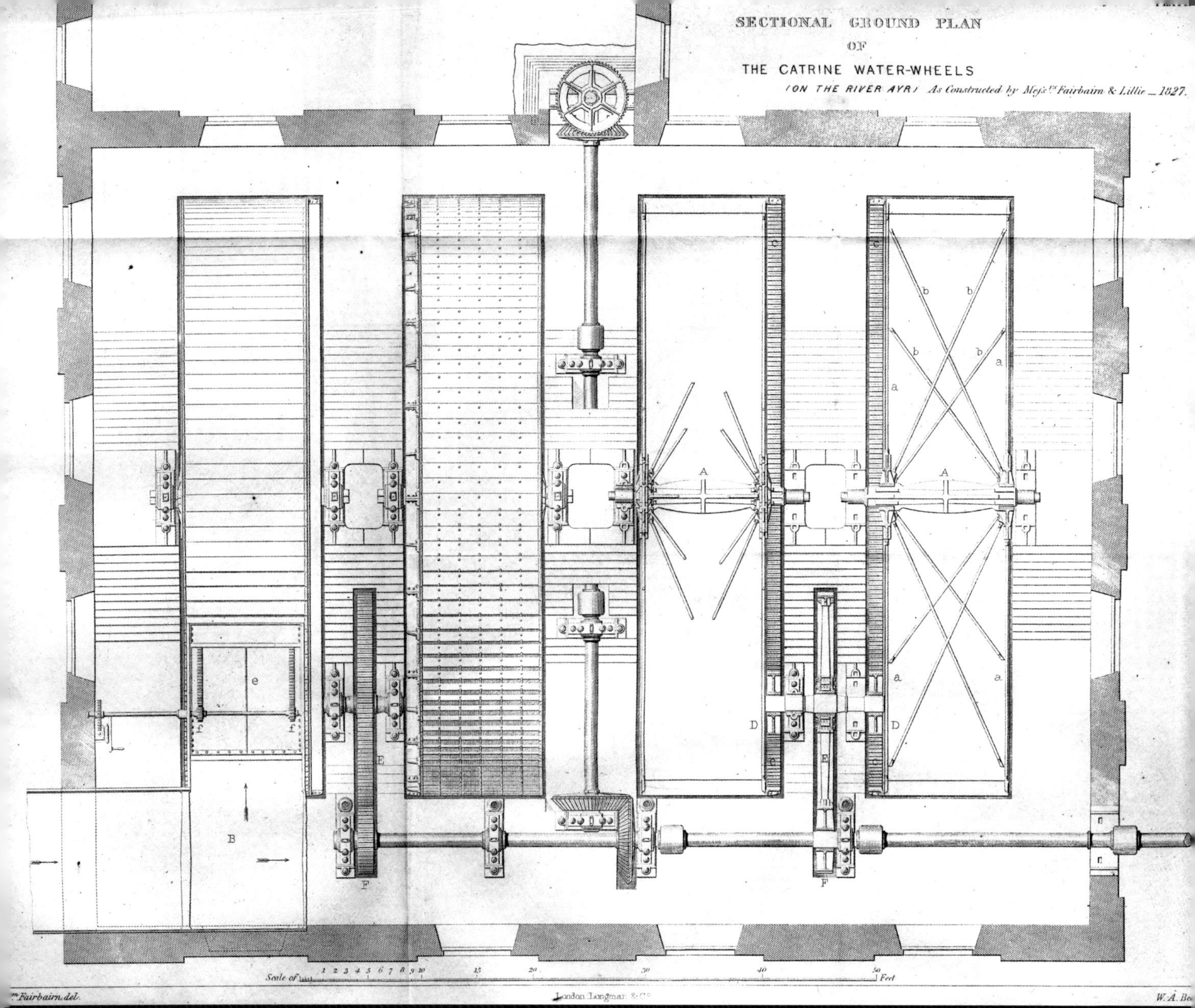

Glenbuck Loch was one of two large reservoirs formed by Finlay & Co to augment water supply to the Catrine Works.

Bleaching Works

Jeremy Lloyd (last manager of the bleaching works): *...We did a lot of work on the weir and the salmon pass because we had to. It was falling into disrepair as you would expect...and we were told – the anglers came along with the Water Board* [River Ayr Salmon Fishery Board?] *and said we got to do it. We resisted it as hard as we could because we knew it would be very expensive. When our backs were to the wall we went to a company, whose name I can't remember, who specialises in these jobs. They looked at it and came back with a proposal and we were horrified. It was a lot of money... This was to build a fish pass, and reinstate the weir. Well we weren't that fussy about the weir because we weren't using it. The weir was OK as far as we were concerned, but it did not suit so we had to do it and £60,000 comes into mind, I can't be sure. It was a hell of a lot of money and Hugh Young the maintenance foreman who was involved, he looked at the stuff and said "Yes I can see it's 60K worth but I reckon we can do it a damn sight cheaper and...the Board said yes if you think you can do it, do it. We did it in the summer holidays when the mills were closed. We accomplished it in a fortnight with our own people. We said we will knock down some of the stuff that's particularly bad until we get to the hard base and then we will put gabions in – I didn't know what a gabion was... They came up with a drawing and they happened to leave one behind, so we had a fair idea of what was going to be necessary. We spoke to the 'water people' and they said yes if you can do that then carry on. So we set about it...these gabions cost next to nothing and we ordered x amount of gabions. They were four feet long so we worked out how many were needed. We found they cost buttons and then we had to get some rough limestone to load into them. We found a little trucking firm, very little money to us. We got to the level we should be at where we stood the gabions in and I think they lasted pretty well. We did it for a couple of thousand I think – it was so cheap compared to what we were in for.*

I once got into dreadful trouble with Kays. We were dyeing a lot of cloth for them and it faded. They did have a good line and they tested this cloth and it faded. I didn't think it was going to fade...I'd used an inferior dye on purpose. I knew I could hit the shade, but I knew it was an inferior dye, but I thought we could get away with this, we've got to get away with this because we needed to make some money. But it came unstuck...all the cloth had been made into dresses.

Alistair Plenderleith: *Ma faither used to go roon wi fishing stuff fae Auchinleck. He was fae Auchinleck. He was actually born in Tillabuddy* [Tullibody in Clackmannanshire]*...You don't ken where Tillabuddy is? It's a wee bit on the other side o Alloa...Tillabuddy...aye. See on his side they were a' gamekeepers. He came to Dumfries House to the Marquis of Bute's. Aye. Ma faither used to bum to us that he had a hurl in the Silver Ghost that...he had at that time... After he left Dumfries House estate he went to work in the Barony...and that's where he met my mother...* [who was working] *in the...Bleach Field, aye. Ma faither got a hoose in Catrine along wi ma mother. Thats how it a' started... That was up at 33 St. Cuthbert's Street... They a' had to dae wi the mill or the Bleach Field cause they were tied hooses at that time... The wages was very, very low...aye but the rents were very cheap. You got enough tae dae you. They were happy days. You didnae make a fortune nor nothing like that, but any family coming up was guaranteed to get work. You could go into the mill or Bleach Work. Either that or go to the mines. It used to be a coalman joke in Catrine – the miners stood at the brig they had bigger wages and the Bleach Field workers a' went tae Blackpool! Ken, they were kinda savers... There was a wee firm in the Bleach Field and the mill where you could pay half a crown a week, or something like that...you got holidays and that. There was a guy by the name o Bobby Cairns...he kinda run this, aye.*

The Bleach Works made cotton and that, sheets and towels and all these things. We lived across the road in St. Cuthbert's Street across the pond, aye... Well, it was to hammer the cloth into...ken the cloth came in [noise of paper sliding back and forward] *and they made sure it was a' flat. The beetles came doon...everybody that worked in the Beetling Room was deaf...it went 24 hours a day. At the weekend when they stopped and you went to your bed at night you couldnae sleep because we were that well used to them going all day, we just took it as a natural thing, ken...just like putting the telly on then switching it up when you waken up.*

My father worked as a carter, he drove a horse and cart. It took dross into the fire doors at the station, you see, and to the mill... The stories aboot the horses were hilarious, ken! ...They were Clydesdale horses, aye. There were some beggars among them. There was a really bad yin at yin time and it ran away. There was a brig across the water up at the...where the whisky bond is and it was just a single yin, ken, and it run away while they were undoing the dross fae the lorry. It met my faither's horse. He was coming doon the brae into the Bleach Works and met the' heid-on on the brig. They spent a day cutting them oot o harnesses and a' that. Oh, it was a bad beggar, ken! ...They had a' different names. My faithers horse's name was Chance... There was a chap called Jimmy Camel fae Catrine and Sanny Cummings he was the headman...this Jimmy Camel was put in charge o this horse this day when Sanny Cummings hadnae come oot. He was banging...the dross into the fire doors when it took him by the hand and shook him, lifted him right off the ground and shook him by the hand. So he had to go to the hospital, ken. So the heid o the Bleach Works department at that time was Geordie Wilson, so he suggested to ma faither that he jumped in the cart and ta'en the horse roon to the stable. My faither said, "Aye, that's alright. How do I put it the stable wi a cart on?" My faither was used to horses so he just took it roon and put it in the stable. It was another oor before someone appeared to see if he was alright! They were the kind o things that happened, ken, in these days. He was a bad horse, a really bad horse! ...He was a bad swine...when you'd to feed him you went in wi the bin to put it in his trough you always kept the bin in front o you. When you were coming back oot you had to reverse back oot and keep the bin in front o you, cos he would wait for you going by...

We had bad days too though...well there was a wee boy got drooned up the water, Cairns they cried him, Alec Cairn...he wandered away and went into the lade up the back. He was only a toddler ken. There was a chap by the name o Jones. I think he lost an arm in the Beetling Room at that time...

I went to work with Finlays till I was about 18, then I had to go to the National Service. Then that was the end o Finlays...I never worked in the new mill. I worked in the Bleach Field, only in the Bleach Field...I did the pletting: made cloth intae sheets...you measured them a length, maybe 36 by a 72 thread, ken 84 or something...all different sizes. You plated them intae a yard or something like that but they were double, ken. You cut them up, cut them up and they went upstairs to the shoeing [?] *machine and that…aye, that was really the end. They came up fae doon stairs for the finishing. They came oot as the finished product and went abroad… There'd be about six or seven* [doing the same job] *at that time. There were machines for doing it too…it just went back and forward…in the Bleach Field there must have been three or four hundred…there were buses came fae New Cumnock, buses came fae Auchinleck, double deckers tae. And a' the folk in Cotrin. There would be about four or five double deckers came in. Countlaw a' these places. Burnbank, Burnpit, Muirkirk. They all got a job, ken…aye, happy times aye…I went to the Coal Board works up at Lugar. I was there 33 years…a store man…bits of machinery. You supplied a' the pits in the area…the wages were a lot better. You could get plenty of overtime tae. It was a different world, ken…I mean when I was in the Bleach Field…I'm no saying I'm right in saying you got about £2 18s* [a week]*…when I went to the mines and that £9, which was an awfy amount of money then, ken. It wasn't an awfy amount of money but it was treble what you were getting at the Bleach Field.*

Jim Bunting: *Aye, my grandfather came to Catrine. He was head-hunted really, to start up there. They didn't have a dyeing department as such in the Bleach Works and that was his job over in Muckamore in County Antrim…he came over here to start up the department…that was in 1932…really up until the 60s the company was really quite profitable…it was a big, big employer in the area. It used to be, at 6 o' clock at night, the buses would be waiting outside the mill to take all the workers home: maybe six double deckers. They came from New Cumnock, Muirkirk, Cumnock: all over the place…*

Lara McPyke (neé Bunting): *My great-grandfather, my gran's dad…came here as the dyer…in the Bleach Works. So mum and dad's house up in St. Cuthbert Street is still called the Dyer's.*

Maggie Bunting: *I came from Ireland. I came from County Antrim, two miles out of the town of Antrim. My father, he came here to start the dyeing and that's how we landed in Catrine. But it's been very good. I've seen a lot of changes right enough, but its still more or less, just roughly, the way it was. We came to St. Cuthbert's Street to the house that my son lives in now. It was very nice and the people were really nice… I was 14 when I came here…there were six girls of us…"the Dyer's lassies".*

Jim Bunting: *Apparently it caused quite a sensation in the town when the family arrived with these young women – six young women!*

Maggie Bunting: *…A woman met my father at the water dyke one day and she said, "Good morning Mr. Dyer"! …We came here in 1932, so I never was at school here…I started work in the Bleach Field in the Sewing Room and that's where I finished up, the Sewing Room in Catrine…I worked there from 1932…I worked there till 44. Then I left when I was married and Jim was coming. Then I went back to work at night in it, from 6 o' clock to maybe 8…it was a good place to work.*

Lara McPyke (*neé* Bunting): *…I suppose that was quite a big job, really, in the Bleach Works…Billy Dick* [another interviewee]*…said that as a part of his training in the mill he had to go and look at all the different jobs that everybody did. He said that was one of his most vivid memories was of Papa Davy throwing mixture in, just guessing them. It seemed so, kind of, random and ad hoc but it came out absolutely…it wasn't measured or anything…*

Jim Bunting: *…Most of his work was blinds, for window…a lot of that was obviously for through the war…blackout blinds… I was the first baby that was born here…I was born in the house I live in now up in St. Cuthbert Street. Fae I was a wee boy…I would be about 5 or 6…whenever I finished school I would be straight down at the Bleach Works and was in with all the machinery and everything… I was in there all the time, aye…it was a fascinating place, the mill…it was…really huge. Where my grandfather worked, they dyed the blinds. The blinds would go through the dye and then it would come up and be led over a whole set of heated rollers in big drums…it was quite dangerous… I remember men getting their hands caught in the drums and…it was quite sore, you know, to say the least…*

…The horn would go you could hear it all over [the village] *– at five to eight in the morning…and then it went at eight o' clock and the five* [minutes] *was to warn folk it was time you were making your way to the Bleach Works…it was a horn. Steam operated…it was the horn for the Bleach Works…a bell they had at the mill.*

Bleaching Works

Robert Dalziel: *I'm Robert Dalziel; I was born in 1946 on the 1st of March and lived in the village for 23 years. My family have connections in the village going a lot further back than that, several generations…my grandfather Dalziel was a foreman in the mill and they were consequently one of the more comfortably off families. They were able to buy their own house, just next door to the Institute here at Rowan Lea in Catrine in 1904… His wife Mary Heath was quite an interesting personality from the village because she was English, came from Devon, and in 1895 became the first district nurse in the village…she lived to the ripe old age of 92… One of their daughters, Marjorie, married John Hogg who was the manager of the Bleach Works for a long time…he was a remarkable man and very much a self-made man…he could count up three columns of figures at a time, without any bother he could keep going as long as you like! They lived in…Broomknowe where my father was the gardener because it was part of the Bleach Works and for part of his life my father worked as the gardener in the Bleach Works. Probably my Uncle John would get him the job I would imagine. …There* [were] *actually quite big gardens…Broomknowe itself had, which was the manager's house, a huge garden, still has. You can hardly see it in the centre of the Voes up there, and there were quite, well not a garden* [but] *wee corner garden areas and there was a huge greenhouse which actually sat beside the Voes. That's long gone…they had* [a] *great heating system which was actually led off the Bleach Works heating system so the greenhouse could grow absolutely anything. It was enormous! It was a huge long thing…he brought on lots o plants and he grew vegetables as well and they brought on all the plants to bed out on the gardens and that's why he did it, and of course the Mill had a garden at the side of it as well, the New Mill, and that had to be tended and looked after. Plants and things in it. So* [there] *was quite a lot to do actually for a gardener there…*

…My father moved from the Bleach Field. I think he was somewhere between £5 to £6 a week and he moved for £1 a week to work at the builders in Mauchline, and even paying a bus fare it was still worth moving!

View in Catrine Bleaching Work Gardens, October 1859 – "J B, Mrs. B & Agnes".

Bleaching Works

Mary McCluskie: *It did the P&O liners…my sister worked in the Bleach Works and she only got about one* [shilling] *and six* [pence] *for doing a dozen pillow cases…that was all with P&O stamped on them. They did a lot of work…they were good sheets. Everything like that you always got your diapers out off it too for the babies. It was good.*

Ruth Sharp: *…Four years* [after she was born] *we left there and we lived in Riverside Villas down here, just across the way from Co-operative Avenue. Then when my father became manager of the* [Bleach] *works we went to Broomknowe which was next to the works, the big house next to the works. We lived there for 25 years. It was a lovely house… It was built by Morton, the previous manager… Of course Finlay paid for it. But, it was a beautiful house. It had the signs of the zodiac on the top, small windows. There were 12 of them, and when the sun came through gave lovely patterns in the rooms downstairs. The last time I was up they were all away except one. I don't think they could take it out.*

[My father's name was] *John Renton Hogg…he came here* [from Coatbridge] *when he was 19…he started off his career in Stewarts and Lloyds as an office boy. It was from there he came to Catrine…he came as clerk to the then general manager who was a Mr. Morton. Well, several years after that the Great War broke out and he was a Territorial so he disappeared from Catrine. Then, of course, he came back after the war…there were two managers: there was a Mr. Grundy who was the manager of the mill and my father* [manager of the Bleach Works] *at the same time…he was always an incomer, you know. No matter how long you stay here! …When I was smaller…everyone was related. Big families were related, and you had to be very careful… Maybe if somebody got the sack in one, no-one would speak to you…*

…There was this wheel but it wasn't used. They gave it up, maybe early 30s, and it wasn't used but it was right next to our house. The water gradually grew, turned full and the buckets turned round every five minutes. Through the night even. So you'd to get used to sleeping with it…it was not as big as the one at the mill, it was a big double wheel…it was taken away. It disappeared during the war when I was away…quite a narrow wheel. There was a cundy [?] *from the Scone Voe through hatches. They pulled up the hatches to let the water in. The water flowed in there and the buckets filled and it went round. There were two beam engines that gave steam from the boilers, big boilers , and that's where the dross was used from the carts.*

…There was a man hired in the works for the rats. He said he could get rid of them. They tried everybody, even professionals. They ate the starch and they were big…there were a lot of them so they decided to get rid of the rats…pandemonium. These rats, they didn't take poison, they knew not to eat it, they wouldn't take it at all. But…he was a mole catcher to trade, he said he could get rid of them, and he got rid of them alright! He was cruel. He caught one big rat and burnt it along its side and let it loose and all the rest moved out. And that was perfectly true. There is an ending to the story…it was a horrible ending. That same gentleman worked in what they called the pot shed and the big pots were sealed down with steel clips and the cloth went round a spinner in the middle of them. It was brought up to a big temperature to clean out all the oouse and everything, you know, and this day he was working with the other men in that building and the pot exploded and went up! The lid came off. The cloth wound round him and scalded him…he died!

…Only two accidents in all that time, in 25 years. The accident that was most plentiful were the girls at the sewing machines. They worked piece-time and they sewed their finger and they used to come in and hold their finger up with the needle right through it! We had two men that looked after the medical in the works, and they used to go and get the doctor if they couldn't get it out and they would cry…Right through the fingers! There were about 200 worked in what we called the shaft. The shaft went right through where all the machines were. There were four shafts so there would be 200 workers during that time, during the war.

How many was there normally at the Bleach Field?

Well, it varied between 350 and 500. It depended on trade and one thing and another… I eventually came out of the forces and I became the pay clerk there…[Returns with photographs] *Now, this was taken in 1929 when my father became manager… Now I know who all these men are…*[pointing to them on the picture] *This one here was the foreman of the engineers…he was a Mr. Hood…wait a minute, sorry, not Hood. That's Melrose, Tom Melrose: he was the electric man. This was the head engineer in the mill, Peter Craig… That was my father. Now this one was called Fussy Gibb, but you don't use Fussy! I think it was James was his first name. Either James or John, but James is good. That was the director Dalgleish who took the photograph… That was* [taken] *in the Finishing Department; where they finished the cloth before it went upstairs… My father was born in 1890…he would be 40, nearly…* [Referring back to the photograph] *But the hatch* [hat], *you know, this was always a laugh in the district. The hatch, the bowler hats that they wore…*

From left to right: ??, James Gibb, John R. Hogg (Manager), Peter Craig, Tom Melrose, Peter Thom.

That would distinguish them as...management?

John Sharp: *The office workers wore* [bowler] *hats.*

Ruth Sharp: *This man here, Peter Craig, he was getting towards retiral then. He was a well-known man in Catrine then, Craig. And Tom Melrose, and Peter Tom. There are two Peters there. He was the engineer manager in the Bleach Works and he in the mill.*

Ruth Sharp: *His family are down in Cornwall now, and Tom Melrose: he's in Linlithgow... There was a girl who worked here who lost her scalp on that machine...she became a school teacher. The works man that saw to these things, clamped it back on her head...the doctor came up and said he did a great job...she was Mary Simpson.*

John Sharp: *She was a school teacher to me when I was a wee boy.*

Ruth Sharp: *That's my father in the home guard* [left]*...and that was his retiral photograph* [opposite page]. *That was Mr. MacDonald. He made the presentation. He was the foreman of the lapping department. And this is a clock that the works gave him. The office staff gave him a wireless... Mr. MacDonald, my uncle married his niece, so he always said he was related to me every time we met on the pavement. He used to give me a sweetie!*

Who are these people in the back?

Some of these are just young trainees. Mary Plenderleith, she married a...local farmer...and this is another Plenderleith. That was a cousin of hers...he was called Johnston, the fella at the back. He worked downstairs somewhere. That's all I can remember.

...During the war there were 500 employed in the Bleach Works...there were a lot of women. They did the finishing: the sheets, pillow cases and that. We sent them out to displays in big shops all over the country to put their initials on for nothing...it was very famous, Finlays. The main business was in India...in Bangladesh...this was just a very small part...they owned the consolidated tea and lands I believe...and finally, funnily enough, India and Japan flooded the market with cheap goods put them down eventually.

...I remember one incident in Broomknowe. We lived up next to the voes. The voe next to us was called the Scone Voe. It was a wee voe the shape of a scone! But very deep. That was the one that held the water down to the big wheel we had at the Bleach Works. One day we had three carthorses that pulled the dross from the station to the Works. These big Clydesdales were put in the field at the weekend, and one escaped. It got its way up to the voes. Between each voe there was a narrow strip in between to separate them, with grass on it. Lovely grass. And it fell in! It swam and it swam for about half an hour before anybody knew it was there. They tried to get it out, it was a Saturday, but couldn't get it out. Oh, it was pandemonium! But anyway, my father was shooting up at the Target. He was a great shot. He had three gold medals for Ayrshire. He shot at Bisley, you know. But anyway, they went and got him but they couldn't think what to do so he says, "Take out the big door into the Works. Take it off the hinges." He says, "Slip it in sideways and lasso the horse!" So the head engineer got the [rope] *round the horse and pulled it out. Oh, the poor animal! We had to send for the vet at Cumnock, Shannon, and he got this horse into the yard, and I'm watching it. It was called Chance! The vet says, "Send somebody down the street and get three bottles of Bass" and they poured them down its neck to bring it round. And it was fine! It lived to be a good age.*

Anne Fleming: *As he* [her father] *got older he wasn't so fit. He couldn't concentrate the same and he'd worked in the Bleach Works before the war and they kept their jobs open for them. So he went back there and he worked there till he had to give up due to ill-health. He was in the Cutting Department: that was cutting the sheets, pillow cases, the towels and stuff…it was like hand-cutting in these days. He was like the deputy foreman and they were going on to an electronic guillotine. Because he had epilepsy he wasn't allowed to work it…the cutting room, that was always his first love. The pattern was just the kinda, "Och well kinda I've been demoted sorta thing"…we used to say "Cut everything wi pinking shears"! …All these wee bits of cloth had to be cut out. So this* [produces a pattern book] *is when he was moved into what was called the Pattern Making Department and he made up these. It was to give out to* [sales] *reps to sell…they had striped stuff and everything else like that. They did tartan towels and they went all over the world… The raw cotton came in here to the village, to the mill, and it was all processed there. It was taken up to the Bleaching Works, bleached, dyed, whatever, and made up into sheets, pillow cases, towels and then it was exported to…all over the world really… When my mother was young…she was a machinist and…they would put initials on your towels or for hotels and that the Royal Hotel, or whatever and she did that freehand, script writing they called it on the machine. Before she was married – they were married in 1937 – they started sending the girls out to what they called displays. They went out to all the big stores like Selfridges and all these places. They went to South Shields, Sheffield, all over the place and she was one of the older ones so she always had a young trainee with her. They stayed in various degrees of digs, which were horrendous, some of them! When you think on it, in 1937…that must have been a big thing…for young girls going away from a wee village like this. They worked in the windows at Selfridges, you know, in London and that, actually doing the demonstrations…and to be responsible for another younger girl as well. Some of the digs they got they'd to put the dressing tables against the door and things like that!*

[Referring to a photograph] *That was her as she got older. She actually got a machine down into the house at Mauchline Road and the lorry used to bring her doon stuff. There were very few of them could do this initialling freehand… She worked from home, aye…they had white overalls with the tartan slashes and that and Finlay and Company. You can see she's doing the initial there…I don't know how many more of them did it at home at that time but…it was after…my grandmother was away in the hospital that they'd asked my mother if she…couldn't actually go back to work because she'd to visit Granny all the time, but she could do this in between and they…were so desperate to get her that they would install a machine in the house for her. She phoned them up and they came and collected them again and took them away…*

SINGER

The New Mill

Modernisation plans for Catrine were put on ice due to the outbreak of war in 1939, but were revived as hostilities drew to a close and the foundation stone of the New Mill was laid in 1945. By 1950 the weaving shed was in operation. The original plan had been to power the New Mill with hydroelectricity using the site of the giant wheels (where two bungalows sit today next to the bus stop in Mill Street). A recent options appraisal of potential hydro sites in Catrine also identified this as the optimum location for a hydro as it is the place where the maximum fall (and hence output) can be achieved. However, after the Giant Wheels had been demolished to clear the site the problems and costs of ongoing repairs to and maintenance of the tunnel bringing the water from the voes became apparent. So the easier option of siting the turbine house in Laigh Road from where it could power the bleaching works was adopted instead.

The New Mill prospered in the 1950s but by the late 1960s was struggling. It closed in 1970. The building later became a furniture warehouse and at one point was sold for a nominal pound. By 1985 it was lying empty and it was demolished late that year.

Although the removal of the Old Mill and the New Mill has created the large open spaces which help the centre of Catrine breathe and make it so attractive, it's worth reflecting for a moment that this delightful ambience has been achieved at a cost of many local jobs. A ten year battle to save the Old Mill by the Historic Buildings Council was undermined by refusal elsewhere in government to identify another possible industrial or commercial use and a local politician's desire to see a straight road running from St. Germain Street through to Mill Street instead of the three turns about the square. If the Old Mill had been conserved today it would be luxury apartments, or a variety

of work units, or perhaps a visitor attraction on a par with New Lanark. The New Mill was a thoroughly modern post-war building constructed to the highest standard that today equally could have been apartments, divided into various industrial uses, or a much-needed in this area conference and exhibition centre, or the site of a world-class museum attracting visitors from all corners of the globe. All the jobs these would have offered were thrown away by a lack of vision. That this is the case is evidenced by the eventual regeneration of other disused buildings and sites associated with the mill which now form the backbone of local employment. Catrine Bank House (later Daldorch) has put Catrine on the map as a residential school for autistic children. This has brought new skills and employment to around 400, mainly local, people. The former bleaching works is now the site of Glen Catrine Bonded Warehouse where around 150 souls are employed. Smaller employers are SB Optical Ltd, housed in the New Mill extension and Stenlake Publishing attracted to Fisher's empty premises by its size and low price. Besides the potential jobs of today lost by the reckless destruction of the buildings' demolition, a skilled workforce was lost also. The accounts that follow demonstrate the level of skill that was required in the work of the New Mill.

Blow Room

Billy Dick: *Everything was done through Finlay and Company. If they did it, it was done, end of story! They actually sold the mill in the end for a pound. They sold it to…they no longer exist now…a big company in Ayr. They stored furniture in it. Eventually he disappeared to America…he sold it for a pound to the council who flattened it, ken…there was talk at the time. For instance, the academy wasnae built at Auchinleck. Now, they could have used it…it would have been ideal…take my word for it, because I worked in it…they could have partitioned it off into classrooms. They had the weaving shed down in the bottom which was a vast place that could have been used for games halls…the one thing that went against it was that there were nae playing fields, but at that time the farm across the road could have been bought. But it never came to anything…and they were going to be building another hospital, believe it or not, although they did away with Ballochmyle. I can imagine…they wouldn't want an industrial building to make a hospital, but there was great potential. It was a new building…I saw it built…that was a great big five storey building with glass right up the front of it, very modern building, built mostly with government money…Finlay and Co were about out the game – this is hearsay from ma father – when the war came along. There were cotton sheets and bales of cotton lying everywhere…the war came along and it just disappeared like that! They made a fortune.*

…As I probably said to you before, the advent of air conditioning ruined it [cotton mills require certain levels of humidity and when air conditioning became available it enabled India to build a home cotton industry that ultimately caused the closure of the New Mill at Catrine]. *You couldnae work…you've got to have humidity and heat, because it* [cotton]*'s very brittle.*

Alfie Gionetti bale mixing

You take a cotton thread I'm talking about a thread like that [demonstrates by holding up a hair between his thumb and forefinger]. *See that? Well that's where it all starts...I could...tell you where that come from in the world...from its length and its smell. You burnt it. I learnt that at the technical college up in Glasgow (it's now Strathclyde University). It had a weaving shed in the very top flat, because the west of Scotland had a lot of big mills. Huge, big mills in Glasgow. None of them exist at all... Most of the cotton in my day...if you're going to the top of the tree it was Egyptian cotton, very yellow. That wee sliver...if you could get it two inches long that was good, but you couldnae use that...it was too dear. You mixed that wi stuff that came fae Russia, stuff that come fae America, stuff that came fae India. The South Sea Islands and Egypt cotton were the finest in the world because of their climate, ken. You got that in, the bale came in, the bale was the size o this desk. It was packed; really rammed in! When you burst the* [bale] *it went to the ceiling. Whoosh! And that was pulled off in layers and thrown in to a blowing machine, cried the Blow House, and it was just a great big cage three, four times the size of this* [room] *with air blowing in to it, and it blew all that up till you got cotton wool. Just flying aboot there. That was mixed wi the cheaper stuff that was maybe only an inch, right. So that all went in there and got tumbled up. It got tumbled up for hours and hours and hours, right, and that came out of there and went in to what they ca'ed the carding. The carding was a great big machine wi you ken what velcros like noo? Well this was mad' o metal. One went that way, the other went that way. A big drum, half the size o here* [the office] *and a small drum. One went faster than the other, and somedy fed that in what they call a lap...they fed that cotton in to that...and just like the old ones you'll have seen on some of the*

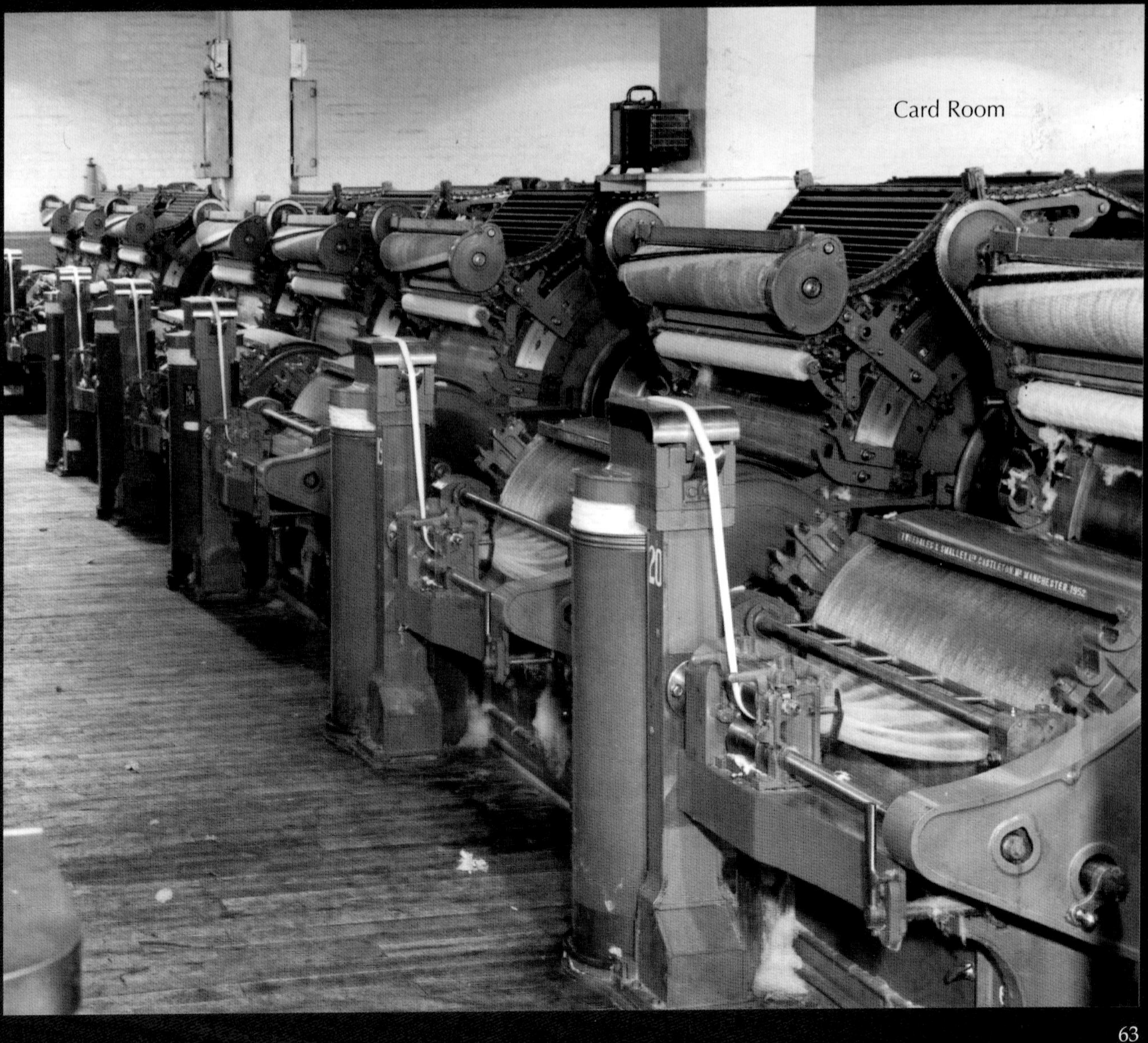

Card Room

television programmes, where the old wife's sitting wi a comb that way and a comb that way, going like that [demonstrates with hands parallel moving in opposite directions]. *Well it did exactly the same thing only on an industrial scale. And it laid it all on one line, right? And that line come in and it come to the front o the machine, and it got narrower and narrower till it came out like that, and it came out in what they cried a rove. Now, a rove was about that size* [demonstrates] *but it was all running the same way, right? You went up the stairs to the next flat…a huge, great lift, ocht the size o the library, and it went up to the next flat and went in there to what they cried the roving. By this time it went into a can: a big tall can like this* [demonstrates with hands]*…and coiled roon and roon…exactly the size o a rope! Roon and roon. There was a spring in the bottom to ease it up, and it went into this machine where a series of rollers…that went faster and faster till you got a thread. Now depending on the speed and the size of the rollers you put on, you got the thickness of the thread you required…the faster it was going, the thinner…it got, aye. And the longer you put it in, obviously, it went on to another stage. That came on to a bobbin, or what we cried a cheese… A cheese: shaped like…a cone. This is you trying to get it on to a conveyance to be woven. This was Finlay and Co doing the whole thing. Other companies…didnae do any of that. They sent that thread to sombdy else, who put it on to a conveyance which I'll come tae for to be woven. Cos it a' ended up at the weaving. The weaving was where it a' come together. They* [other companies] *would do that and sombdy else would weave it, and then sombdy else would take it away and bleach it. But there was an awfy lot in between that. Right, we've got to that thread at the roving and…then it's passed on to the cheese or cone. Now you've got to get that onto a small bobbin…you had counts o that depending on the thickness of the cloth you were wanting. It went from 7s to 32s. That was just a standard…32 was very brittle; a 7 – you made flannelette out of 7…because it got teased up. These threads went onto…the next layer…and they spun it…*

Margaret Dick: *When I went in that first day there was a Weaving Mistress. She takes you and shows you where to stand. They show you things to dae and learnt the weaver's knot. You'd to tie a weaver's knot and I'd already kent that because ma sister had shown me how tae dae it. Then you'd to learn to fill up what they called the batteries –*

Weaving Shed

that was putting the bobbins in. It was an automatic machine for the shuttle. Then you were put along with a girl and she'd to show you the ropes, but the Weaving Mistress always came and ta'en you at some time to show you the ropes…she was more of a headmistress, but after you kent your job she was guid to you. She was just being firm so you would get it in, but I grew to like her.

Billy Dick: *The weaver's knot, why it was called the weaver's knot? Was because it didnae slip and it was small? It was able to weave oot through all the spine things* [heddles] *that was in the loom. The weavers had to tie their knot…and it pulled. It didnae slip unless you made a mess o it!*

Margaret Dick: *You had to get it into your heid. There was the heddles up and doon. The threads oot through. And they had the wee, tiny holes and you had what you called…a cleek! And your scissors. Billy made me my wee sheath, it was a bit o leather with a hole in it and you stuck it…and tied roon aboot you, so when you needed it was available. And the wee hook; it pu'ed the threads through…when it broke. And you'd to learn a 1 and a 3, and a 2 and a 4. That was the…kinda…you put two together and you pu'ed them through the heddles…and through the reed.*

Billy Dick: *That's what beat the cloth up, to make the weave.*

Margaret Dick: *And then you had to learn also, there were huge, big machines the length of this living-room; you'd to learn how tae put them on… When I got my own row of machines there were 18 when I came in in the morning, I liked to be in about quarter to six. We started at 6am. But we had to turn clocks from A shift to B shift to make your bonuses, right…I had a' that to dae roon aboot 18 machines and then you had to go and switch them on and make sure that the shuttles were well up in their boxes so at 6 o' clock when you started them a up…they were just ready to go.*

Billy Dick: *The reason she talked aboot the clock because you were paid by the pick. Every time that shuttle went across there, at the end of the shift they counted the number o picks that you had done, and that's how you were paid. A wee girl from the office came down and wrote…about twenty minutes to two, she wrote down all your figures and that's how you were paid!*

Margaret Dick: *Aye, your bonus. Then on a Thursday, eh, Bert McDowall that's Billy's cousin he came doon from the office wi a tray, like what you would get in the pictures wi the ice cream and stuff on. He had a tray, something like that. On that was all the wee, brown envelopes wi your pay…you'd to sign for it every Thursday.*

Billy Dick: *…Most girls, if they found it too much at the weaving, they finished up what they call battery fillers. That's just putting the stuff…*

Margaret Dick: *…The bobbins in…*

Billy Dick: *…But most of them, they were all picked because they were fairly strong and big at the weaving. In all walks of life there were some better than others.*

Margaret Dick: *But they didnae get rid o them, Billy, they found them a job. Either remained a battery filler or…*

Billy Dick: *What happened wi companies like that, when you became too old you went up the stairs to what they cried the picking. That was* [where] *the cloth was run off a big roller, and it was run over, and they watched for any defects and sorted them before it ever went to the Bleach Fields.*

Margaret Dick: *They did keep on…there wis yin or two people working that were kinda simple, and they got, like, menial jobs like filling up the cans.*

Billy Dick: *They brought some in fae a school, because they was a lot of repetitive work and you could teach them the repetitive work, ken. Cos an awful lot of things in weaving, even when I finished up in the carpet thing, there was lot of repetitive things. You can imagine standing tying something like 4,000 ends in the back of one beam, and there were two beams. You'd to stand and tie a' these… You'll see a proper Hattersley loom at Moffat.*

Margaret Dick: *Yes! That's the kind that we worked. Go and see that man and he'll tell you all aboot pulling ends. We quite often just go to reminisce or talk to the guy…I'd love to get back in and say, "Can I have a shot at that?" Aye, you should go and see it…you'll hear the noise of just one machine!*

Billy Dick: *Well, you're talking about 126* [machines/looms] *in that one shed, and all going at different speeds.*

Margaret Dick: *But you got used to it…you went in and…it didn't bother you… I started at 15 and you werenae allowed – I was on day shift – you werenae allowed to go on shift work until you were 16… I'm no bummin but I must have been quite guid because about three month before I was 16 I got cried into the office. There was this group of machines that I was to get. Would that be all right, and I said, Oh aye, I'm having them! So I got this row o machines. There were two older women in the next couple o rows and I used to help them. I hurried up and did ma ain job, and then helped them oot. They were tiny! And this wee yin used to come and say to me, Margaret, could you come and help me to pu this through? Her wee arms couldnae reach. It was too far!*

Billy Dick: *…When I started in there a weaver only looked after two* [looms]*, and they were kept going because you'd to do everything by hand, but they became automatic very rapidly. And these rows o 18 looms…were divided up into 62 and the tenter, the Scottish Power Loom Tenter was the man who maintained them, like myself you had 62 to look after. So you had like four rows of looms and a half row and you had a neighbour and you worked with one another…they really battered on! The weavers, I would say, really had to work…if you were lazy, you hadnae a chance. In fact, if you were that way inclined you generally just disappeared into the sunset! …Every loom had a wee red light at the top of it, and if it got knocked off for some reason, you just made a bee-line for it.*

Margaret Dick: *Even if your machines were all going, you still had to walk up and make sure the materials were coming oot perfect, and you'd to walk roond the back o your machines and make sure that there wisnae things clogging up the threads. We had to cut the collars – these were the extra bits of threads. We'd to cut these and make sure they werenae getting too thick. These were put up the back and that was what you tied your knots wi.*

Billy Dick: *Any extra you needed, these extra threads were put in there in case something went wrong. When they wound the thousands of threads onto the big beam at the back they always put in half a dozen or so extra. Of course, they wound thereself roon and roon and roon till it became…*

Margaret Dick: *…And then you also had to watch, they put a mark on the threads, and when that was woven oot through…that mark came up on your cloth, you'd to go and write it up on the board for the chap to come and cut it off and take that roll of cotton away…*

Billy Dick: *…25 yards.*

Margaret Dick: *…to be examined up the stair. Then I remember tae when they brought in the candy stripes. We thought this was wonderful! Working with colours. Instead of just the plain white, you had your coloured candy stripe.*

Billy Dick: *The bulk of the weaving was done for…Finlay and Co's name come through weaving jute…it was so heavy and so thick it was used for sailing cloths. When I say sailing cloths it was used for sailing yachts. That was away back in the days of the clippers and things like that because Finlay and Co were on the go then, but the advent of lighter stuff that was waterproof and windproof did away wi that. Most of the stuff was made for government, sheeting for the forces, things like that, what we cried AMS Ministry of Supply, and that used to keep half the weaving shed going for long and weary.*

Margaret Dick: *…The signal to get the tenter to come and look at your machine…an empty bobbin: if it broke down your machine, there was a wee bit of metal stuck oot the top. You got an empty bobbin and you put that up on the top of that, and that was the signal for the tenter to come and sort your machine.*

Billy Dick: *"Here's that woman again! She cannot keep thae looms going."*

Margaret Dick: *You cannae help if a machine breaks doon…and then sometimes your shuttle got so rough they were catching and pulling all your threads so you had to get the tenter to come.*

Billy Dick: *You really need to get to…I wish I could get you to some weaving because there's so little of it now. To understand the amount…how fine the stuff was, how to handle it and no get it dirty. In a factory where machinery is going it has to be oiled all the time, it had to be kept* [clean]. *The floors were absolutely spotless. There was a man went roon aboot all day long sweeping…and that's all he did all day long, picking up the fluff.*

Margaret Dick: *Did Linda* [Smith/Wilson] *tell you an all, on Fridays, if you were on back shift and you were going to the dancing…? Well I did dayshift/backshift week aboot…and on the backshift on a Friday night if you were going to the Auchinleck dance you took your clothes in that you were going wi, and at quarter to 10…we all used to make a bee line for the toilets, and I've seen some o the lassies standing wi their feet in the sinks and everything! Putting on your tights and your make-up and everything coming oot all ready for the dancing.*

Billy Dick: *The number of girls…when I was a foreman they would come to you about 9 o' clock at night on the 10 o' clock shift; Oh, I'm no feeling very well Billy! Oh, is that right? Your lipstick's looking well! Ken, you kent fine that they were going* [to the dance]. *As a rule, if it wasn't too often, you kinnae…is your pal there? …If you keep them going…*

Margaret Dick: *You tried to sneak some of your machines off a wee bit early…and yet it was 10 o' clock you were supposed to start putting them off. But maybe the bus was at 10 past or something. You'd to hurry to get oot.*

…You explained to me earlier that you met at the mill itself. You were working as a weaver, Margaret, and you were the…

Billy Dick: *…Tenter.*

Margaret Dick: *I had a great big pony-tail in thae days, and he just liked my long hair I think! He keeps talking aboot it yet! I didnae really like him to begin wi…it was during a Sunday School trip…that's when we actually…something clicked. I was an awfy shy person and I wouldnae go near him, because I always blushed. I just kept my distance away and if I needed my machine sorted I would put this up* [a bobbin on the piece of metal that stuck up] *and I would run away! He just had to guess what was wrong with it.*

Billy Dick: *The whole thing about the mill was it was close that way. There was a lot came from Muirkirk and New*

TWEEDALES & SMALLEY
15

14

Cumnock, not Cumnock surprisingly enough, not even Auchinleck, just the very odd lassie. They a' come from there. The buses arrived there in the morning and they a'…

Margaret Dick: *…piled in…*

Billy Dick: *…and when you went…I went in when I was 15 years old, two days after my birthday, to start my apprenticeship…I had been used to going in and seeing my father, and I knew aboot the noise and things like that, but the thing that struck me most was the language. Very, very coarse…you soon got used to it…some of them were terrible!*

Margaret Dick: *Oh there was danger there, because the shuttle sometime flew oot the machine and hit you. There was a lassie lost her toe, something dropped on her toe, and she lost that. And then you got folk losing fingers.*

Billy Dick: *There were very few to be honest with you. For all the amount of machinery that was there. Nothing like the pits were.*

Margaret Dick: *…Then one day the lassies fae New Cumnock and that never turned up to work, and it turned oot that that was the time of the mining disaster, the Knochshinnoch disaster…they didnae come into work. Some of their relatives were involved in it. We just had to try and get on the best we could without them.*

…It was a good wage, compared to my sister who worked in another part of the mill. She was in the winding. I got more and she used to resent it because I made more than her…

Billy Dick: *The likes o in my trade there was electricians. We always got paid more than electricians because it was such an obscure trade, ken. There wasn't that terribly many of us. When I said I got £2 and that, that went up so much…your five years of purgatory as far as wages were concerned was as an apprentice. You were in debt but you had security…was an indentured apprentice, which meant that they had me for five years whither they liked it or no. And it's how you did your work and how you progressed in it. We were very parochial because you didnae get movin aboot…we were a' here. The way the village, as you've seen, is split, ken…*

Margaret Dick: *What I didnae like aboot it though the likes o the lassies that were the weavers and that when you got married that was it, you were out. Married women werenae expected to work. It was a pity…yes I had to leave.*

Billy Dick: *We moaned and groaned, but no…there were very few that didnae get on. You had to get on because every depended on everybody else. The menial jobs…the girl that brought the weft out to the loom if she didnae bring it oot your loom didnae go! Therefore, if you loom didnae go your pick meter wasnae going; you werenae gettin a bonus. Everybody depended on everybody else. They were quite good at that, at helping one another out…I wouldnae stand by and watch…I could see the chap up above me having two or three breakdoons at the one time and I would go up and dae the simplest thing…it was very much a girl performance…and wi young men there was the usual…banter went on. But never anything really bad.*

Linda Smith (*neé* Wilson) worked as a weaver in the New Mill from 1965-1968: *…I started when I was 15, and the domestic science teacher says, "Where are you going to work Linda?", and I says, "I'm going to work in the mill". So, I started off in the mill at 15, and it was Bobby MacDonald that I met that morning, with another girl, Anne, and we went straight in and we were to battery fill. You know battery filling for the looms. I found out these were my looms. Nine on one side and nine on the other. There's the batteries. See the batteries? That's the batteries on each loom. An there was an A shift and a B shift, and I think that's the wee clock there. I was the A shift, and you had to* *remember when you come in…you started at 6 in the morning and you finished at 2, and that was one shift, and the other shift was from 2 till 10. I was the A shift A or B shift, but I was A…when I was 15, but I wasnae on these looms at first. I was on, just beside here there were nine looms…sitting, and I started battery filling and learning and even going around and helping the buddy that was there, ken. There were battery fillers plus you were to do that line, the lady that did that. Well I helped. I done the batteries. But it must have been Janet Harkness that seen me, and says, "Oh, she doesnae smoke"…Janet Harkness was the Weaving Mistress. You got to know her quite well because if you seen her coming oot a door you had to look at her twice cos she was that straight and, her shoulders back. She was like a wee, kinda, army man! You would think coming towards ye! An after a wee while at the batteries, eh, she says to me, "Linda, I'd like you to come into the Training Room". The Training Room was…just a wee room wi two looms in it. And they took you there to see…they timed you, to see how long you did when the yarn broke, eh; how long you took wi the cleek, to go through the needles. Everythin was timed. So she must have seen something in me cos I was quite quick. I was going quite quick. And that's what they wanted. They wanted everything going smoothly; the looms getting seen tae; watching your cloth. So everything was all timed, and you'd to do it in ten seconds, or* [something like that]*, and then she would break a bit o yarn and the loom would stop, because you see they needles there they needles would drop…so that said there was something wrong wi the yarn. Or if there were wool or ouse roon aboot there. And that's the wee bits o yarn you used to pit doon and to make your wee cross and to join up the yarn together…wi the nine looms, I learnt…say if the lassie went to the toilet, well I was that way that I wanted to make sure I did ma work. I didnae want to get into bother fae the Weaving Mistress! They were a' roon about. Though you thought they wernae there, they were there, and they checked you. Especially Janet! If you seen her walking towards you, you thought, What have I done? Have I done something wrang? What's she coming to me for? But…she must have thought, she's going to do well, so I'm getting her. So I went into the training room, and she would time us. I must have had a good time…*

Was it mainly girls that worked in the mills?

Well, the yarn…see there's a build up there, a roll there. When it built up, it was the boys or young men that came…to take that away. They took that away up to the Checking Room: where they checked your yarn. They knew where it came from, and if there was anything wrong… If you weren't watching your cloth at the front and there was a mark on it, that could have went for ages, because, if you weren't being vigilant…there was extra yarn that went aroond aboot the thing there, an you'd to cut that as well, and then start another bit of thread round it. And the yarn you took off the extra bits there went on that wee bit there…the other thing was the shuttle. You'd to watch that! In the three years I can safely say I wasnae hurt. You'd to go between these looms…as they were moving, if anything went wrong you put a bobbin up, an there was a wee light…a light on every loom. An when you put your bobbin up, that let the tenter know. He'd maybe be looking after five or six rows, and he would look doon, and if the bobbin was up, he came to see what was wrang. Sometimes the shuttle got…you'd to rub it doon. Say there were bits of wood sticking up. If it was moving back and forward like that [gestures with hands]*, if it had a bit o wood stickin oot of it it would break the yarn. So you'd to keep this going. Billy Dick says, You're going on to these looms!, cos they needed somebody for the A shift. I think I was just 16 then. And he says, You're going to these looms Linda, and I says, Oh but Billy, I cannae dae a' that! Ken, I was kinda greetin! I says, I cannae dae that. It's too much for me Billy! He says, Linda you got…92-93% oot the hunner: you'll be good! So that's me. I was thingmd into the 18 looms after that, an because I had been put into the Training Room some of the battery fillers…went to the office to object. They werenae against me* [but they thought] *if they had been on battery fillin' for so long, why should they not get a chance at having looms. So they went away into the office and they came back oot wi their books. I don't know whither they'd cheeked up to Mr. Niven or what they'd did, but they said to me after, It's not your fault but we should have been in the training bit quicker than you were. I had just started at 15 or 16 and they had, maybe, been there two or three year at battery fillin…I took it as…I was looking at them and thought it was terrible. But it wasn't ma fault. What could I dae? Janet said, You're on thae looms, and that's you you were tae dae it…well I says…I never*

3

2

smoked and if I went to the toilet it was just the toilet and back oot. I didnae sit and gossip or try to…be lazy. You had to be quite smart at it a' because the Weaving Mistress looked at you, you had to gi' them respect…like school teachers, telling you off. And…if the loom was going and the shuttle flew out sometimes there were accidents with that. I never got hurt at any time, but if that came out and you went out to about the middle of where the Weaving Shed was, you had a pole wi a blackboard and you wrote down whit number your loom was: 265 - SMASH. But you seen them comin…quite a lot o the yarn went away, so that meant that was stopped for quite a wee while the Weaving Mistress came tae sort it. If she was over-worked you got, "For God sake! What happened here?" "I don't know: the shuttle just flew oot!" The other thing wi the pin going up, Tommy McComb was a tenter – they sorted the looms Tommy McComb and Archie Ferguson, Stoker as we called him, he came up…I used to be frightened. Me just 16, you were to do what you were told. I said to Stoker the other day, I was feart o you Stoker! I says I used to hide behind the looms an say, Oh here he comes!, and he would look doon and I would be hidin behind a loom and he would sort it, take the shuttle away, take it tae his wee bench and rub it doon…and a lot of times it was smashes, but we couldnae help it…

…it would just come off by itself?

Aye. You'd tae make sure you'd to take out the shuttle as the machines goin like that [demonstrates] *moving back and forward, you'd tae make sure when the shuttle was in…if it wasnae in the right way it smashed. So you'd to turn the machine right roon again…an in fact I cannae hear right tae this day…*

…it must have been very…noisy?

Well, you made signals or things: what you were doin. I think you learnt sign language…when you were going away or going oot, here was nae use shoutin tae you: Is that right Linda? or, That's right!; Are you going oot for 5 minutes?; That's right; Well I'll keep the batteries goin. Everything was shouting! I think to this day you were getting dust…going into your lungs…you would holler…we did a lot o things tae for…we did tricks wi one another sometimes. Somebody had a thing like a dog's dirt an they brought it in and put it doon on the thingby; they're saying, where did that come fae? They would think it was rats or something…must ha been a big rat! Ken, there were a lot o, like the pits, camaraderie between a' your workers. Everybody helped yin another. If one didnae have something you helped. And then some o the times we were up at the dishtowels away at the back when I was older – somebody hadnae come in for their shift…the other week I was back at ma ain looms again. It was harder to dae the dishtowels. You had a 1 and a 2 and a 3 and a 4; and a 5 and a 4 and a 3 and a 2 and that was the bow. You got a box pattern for the dishtowels. Whereas with the ordinary yarn it was a 1 and a 3 and a 2 and a 4. You'd to keep that pattern…

Is that the sizes…what is 1 and a 2 and a 3?

Well, the needles…that was for the cloth. The other one which was a 1 and a 2 was to do wi needles. The needles went through thegither…as you pulled the thread…it went over. You joined a new thread, and you put it through that bit there…then you lifted up your yarn and parted it and you put it through…

What's parting?

Just parting the yarn…as you put the hand over the heddles you parted the yarn where the needles…just there…you put it through the needle…

When you talked about the shuttle, going up and down, and you never had an accident do you remember any incidents or accidents?

Aye. Some got their hands checked in the looms, there. That there [referring to image], *they rods there were between all that there, so we'd to come in and oot they…say you went between two o the looms: your overall could catch. Or else you could be doing the looms there…and sometimes, it just flew oot. The shuttle flew and you'd to get oot the road. But I hanae mind o that ever havin that wi ma looms. They were really good, so they were.*

So you enjoyed your work?

Oh aye! I would even go back to it to this day. I would go back. That was 1965 I started; by 1968 they were telling us it was gettin closed. So…the new mill that I was in was built in 1950 and it went to 1968, so it was only, eh, 18 years that it run…some of them were joyous and some of them, when we heard it, were, oh, we'll no need to work! We were all silly I think we were all silly, some o us because we had to go oot and get work after that. I think I went to…the shoe bit at Kilmarnock. I did machining there but I didnae like it. I liked the mill. It was a good place to work.

…You got your wee break. You didnae get long. And you could come oot the side o the mill, through…that bit and in tae May Cook's in the square, or Mr. Ferguson the baker… May Cook was a proprietor of…a tearoom. And we would come out of there and go into Ferguson's…and get hot pies…the man done all his own pies an everything. Great pies to this day! The tearoom was good. You had quite a lot o wee shops an things. Then you'd be back in from your break to start the looms up again, because the Weaving Mistress was going up and down they watched you a' the time. They watched for the light goin on and hoped for an easy day…the percentage you made that went to the tenters: that was their wages too. If you hadnae a good day wi your looms, or it went no good for one week, their wages would be low. So that's how when Janet was testing me, they're watching how fast you're goin an how fast you can get the yarn back on over the heddle and get that machine back on going. You were going up an doon looking at the yarn all the time watching the needles were working. Hell mend, if you let thae needles, didnae work and you werenae watching coming oot there the Weaving Mistress checked and asked where you were and what you were doing…somebody no doing what they were telt, they would get telt…if they were coming in late they would say…well they wanted to know if you were going to be a good worker and attend the times an everything. Different shifts: you could lie in on the 2-10 shift, but then you had the 6-2 where you were up at 5 in the morning, to come doon the brae, eh, and it was still dark, some of the time, coming doon tae your work. It stopped at 10…when you'd to start at 6, what I did was, if you get in there at half five, I went round the looms to see that they were all working. Because say you were just finishin at 10 and something happened wi a couple o looms. You could put that straight on so you can…I was always that way that I would make sure everything was right. I would put on the loom an' make sure everything was working alright. Because you could staun there, you could have 5, 6 lights goin, an' you'd to get roon a' that and it'd be a' different things. It could be the shuttle not working right, it could be the machine no going right or anything, the yarn could be goin in below…I did no bad, I think I was making £9 something, and that was good! A week! About £9/£10 I was making, and that's when I was 16/17. Oh that was good, that was good! …Friends come over to where we lived in Shawlands Street, and I decided to go to Niagara Falls, Canada. I saved up my money…and I went on my holidays for three weeks in 1967…at that time it was about £72, that was a lot of money in 1965/66/67, £72 to go to Canada.

Evelyn Campbell: *…The mill used to have a big dance hall up in the top and they held a lot of different things for the village, ken, no just for the mill. Ken, there was a dance flair and everything up the top o it: canteen… That was with the new mill.*

Robert Dalziel: *It was a busy village, a very thriving village in those days, although, I suppose, unbeknown to us the textile industry was in trouble. To all outward appearances in the late 40s and throughout the 50s it seemed to be quite a thriving village, but I dare say they were struggling to get orders much of the time. I do remember later on in*

the later 50s there wasn't always work. I can remember my mother sometimes working and sometimes not working. I think that must have been when orders were scarcer in the mills and…might lay off the weavers for so long and then take them back on when more orders came in… I think in the end my mother had a wee spell in the mill when she worked in the packing room rather than weaving…she worked there for a while cos I remember she was lightening fast in parcelling up presents at Christmas!

Ruth Sharp: *There was a new mill built…and of course it was a bit of a white elephant when it went down…the mill was built…it would take two or three years to build…it was built by George Reid of Catrine.*

John Sharp: *25 year ago it was knocked doon…85 that was knocked doon. A crowd fae Glasgow came up and they demolished it. They stayed at the Old Mill Inn doon there. The mill was a beautiful building… After Finlays went doon, Carrick…furniture business went into that for about two or three years. A' the boys worked in it. They'd be a lot anyway. It was just furniture and beds and stuff like that they kept there. Once they went doon that was it by forever.*

Evelyn Campbell: *…And then when the new mill* [got] *demolished there was nothing* [done] *with it. The kids were in it. You should have seen the street with toilet rolls! …They flung everything oot it!*

Barbara Devlin

James Taylor the mill manager.

When the Mill and then the Bl

Maureen Kiernan: *...Up St. Cuthbert's Street this is where Catrine really got its name as Queen of the West up at the voes...everybody took a pride in their gardens and everything up there. Where the sandstone houses were was okay, but moresay where the company houses were (that faces onto the voes where the swans are)...they used to hold wee flower shows and everything...everything revolved aroon village life...you just think about a' those things and maybe a lot of folk hasn't got memories o that noo. Most of that generation is away...*

Evelyn Campbell: *...They* [Finlays] *maintained a the river, cut o the hedging...*

Sean Campbell: *That's hoo this place was ca'ed the Queen of the West. You could have walked anywhere on the pads* [paths] *and it was spotless. No noo.*

Mary McCluskie: *I have to mention Mr. Taylor, the manager of the mill...he did an awful lot for Catrine...he kept Catrine lovely. The gardens and the steps up to the church, he sorted all those, and the steps up to* [the] *Memorial, he kept them in good condition with his workers...the reservoirs was the same: he kept them all clean. We used to swim in the reservoir, I'm going to call it voe, for we never, ever, called it that* [reservoir]...

Alistair Plenderleith: *They continued...they were the last to shut... A lot of people moved oot, a lot of people went to England tae... Some of them came back in later years ken, but a' the kinda aulder stages of the Bleach Field just stayed. That was it. You got a wee bit pension and their auld age pension and that was it...there used to be a thing at work...Down Your Way I think they cried it. Wilfred Pickles ran it. It came tae the mill. It was for factories a' o'er Britain. It was a radio programme. About one o' clock or half past twelve. Wilfred Pickles show. Her that used to be in Coronation Street wi the* [hair] *net was there. Ena Sharples and a' them came...aye they entertained people. Maybe find oot yin or two names that worked there and cracked a wee joke, ken, and that was it.*

How did things in Catrine change after Finlays closed?

...Well, friendship kinda fell oot at that time, ken. Some people went yin way, some people went another. Some got married...a lot of envying people...people that moved away and that...some thought they became better than you and moved intae a different kinda society, ken. But we've long memories! There were two or three boys I went to school wi and I hadnae seen them fae I left the school...two or three o them went intae the Merchant Navy and they moved on, ken...[Folk come back to the village] *and say, "You don't ken me!" I say, "Aye I ken you!" But eh, it was many moons fae I seen them.*

Maggie Bunting: *The raw material came in at the end of the mill...the raw cotton came in and it came up through and came out the finished article: sheets, pillow cases and that... It was all done in Catrine.*

Jim Bunting: *Yes exactly. The mill, it had all the machines the looms and all the rest of it and they prepared the cloth there and then and it would come up to the Bleaching Works to be dyed or sewn or whatever...it was all Finlay. Finlays was Catrine...they maintained the roads and everything, the steps up to War Memorial. It was always the Finlay men that looked after that...when Finlay went away there was a big decline in the village. You know, you missed them you really did.*

Lara McPyke (*neé* Bunting): *...Other villages it would be the council that would do things like that, but if Finlay did it here there maybe wouldn't be the same...the likes of these houses were all council owned...nearly every house in the village was owned by the mill...the house my mum and dad were in, it went to the council; it was a council house...the St. Cuthbert Street ones and the ones along the Newton they were council housing...once Finlay would leave, obviously they hand them over to the council...so these houses in any other village would have been privately owned for generations become council houses...that would have caused a big shift for folk when Finlay left.*

Jim Bunting: *...It took quite a while, you know, for the village to overcome that. For a long time it was pretty run down, but once the Square was built and things like that...*

Volunteer Arms ("Honky Tonk").

Harry Houston: *…It was a death-blow to this village because Cartine was a mill village. If you just go up and browse through the grave yard up there you'll see Catrine had a school long, long afore they had schools, they had lights, they had education and loads a things. A' the hooses were a' at wan time – mill hooses and fae that you had workers working in them. You had building works in them; joiners…it was the community. If you look and see the weir and the voes and the tunnel, that was a' maintained. Noo it's falling to bits and we're trying to get money tae dae something aboot it. From that aspect it's never, it's never come back… I think a lot of heritage was ruined in Catrine, ken, when they ta'en doon the wheel and various things. When you see what's happened at New Lanark, Catrine was a far bigger place than that! So that was somebody that thought different up there and you see the two places noo… I think if you had asked the people of Catrine at the time if they wanted to keep the wheel or scrap it you would have had 90% would say keep it, because people came from a o'er to see it…even then people were amazed at this. So it wouldn't take a genius to think, we've got something here!*

…If you look at the guid they done initially and the ideas, ground-breaking in a lot of ways with wanting their workers to be educated and to gie them medication. You'll have heard about the ambulance Bonnie Jean? That was another thing that you've got to gie them credit for. Way beyond their times then, that's never been an issue…the issue was once they became more competitive then things would change…plus they werenae just sourcing the mill, they were doing the village and a' the roads, so that was a huge thing…in 1950 they built the pumping station as well. It was a Glasgow crowd Wilson, Kinmond and Marr that done that…so it was all progress. They built the new bridge as well, the wan at the Bleach Works…the original bridge was mair for horse-drawn stuff. It used to have a couple of metal rims going up the middle of the road, obviously, to take the carriages… Where it was done before with the mill, naebody does it.

Anne Fleming: *I'm a Finlay's baby, but there was no way I wanted to work with them because you had Finlay and Company breakfast, lunch and dinner… They* [parents] *probably would have spoke for me and got me a job in the offices but I didnae want that.*

Maureen Kiernan: *I think Catrine is like everywhere else noo: we're built up with a housing scheme and it's just no the same. The friendliness: aye, they're friends but it's not the friendliness that used to be when I was younger. You could put your key behind the door and you just put your hand through the door. You couldn't do that noo…you don't know folk…you don't see…everything would be centred round Catrine because you would have the mill, you would have the Bleach Field…then you had the miners, but the mill at one time there used to be…10 or 11 buses sitting there waiting to transfer folk away to Auchinleck, Cumnock, New Cumnock even up to Muirkirk that worked in Catrine Mill…it would be mainly women because it was like the finishing actually went on there. Then they latterly got to bring some material from Deanston Mills through to the Bleach Field to get bleached and sewn up and everything else. Catrine Bleach Field was a lovely place because they used to go away to big exhibitions in London and everything else…at the Festival of Britain, they had a big stall there, Finlays. Finlays was well-known through the world. They used to do beautiful embroidery. We've got…a pair of towels up the stair. My mother had bought them for my Granny Kiernan before my mother was married. If I say to you I'm 74 and they towels are up the stair. They were bath towels and they were…white towels done with green and the initial K on them…you could get your towels initialled in the Bleach Field…they were made to last. We've got quite a few products of Finlays…I don't know if we've got the cotton sheets you don't see many folk with cotton sheets but Im quite sure when we had that exhibition down there, the stuff that came out from Finlays was unbelievable… When they built the new mill they had a shop where you could go in and buy your products in the new shop as well.*

Ruth Sharp: *Well* [the people] *they always thought maybe the wages weren't very high…but they had different perquisites that they got. Their houses: they could buy them at certain times. This row, Co-operative Avenue, belonged to the Co-operative first and then Finlay bought it. Now it belongs to the council…they did look after their workers, but maybe the wages were a wee bit lower than some places. But that was because of their Indian* [manufacture]*…Mr. Taylor, the General Manager, he came from a big factory of theirs in India to take over here. It took him a wee while to settle that they weren't Indians!*

Ruth Sharp: *Yes…they started off with five shillings* [pension] *away back in the days of my grandfather. He was…the finisher in the mill. He helped to finish the cloth. He said that he got five shillings from the Works. Well, when I left I think it'd went up to fifteen* [shillings] *each, for the pension at the works. A week! It was quite a sum of money…they didn't need to pay into it, it was just given to them. I remember when I was very small going out with my mother to distribute packs of tea from the big tea plantations from Finlay, and it was a present to all their old age pensioners. She was offered the Works car to go but she wouldn't go in the car. She walked with her basket because she knew everybody. She was a local lady. We took these round to all the old people and they all had their free tea…latterly, the tea that we were offered from these places, we'd to pay for it. It came in big, 5 lb packs. So they were quite good that way. There was quite a bit done.*

John Sharp: *You had an awful lot of miners, you had everybody that worked in the mills, the Bleach Field, the hosiery they came fae everywhere! …And the next thing it was a ghost toon. A' the works stopped. They came fae Cumnock: everywhere they came fae to work here. Bus loads. There must have been 5,000, easy, workers here and you had the wee hosieries, you had two o them, and everybody else who worked in Catrine all gone.*

PART THREE – BALL

After many years of having been leased out, Ballochmyle House and grounds were sold to the government in 1938-39 as a site for an EMS (Emergency Medical Services) hospital. It was built to the standard plan for EMS hospitals. Two blocks of eight wards and an administration/lab block were finished by 1940. Each ward had 40 beds. The mansion house was used as a staff residence for doctors, nurses and technical staff until later that year when the nurses' home was completed. The first patient was admitted to Ballochmyle on 20th October 1940. A further two blocks were completed in 1941, as was a second nurses' home nicknamed 'Siberia' by its residents on account of its inadequate heating. By December 1940 a plastic surgery and jaw unit was at work. The unit trained officers of the Royal Army Dental Corps.

Jack Mustardé is perhaps the best known doctor who worked at Ballochmyle. He qualified as a surgeon in 1940, but was taken prisoner at Torbruk in 1942. After having been transferred to Italian custody he was repatriated in 1943 due to illness. After he had recovered he specialised in plastic surgery at Ballochmyle. Besides becoming a consultant there and later at Canniesburn, Mustardé also wrote two books on plastic surgery. In 1992 he visited Ghana and discovered the West African country with a population three times that of Scotland didn't have a full-time plastic surgeon or suitable facilities, so went and canvassed the president, Jerry Rawlings. The president persuaded Mustardé that he was the best person to help and in 1997 a Burns and Reconstructive Surgery Unit opened in Accra. Subsequently, equipment from Ballochmyle went out to Africa.

My dad died in this hospital 20 years ago and it' s sad that the place he spent his last minutes is now a luxury housing estate. It was a good hospital.

This poignant comment doesn't come from the Memories Project but a simple post on a web site by Siobhan of Glasgow. Mixed feelings surround the housing development, above and beyond the loss of a facility which had offered significant local employment and links with the community of Catrine. Ballochmyle Hospital closed in 2000.

Jim Bunting: *I worked in the Path [Pathology] lab at the hospital, aye…I left school and kinda bumbled into that! …I just sorta fell into that job…when I first started in the lab we had to work on Saturday. Worked Christmas day as well! …When the new hospital at Crosshouse was built there was a brand new lab in there, you know. The lab at Ballochmyle was just in an ordinary building. It wasn't a proper lab as such.*

CHMYLE HOSPITAL

Lara McPyke (*neé* Bunting): *I remember as a wee girl going in and seeing all the…specimens! My Dad was showing us birds, black lungs and everything! Ohh! They used to be in, literally, big glass.*

Jim Bunting: *…It was a pity Ballochmyle closed because it was such a good hospital from the point of view of recuperation of patients…it was out in the country and they had verandahs on each ward…it had a great community spirit about the hospital. It just outlived its usefulness, you know.*

Lara McPyke (*neé* Bunting): *I suppose it's better the lands being used than not used really. Especially the big house. It is miraculous that it has been saved, I think, miraculous! Lee and I walked up round there a lot, you know, and it was really bad…there was no roof on it or anything. It's such an amazing building…at least it's been preserved. At least it's there.*

Jim Bunting: *That's where all the young doctors who did their stint at Ballochmyle were housed in the mansion house, aye. Until it became unfit for use* [laughs] *put it that way!*

Maureen Kiernan: *It was requisitioned during the war…they built it…used the grounds and built up the hospital on it. They were all single-storey…that was used for doctors and surgeons…they lived in there. The operations were done down the corridors and…it was a plastic surgery place…it was a plastic surgeon, Mr. Tough…then it was Mr. Mustardé. Although a lot of the equipment came out off Ballochmyle, Mr. Mustardé took it away to…the Third World. The plastic surgery would be done in Ballochmyle. It was world renowned. It was servicemen that would maybe get burned or anything like that…they wore blue uniforms, but they would be allowed into the village, if they were fit to get out. I know one man who married a Catrine woman, and his face was a' burned. They would come down…Jacob's Ladder and right through the gatehouse and up to the pubs. They wouldn't have much to drink, but it took them out. Ballochmyle, it was a fantastic place. Fantastic surgeons in those days…I would have preferred seeing the hospital there. It would be much, much nicer if the hospital had been kept there, or what I heard at the time…turned into a sports facility for the SFA, but the money kinda went haywire… There were two gatehouses into Ballochmyle at that time. There was the first gatehouse and then the second gatehouse. They had church services and a' up there in the canteen. If we couldn't get on a Sunday morning up to the Birnie or something, we would get the bus and go to the canteen. It was set up for the Catholic church and then when the Catholic church moved out, they set up for a denominational service. There was a lot of employment at Ballochmyle Hospital. So we lost all that as well. We lost Finlays, we lost the pits…that was it…it was quite sad cos a lot of folk had to move away. There were still a lot of coal mines down in England so a lot of folk in this area moved down to Derbyshire and to Nottingham…but everybody seemed to find employment. It maybe wasn't what they were used to. They moved away to get employment, cos they were quite young. Ballochmyle was there and men could get jobs as porters or ambulance drivers. I mean, it wasn't as if you had paramedics in those days…the hospital was a Godsend because it employed a lot of the women.*

Anne Fleming: *I left the school in 1955 and was lucky enough to get a job at Ballochmyle Hospital as a short-hand typist/secretary to the matron at that time… I did the first three years at Cumnock and then did a year in the*

commercial class, which was short-hand typing, English and bookkeeping. I got my Scottish Certificate in that. Just before I left the school, during the summer...holidays, the girl that was the clerkess at Catrine School had applied for extended leave to go to Canada, and because I was the only one in the commercial class from Catrine, they sent me to work at Catrine School as the secretary. That was getting the exams and the prize things all sorted out...that school's no longer there...Mr. Carruthers was the headmaster...I would have liked to have kept on that job but the girl was coming back and at that time you could have applied for umpteen jobs and get interviewed: Saxone, BMK, lots of these places in Kilmarnock. I ended up taking one that was in Galston. It was a hosiery. The Balmoral Teashop is still there. That's where I started working and I was there for three weeks, it shut down for the holidays...and then I went for three weeks, but my name was in at Ballochmyle...and they got in touch and I started there that year in the September. I was a week at the front office till they decided where you'd to go. It was a Miss Jean Neil from Catrine who was the administrative boss at that time and she decided where you were to go. So I was put across the corridor into the matron's office. So that was 55. I was there till 61 till I was pregnant with my first child. The next year...they contacted me to see if I would like to come and work in the telephone exchange as a sort of relief, one day a week, supposedly...mum was the babysitter or whatever, and I did that for a year...I left after a year when I was having second baby and then I wasnae back till Ian was three. That was in 1972...22 years later I left due to ill-health or I might still have been there. In that block/office I went across the corridor, back across the corridor...and ended back in the office where I had started...it took me 40 years to do that! So Ballochmyle was really my life and it was sad the day we were at the closing ceremony...about ten years ago... Some of the wards moved gradually fae Ballochmyle to the Ayr Hospital...the first thing they took away was the casualty...we had a casualty department. Then it was the blood...and haematology department. It all went to Crosshouse. So we were what they termed a Satellite Division. In the exchange you weren't just answering the telephone which a lot of people didn't understand...we were there 24 hours so we had the fire alarm service, we had the cardiac arrest phone and if Prestwick Airport was put on standby for a plane, we wouldnae have taken the casualties, but we would have taken patients from Ayr County as it was...so we had a standby procedure. So it was the telephonist that had to go a' through this list of people to notify...plus you had to continue answering your calls at the same time, although that took preference. With the lab being moved, if people were needing emergency bloods done at night...had to go to Crosshouse, so we were the ones that had to arrange that: arrange taxis to takes a wee vial of blood to Crosshouse. Each department had a different set of rules. The haematology side was different from the biochemistry side and all that sort of thing, but it was interesting... Even further back when it was the war time they had the big burns unit...you had photos of like...this Polish chap stayed in this street and he was badly burned and he had been treated at Ballochmyle. And the big facial unit and that. We had dental, we had everything! It was a teaching hospital...the nurses went through their training there.

In these days when it was day matron, she wasnae big but, by jings, she could...I've seen grown men go out of the office crying! She had a wee poodle dog and it sat below her desk and if there were two of us in the office and if we got buzzed to go through, she had a flat within the building...and if she buzzed for someone to take the dog through to the house you knew someone was in for a row. They had to come with breakages; if they broke a glass medicine dish or a thermometer you'd to come to the office to report that...and you got a row for it! You knew someone was really in for it if the dog got moved because it glowered from below the table! She was in charge. There was her and the medical superintendent was in charge of the doctors, and there was the steward: he was in charge of the porters and the gardeners and things like that, but him and matron, they collaborated, maybe, every month about the menus and things and they had the staff dining room, which was very much by creed...matron was here, and if matron was in before you, you'd to excuse yourself as you went past her. Then it was the sisters, the staff nurses, the students and we were deemed domestic/technical staff. You couldnae go much lower than that! But it was very much class... They had big dances held in the nurses home...the first time I took Jack, he was interviewed by the assistant matron and nurses' home sister. "Oh, this is Jack. We've heard of him!" He'd to be eyed up and down, and I mean there was no drinking; no bar. There was drinking but it was in the nurses' rooms, unofficially. It was very much them and us. The doctors, the consultants and all that sort of thing…I worked with nice people. I keep in touch with some of them yet…it was like a big family, Ballochmyle…you had the nurses' home, the mansion house for the unmarried doctors and the annex…and later on…these mobile homes. They had a tennis court and all that, they had the teaching school for the student nurses…then you had the prize-giving day which was a lot of work for us. You had all the certificates and they got their Ballochmyle badge and that sort of thing. It was a big day. Every second year they had a big sale of work which was for the benevolent fund for nurses in Scotland, and we used to have to send out letters to all the companies, the factories up the valley, the hosieries and all that sort of thing. They were very good at sending donations. They made a lot of money then. We had concerts from time to time…the students put on reviews and things like that…one wee male nurse who was quite tiny, they had him dressed up as a baby once, just with a nappy on! Then one year there was a line of underwear on the flagpole! There was a row about that! They had gardens at the hospital as well. They'd about eight gardeners and they produced all the fruit and veg that they used in the kitchen…and they had walled gardens…it was mainly fruit. There were so many rhododendron bushes. The grounds were lovely…it [the walled garden] *will still probably be there…it was down towards the mansion house side, and the mortuary was away down there, just verging on to the golf course…then my daughter left school, she got a job as a nursing auxiliary up there. This was the line continuing on…she was always Anne Hasting's daughter. We've a thing in the village here: you talk about people with their maiden names…the wee villages tend to do that…even now we talk about, That's such and such…I would say, "That's Margaret Waddle, not Margaret Dick.".*

Mary McCluskie: *…We got an awful lot of cases in there. They* [patients] *used to come down into the village in their pyjamas and dressing gowns and slippers. We just took it for granted, we never thought anything of it. Some* [had] *big cages over their face where they had been badly disfigured, others with their fingers off and that.*

…I was at Ballochmyle working for a while too…I was just a domestic, and then I was in the laundry place…I quite enjoyed Ballochmyle…Ballochmyle was a great hospital! They even [took] *strangers that came from Maybole, Stranraer, all the different places. I always said it was the best hospital I'd ever been in: and the cleanest… At Ballochmyle, in the mornings, any of the girls could tell you when the maids came on they'd to pull out every bed onto the middle of the floor on one side, and that had to be hoovered, then it had to be mopped. Then when they got to the bottom the top was dry for it was warm, and they started on the beds on the other side. Oh, we had a severe supervisor! She used to come in and go along the edges of the things to see if there was any dust…it was really, very hygienic…the matron even checked you if you had open-toed shoes on!*

…When I was at school it was a lovely big estate, and the deer ran wild in it, and the squirrels. We went up there for the Sunday [School] *picnic every year…I think we went up in a horse and cart…and then Reid* [the builders] *gave us a lorry one of the years, and he took us up…happy times… My dad used to say when he was going to the Mauchline pit in the morning the bus had to stop to let the deer cross the road! He said that happened quite often!*

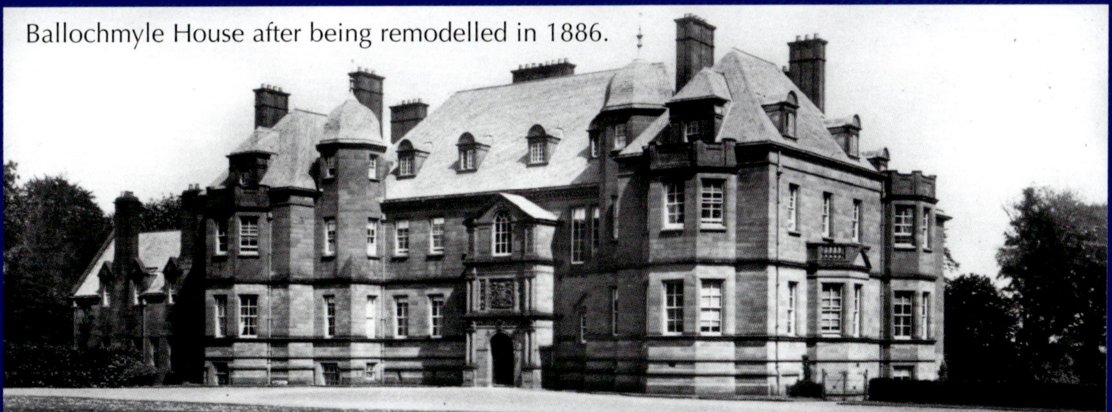

Ballochmyle House after being remodelled in 1886.

PART FOUR – EVERYDAY LIFE

Hor

John Johnston was born on 27th March 1923 at 1 St. Cuthbert's Street, Catrine where he was brought up with his five sisters: *Born and bred in Catrine, aye! Well, my father was a miner…worked in various pits around. He worked on different shifts, so it was very seldom he needed the bed…it could be two weeks before he needed the same time as us. He could be on night shift or back shift. My mother's name was Jean Roxburgh…she worked in the mills at one time, when she was younger. I don't remember her working in the mills…after that she maybe done domestic service for folk, ken, and she went tae tie hay, corn to the farms and big mills things like that. Hard life! …I had five sisters. The only boy…aye, five sisters. I was the youngest o the family. I was the baby… A room and kitchen…well it was common in thae days. There werenae many big hooses…at bedtime it was a struggle! You got by! You had two built-in beds in the living-room and you had a built-in bed in, what we called, the bedroom. Then you had a bed in below the bed, you could pull out, what we called a whurley…and it would go out like* [gestures with hands] *that and you had another bed. A full house.*

Maureen Kiernan: *…I was born in what would be termed the village of Catrine…at 9 Mill Street…we were surrounded by the old mill and various aspects of the mill…it was lovely. My mother was a mill worker. When she was married she got a mill house, and it was only a room and kitchen, but it was a tenement and there was a lot of big families lived in that tenement. We went further down and…I've lovely memories of that side of Catrine…I like the scheme as well, but Catrine in those days was Catrine. I can understand now why it was known as Queen of the West, for it was a beautiful, beautiful village. Beautiful shops; people were friendly. People didn't have much money, but everybody helped everybody in those days.*

Life

Catrine Sanatorium demonstration photographed in Mill Street *circa* 1904.

Mary McCluskie: *I was born 31st May 1924. I'll be 86 at the end of May…I was born in Auchinleck but I left when I was four years old. My dad had a bad accident in the Birnie Pit, so I had to move to Catrine. My mum bought a wee shop…just everything: bread, sweets, anything like that…it didn't sell newspapers, a sweetie, shop that had bread and cakes and things…but she wasn't a good business woman so it didn't pay…we'd a hard life you know, because money was very tight in those days, I mean really, very tight. In fact I can remember having to go into the wash house at 12 years of age. It was outside across the road, and you'd to go into the wash house in the morning before you went to school…it was Miss Begg that was the Infant Teacher. She had two canaries hanging up on the wall, and every morning you went in you'd to say, good morning Miss Begg, good morning Jill and Jack. My mother didn't keep very well. It didn't do me any harm! It brought me up to be a good worker… They were very poor years: really very poor…it's all away now…it was up Ayr Street where the new buildings all are.*

Ayr Street *circa* 1904 looking toward the Brewery.

The War

Alistair Plenderleith: *...You heard what the news was. The parents used to listen to the wireless, there were nae televisions or anything like that. Yin o the memories I have of the war was going up tae the Brae Tops and watching Clydebank getting blitzed. You could actually see the flares in the sky where they were bombing Clydebank...I was just a wee boy watching the blitz...you could...hear the difference in airplanes from the British to the Germans. The Germans was mair a kinda Whooom, whooom, whooom where the British planes was going o'er quicker, ken. That's how you kent. That nicht* [Rudolf] *Hess came o'er tae...he bailed oot...*

Were you scared?

I didnae care aboot it. You were with your mither and faither and that was a' that mattered...I think they were kinda worried about the Bleach Field but it wasnae they bits they were after. It was munitions and tha', where they built ships... There were three or four boys fae St. Cuthbert Street got killed during the war.

I've mind o the [ration] *books: three day and one day. You went to your Granny's if she didnae use them...you got a quarter o sweets! I remember when we got bananas at first...you didnae know how tae peel them! We'd never had had them at ma age...we didnae know what tae dae wi it! ...When you went hame there was aye something on the table...powdered egg in thae days...I actually enjoyed it. In fact I had a notion tae go back tae it, ken. Peas meal...broon stuff made intae peas meal. Peas and broth...you put warm water on it and a bit o butter in it and stirred it roon. It became an awfy colour! You dipped milk intae it. It was...no really tasty but it was feed...*

Mary McCluskie: *The war really didn't touch us. The only thing that touched us was the rationing, because...it's the mothers that should have got medals for keeping us on the rationing we got. They were very, very poor, the rations. I think we went to the café quite often for a fish supper* [fish and chips wasn't rationed during the war], *but if you had money and you stayed in the town, you could go out to a restaurant but we couldn't do that so we'd to make the rations do. Aye, we got coupons, aye, and you got sugar and that. You got a pound of sugar for the full family to do you a fortnight, or that. You went weekly and got your rations, just a wee bit butter. A lot of people went off butter and on to margarine. I don't think it was rationed the same. Lard wasn't rationed and people could bake with lard for a while. Baking wasn't good, you know, but it passed... At that time we didn't have a backdoor, but yince the war came we had one, yes. The man up the stair was a right, good gardener. He kept us going on leeks and that. You fed more than potatoes and vegetables and things you know. We got quite a lot of corned beef, that was about the main beef you got...I think I did everything with it! I made corned beef fritters, I made corned beef pie, corned beef hash: everything! ...See at St. Cuthbert Street...well, they had huge, big gardens up the back a lot of them had hens and we used to take our hard bread up and you would maybe get some apples that they were growing and you went up maybe it would be tuppence – and got cabbage or leeks or something. I dont think the shops stopped* [selling] *green vegetables because they were up there... They got raided quite often! ...There used to be a boy who came looking for me and he always brought me pears. I didn't want anything to do with him, but he always brought me pears. He stole them.*

Sean Campbell: *I went to the school in 43, right, and when the Germans were bombing Clydebank and Glesga, we used to go up the hill and see a' the flares, and I'm no joking! The Queen and the King came into Cotirn when we were at the school...and they wouldnae open their blinds and why they came into Cotirn that was the main line up there. They got telt there was a Messerschmitt following them and that's why they came off the main line...see up the hill top there was a shed in the middle o the field and it was a...*

Evelyn Campbell: *...look-out post...and there used to be one up at the cemetery...it sat on stilts.*

Apparently there's a wreck of a plane...over the brae heading towards Sorn?

Evelyn Campbell: *Aye, it was supposed to be at Blacksidend.*

Sean Campbell: *Aye, it was a Spitfire. You can see the mark* [where it crashed] *yet…ma brother's got a bit of Perspex off it.*

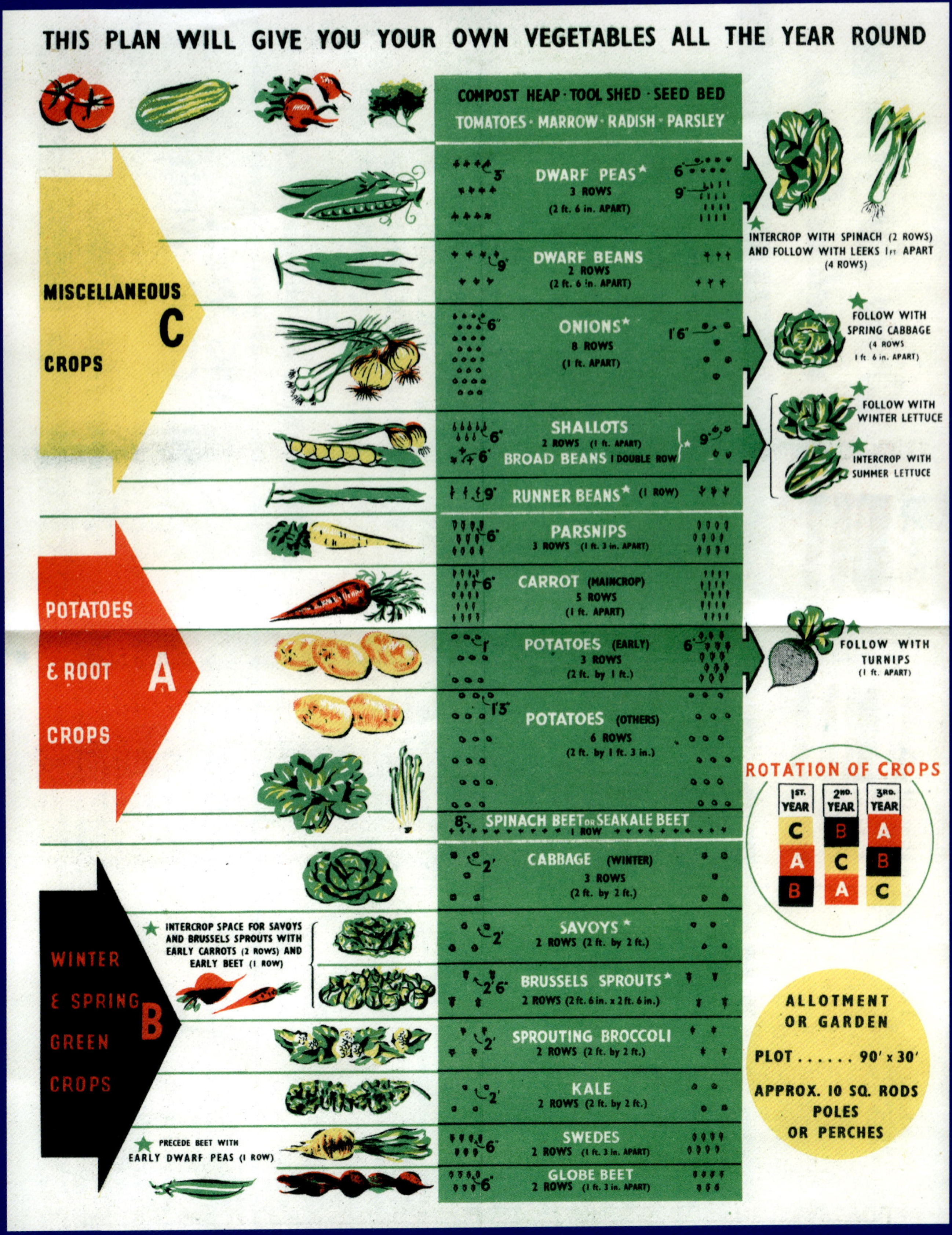

Shops

John Johnston: *...I used to work in a barbers shop. Soap boy. In Catrine. I could ha got maybe 2/6 a week for doing that. Soap boy washing the floors, soaping the men for the barber to shave...I was doing that while I was at the mill too...you went in at night and at the weekends. Say I finished at 10 o' clock at the mill I could have the rest of the day at the barbers, Tannock's. See as you come to the bridge? See the Brewery Bar? It was part o it at one time. He moved to about three different bits actually till he got the shop he wanted, but that's where he finished up...that's the barbers shop they made into a lounge... There could have been four* [barbers] *working at the weekends...that was the days you went to get a haircut...you could go every week to get a haircut. Short, back and sides. That was quite customary in thae days. There were no long hair in thae days!*

Alistair Plenderleith: *It was mainly the Co-op but they went to wee shops tae, but the Co-op...dividend day was a big day. That was when you got another pair o shoes or something like that. You'd be wondering how much the dividend would be. As I say, it a' helps. We struggled through...there was a bicycle shop we used to attend...Ferguson's! That's the name. There was Wullie McWhir's. He selt suits and threads and a' these kinda things. The Tallys: Emma Sisi... The Brewery Bar was the main pub... Auld Harry Hare had the shop on the corner, a sweetie shop. When we went to school it was Eleanor Henderson. She had a wee shop up by the Newton, her and her faither. It was just a wooden hut! ...Selt everything, aye. You jumped the dyke during school playtime and you went to Eleanor's for a Dolly Barn or whatever it was in that days...back into the school.*

Sean Campbell: *She's fae Mauchline, but her faither got a job in Glasgow...when he came back fae Burma in the war...*

Evelyn Campbell: *...and we bought the shop doon here, then it finished up we had two shops...see where the Pit Stop is, just before that. My dad had the grocer's shop, and just roon the corner there, that was a' shops right up that street. The full Square was shops. We had the drapers shop next to where Hughie* [Harvey] *stays...and we stayed*

in the house upstairs when we got married…Hilditches…[The other shop]*…it was a grocers. When we moved into it when we bought it, it was a fish and chip shop! …My dad was yin o they kind, he would go away up to Glasgow market early in the morning…and get fresh veg, ken, so to sell. On a Friday night I used to go up there and we used to bake potato scones, pancakes, tablet…*

Sean Campbell: *He had a grocers van and would go roon the scheme…*

Evelyn Campbell: *…We got married in '62 and my dad died then. My father took his own life…and then my brother and me kept the shop going for two or three years after that. I had the drapers shop but the big mill was there and it closed down, and the Carrick Furniture shop took it over. So, there were always lorries there, so I changed ma shop into a tearoom and I catered for the long-distance lorry drivers. We were friends wi them for 20 years…we had two big attics up the top of the house, so we had single beds in them, so they used to…ken, they had their breakfast in the morning and they'd maybe be there for a couple o days before they got unloaded.*

Jim Bunting: *…The Co-op was a big thing! 11-58: that was our number, wasn't it? Our dividend number? The store number. What's now the council office that was…a department of the Co-operative. But that was built late on…just round the corner at the top* [of Co-operative Avenue] *there? You know you've got the garages, and then you had Jimmy* [McGavin]*…he was the Co-operative manager. That was his house, and then they built that building beside it. Was it furniture Matt sold in there? I think it was.*

…The Co-operative supplied absolutely everything, didn't they? I remember when I was a boy they maybe had a couple of motor vehicles, but most of them were horse-drawn…and the horses used to be kept on what is the Scouts Hill. That's where the horses were turned in at night. Wullie Bone he…used to come round with a pony and trap with the milk [and] *curds on the back and you used to go out with your tin can and get your milk that way… He used to wear gloves with the fingers cut off and it was gie cold in the winter…straight from the farm…you know the Holm Farm road at the Institute? Well that was a farm, the Holm Farm and when I used to deliver the papers… I used to go into Mrs. Dowie's, that was the garage up there, they lived in the house that Burns came to where he dinnered with a lord* [Nether Catrine House]. *Mrs. Dowie…would say to me, Would you run over to the farm and get me some milk, please? It would be okay if I maybe wasn't going to the football or something like that, but I would run over with the can and bring it back and give her the milk. But you got a good tip for it! You got a tanner or something for going for it.*

Ruth Sharp: *…Away back before my time they had Seaton's, a dressmaking shop…Willie McWhir*[ter]*, that sold everything! …Fishers ironmongery…they had a petrol pump and it was beside the wall of the mill. And then of course there was Dow's the garage over here, now away… It* [Catrine] *was a closed place when I was a small girl…it had a doctor, a minister, Dr. John was the minister. He lived till he was over a hundred when he retired to Ayr…and the farmers, of course, came in with their cars, but there was only about one car in the whole place…Willie Reid's bus…they had a hiring service too. In our old house, down at the bottom of the 'Avenue' here, we knocked down a building at the outside that had kept a horse. They had their own horses, but we'd no horses up at Broomknowe except the ones at the works…Chance liked peppermints and my father used to always keep peppermint for his indigestion, and he would give the horse one and one day he stopped on the bridge…and he ate this peppermint and I says to my father, "How does a big horse like that taste a peppermint?"*

Mary McCluskie: *We had the Bazaar. I liked that, that was Mr. Mitchell… I was waiting for a job in the mill for they werenae starting till after the holidays, so in-between that about a month I'd to wait for a job. Mr. Mitchell in the Bazaar asked me if I would come and help his mum. She was 70, just where Co-operative Villas are, and I went…every morning, Monday to Friday, and I did everything I could for her, and I got five shillings. She was crying*

when I'd to leave to go to the mill for eight [shillings] *and elevenpence. She couldnae afford the other three* [shillings] *and elevenpence and they were a grocers' shop. She would just have her housekeeping money likely, ken, from the business. I would have stayed there for I liked Mrs. Mitchell...*

Mr. Cochran, the chemist, he had a wee outhouse he'd made for his daughter, like a wee Wendy House...and he put a boiler in it, and see during the war years he made make-up and all the mill lassies used to go and queue. And leg tan! ...He was a great chemist. He could have went further but he liked Catrine and he married a Catrine lady, ken. He made camu powders and they came from [all] *places to get these camu powders. He made all they things...and he didn't charge a lot for them.*

Robert Dalziel: *...I can remember right enough being handed things like a shilling and told to walk the street to Ferguson the bakers and get half a dozen tea breads and keep the penny change to myself. Tea bread was tuppence each. If you bought half a dozen you got them for elevenpence...a scone, a pancake or crumpet or whatever and if you bought six you got a penny off so it was elevenpence. I usually bought penny caramels to chew back down the street!*

There were actually two Fergusons who were not related. There was the bottom Ferguson the baker and the top Ferguson the bakers further up the street. They were both good bakers but they both had reputations for different things. The bottom Ferguson's baker – that was at the corner of Bridge Street and the Square – their pies were quite famous...and the top Ferguson's made very nice cakes...

...My mother for a wee while, worked in the furniture shop, Alex Niven's furniture shop in St. Germain Street. In later life when she had packed in the mill Alex had...what we used to call Bryan the Butchers. He took over from old Annie Bryan. He was Niven's the butchers and he took the shop next door. It was a furniture shop and my mother

worked in it for a wee while... Alex would organise carpets for you or get your carpet laid for you as well, aye, and furnishings. It was a funny looking place; it seemed a wee shop from the front but there was only the one window in the door, but actually it was quite a deep shop, and there was quite a big back room as well where he stored stuff.

The Co-op was the big place! There was: a Co-op bakers...there was the Co-op grocers, the main Co-op shop, there was David Cairns' father – David Cairns...lived in the same street as me in the Mauchline Road. His father was the cobbler, Co-op cobbler through the pen where they used to have the stables. That was round where the Co-op butchers was, and the Co-op drapers. There they were, on either side of the pen and that was down about Ford Street. There was also a Co-op further up, one opened up in the new housing scheme...

...The Sisi family were in the chippy, as we called it, in the Square for many, many years. That was a very central, focal point for us as youngsters: you got in the café and had something...maybe sit in, and half peas and chips, sixpence and then you had your ice cream, your raspberry sauce, or you could sit in with your fish supper... There was another chip shop in Ayr Street. It was...Siminini...I think was the name. Probably not the correct pronunciation, but it was also an Italian family who had it but we didnae use it so much simply because it was the further away. Both had a good reputation as chippies – both good chippies, aye! I'm trying to think of other shops but the Co-op was the big dominant area...there was also Tannock's; it was a hairdresser...in the back shop was the hairdresser; the front shop was the toy shop and general goods... Willie Paterson's, a newsagent, he was on the corner of Ford Street and St. Germain Street. He was a great village character! There was Mitchell's in the Bazaar, who was on the corner of Ayr Street and St. Germain Street...Mitchell's Bazaar...it was largely a grocer's shop at the end...loads of shops...Margaret Gibb's drapers...was in the Square, and it was very much ladies' wear and childrens wear. Aitken's the shoe shop, now they had been there a long time in the corner of the Square just along from the café and they made their own shoes...it was a shoe shop that made their own shoes! In fact, I remember Tom Aitken as a youngster: he was still in the shop then and that had been the family shop for a long, long time... There were several

butchers: there was Bryan the butcher; Co-op butchers and there was Parks the butcher which was almost exactly across the road from Bryan the butcher. In St. Germain Street there was another butchers there and several pubs, of course, as well… I think they all got along well enough but the people had very definite views of who was the better butcher or the better baker…the butchers had a reputation for being better at particular things. They used to go to Bryan's for steak pies – they had a great reputation for steak pies – and I think…Parks the butcher was pork, they had a good reputation for their pork. Strange memories! I don't remember it being a sort of cut throat rivalry…you would maybe go to one shop and another day go to another one but the Co-op had the big advantage of the dividend. I remember my grandmother's dividend number was 833! You always got a wee chitty 833 marked on it plus what you had spent, and it was always great days – dividend day – because I always got some pennies from my granny!

There was also apparently a very successful penny library in Catrine, which again suggests that there was a fair degree – a fair level – of education in the village, and Finlay, before Finlay in Alexander and Dale's time there was a school attached to the mill…a long, long tradition of education with the workers and they clearly, from the size of the library at the Institute and from the existence of the very successful penny library in the village itself, the workers had clubbed together to create that penny library, there was obviously the desire for education. Certainly, the kind of books that were in the Institute that I saw as a teenager, I mean, it was books on religious studies, philosophy, engineering. There were all kinds of things there…as far as I know they were thrown out…

Harry Houston: *…There was a cobblers. Naebody got throwing away shoes then. It was a' sewn and heeled. I remember goin wi ma mother to the cobblers and there was a guy Davy Duncan. He was a wee bit older than me. He was learning to be a cobbler. There were piles and piles o shoes, ken, and I thought, God Almighty! he'll be there forever! …I remember Cook's the tearoom…May Cook… There was Ferguson's. There were actually two Ferguson's: there was wan the bicycle shop, which was up beside May Cook's and the other wan was further doon the road…on the corner…it was a drapers shop* [Wullie McWhir]*… Noo, up* [Bridge Street] *there were two or three shops as well.*

There was also Willy Cochran's: that was the chemist, just doon from the church and across from the mill...when you went to the doctors it was Dr. Allan, and that was next to the chemist... There was also the post office just up from there. That's the original post office. Just up from the square there was a church which is noo next to the Royal Bank. It's just a parking area. There was a church there. There was also May Folly's shop. We used to come oot the pictures, the matinee, and go in there for chips. There was the bakers: Ferguson's the baker...the butchers, eh, it was always the Co-operative butchers. Then it was Meg Niven started up a place which Peter Logan has got noo...that was a butchers shop then...it was her that owned it, Meg Niven...her man was the butcher...the two of them done the shop.

Maureen Kiernan: *...Where I lived in Mill Street...across the road...Willie Murray had the dairy and you went there for your milk and they had a wee shop and everything else...on the opposite side of the street, where the Old Mill Inn is now, there was the Co-operative but before that it was a Mr. Dalziel that owned that shop. Then the Co-operative took it on and it was Alec Johnston and Howat Steel, his boy. Then the war came and it was Alec and Howat that had to go away to the war, so the Co-operative had to close that down. We come further up and...what's the Old Mill Inn now was the Red Lion. That was Mrs. Raeside's pub...I always remember if my dad was on the back shift, going across wi a jug to get a shilling's worth of beer. You went to this wee side window, in those days women weren't allowed into pubs, and they opened it up and you got this jug of beer... Then further up there would be Carson's sweetie shop, just at the corner before you come to the kirk...in between this there were tenements. They were lovely houses; they were all company houses as well... You went up to where you'd be going to the big wheel and that...was the doctor's surgery and you come round the corner and that was the chemists. You went further up and that was the post office... Dr. Allan was the doctor and he pulled your teeth! Dr. Allan did absolutely everything! Then Dr. MacCrae came for a wee while, and Dr. MacCrae had to go away to the army. When Dr. MacCrae came back from the army he came to Catrine...on that same side of the street down past Chapel Brae...there's a lovely wee cottage sits there, well that was Chapel Brae. My mother and them only got their turn of the washhouse on a*

certain day, and you couldn't hang your washing out through the back because it was all tenements and they'd to go up there and pay. It was Dalziel that had the shop before the Co-operative and it was his drying green. It was what's known as the Toll Green because seemingly years ago that's where you'd to pay a toll to come into Catrine…just at the foot of Chapel Brae, across from Ayrbank big house. They'd to pay money to get on to dry their…washing… Further up was the Gas Works…in those days there wouldn't be a housing scheme; everything was centred round the village. So everything was gas…gaslight…you always got the smell of gas. In fact I think if you go up now you can actually see the remnants of the Gas Works… Then you come to the side of the street I was born on…big families in the tenements, round the corner…then you came further down and round the corner and it faced onto the river. Mrs. Dick Reed and the Borlands and the Carsons a' lived in that bit of the street…next to us was Skillen's sweetie shop. That was the only shop that was there…there were some more company houses and then it was all part of the mill after that. You went in the Weaving Shed and everything was there. You went round the corner and that's where fire doors were, where Inspex [the optical factory] *is now…then we came to the shops. The mill was sitting in the centre and everything revolved round about the mill. The first shop was Baker Ferguson's. The mill used to work on a Saturday morning at that time, and the mill would stop about 11 o' clock and everybody came out from the mill. During the war years things were hard to get and folk would queue up to get into Baker Ferguson's. That's what it was known as: Baker Ferguson's. The next shop to that was Dandy McLean's and Mrs. McLean's…what a shop, a hardware shop, it was like an Aladdin's cave! This is where you went to buy your gas mantle because it was a penny and tuppence – you didn't have electric. It was all gas mantles…you could get everything from a needle to an anchor in Dandy McLean's! You got carbolic soap, all your scrubbing brushes, everything! Then the next shop to Dandy McLean's would be the bicycle shop: Ferguson's bicycle shop. It was always a busy shop because folk needed their bikes. My dad used his bike when we stayed in Mill Street to go to the pit, the Barony. The next shop was May Cook's. May Cook had a small library and a sweetie shop and through the back shed a wee tearoom…that's the first time I got books: out of her library. It would just be a bookcase just about the breadth of the wall and she had books there; lovely books! …You took them away with you! She stamped them out. Just like a council library now. It was a proper library…she had biscuits. It was all loose biscuits in these days. She had her biscuits and sweeties and you went through the back and that was a wee tearoom. May always made the lunches for the school teachers from the Secondary School. They used to go in there for their lunches… The next shop to May Cook's was a lovely, lovely ladies' shop. It was Nora Brown's. Nora Brown was a lovely person – she was a right gentle person and she always had this beautiful perfume about her shop. It was Oil of Petula: a wee tube of Oil of Petula. You could only get it in the chemists, and she had this sprayed in and, ohhh, the shop was really something! Absolutely gorgeous! Then we had Wullie McWhirter's. I know a lot of people say it's Wullie McWhir's, but it was Wullie McWhirter's. It's just right where…Hugh Harvey lives now* [on the corner of Mill Square opposite the Volunteer Arms]*…that's why the two big windows are there…he had everything in it as well: thread; safety pins; everything! It was like a needle to an anchor in his shop tae. We come up to the pub, but before we come to the pub, if you went down Bridge Street on the left-hand side…there was a sweetie shop there. It was my mother's auntie that had it. It was next door to the side of the Volunteer* [Arms]*, and my mother's auntie had that wee sweetie shop. You went further down and, again, it was tenements. There were a lot of tenements in Catrine in those days because of big families and they couldn't build so it was all tenement houses…the McColls and everything lived in that place. Then we came down to a lovely sandstone house and Nancy Campbell and the Symingtons all lived down there.*

…The pub [the Volunteer Arms]*…which in those days was known as the Honky Tonk…the mill was still there and the big sandstone wall was right round the mill. Some folk used to make that their Saturday night: standing up against the wall watching a' these folk coming out the Honky Tonk! It*

was a pub of disrepute, put it like that! ...It would be about the only pub in Catrine that women were allowed into...in those days women just didn't get into the pubs, especially up at the Brewery Bar. Mrs. Kemp just wouldn't allow them into the Brewery Bar. But they got into the Honky Tonk. We had, next to the Honky Tonk, Margaret Gibb's shop...it was a lady's outfitters which was really lovely...the shops in Catrine were classy shops. They really were beautiful, beautiful shops! Then it was more company houses, then it was Meikle the painters...and then more company houses. It would maybe be just an entry, but it was still company houses. Jimmy Symington, the barbers, as well as being a gents barbers he also did ladies' hair through the back...they did everything in those days. They cut the mens' hair in the front and if the ladies just wanted a cut they went in there, but if he was wanting to perm hair – that was during the war years, in my early days before you actually got your hair straightened and a' this – you went through the back. He had a place through the back, and then he employed a lady to perm hair through there. Then it was company houses...it would be Meikle the painter, Jimmy Symington, more company houses and these houses you'll still see yet. You can go through the entry. Right on the corner. Then on the corner just before you come to Kleboe's house, before you come to Dino's there was Maggie Girvans. Ladies outfitters again! ...Yes, three ladies outfitters. Men could maybe go in and get gloves or a cloth cap or that in those days...wee boys could get trousers or that, but it was mainly ladies. Then you came to, what we said in those days, the tally's shop. It was Sisi that had that shop. They had most of that building actually...you could carry-out or eat in...it was spotless! Absolutely beautiful. It was a busy shop...all they sold was fish and chips and ice cream...and sweeties. That was all you got, but...during the war years you were working with ration books and you only got so many coupons for your sweeties. You would maybe save them up for a month and then go and get your sweeties...it was points and they were inside your ration book. Now, it would be like Sisi's shop, and then you went through the back to their house and up the stairs, then it was Bill Fisher's shop. Bill Fisher sold petrol and there was a petrol pump there at one time. Bill sold newspapers, nails, you name it. In those days you'd to get your wireless charged up with a battery. He charged up your batteries... I went to St. Patrick's Primary School, and in those days we didn't even have electrical light in the school...the new school is in Auchinleck now, but in those days it was what we cried the Birnie. You went up the Auchinleck road and you turned off and you went along. It was where all the miners' rows were at that time. Everything was centred round it. There would be St. Patrick's Convent...you went down this lane and it was the convent, then it was the school, the chapel house and the chapel. So that's where everybody went...it was Alec Gemmel's private bus used to take us up there. We brought the batteries down...the nuns could actually put on the wireless to let you know what was happening during the war...it was Bill Fisher that charged them up...there wouldn't be a lot of Catholics in Mauchline at that time. When the pits shut down there were a lot of the miners went to Mauchline Colliery, so that meant they came from Hurlford and everything. That was when the influx came into Mauchline. We didn't have a church in Catrine in those days. That's why we'd to go up to the Birnie, but there was a private bus laid on a Sunday morning as well. That bus was always packed tae!

Then he [Bill Fisher] *had the shop next to it. This is where all Stenlake's property is the now. He had the shop next to it, as well, and it was his daughter* [Edith] *that was in it. They sold china, like beautiful dishes. We've got beautiful dishes through there in our other display cabinet, that came out of Bill Fisher's shop...that was at the front, at that side of the shop, but at the back of the shop, on the left-hand side, there was another small library. That was all in that wee area...then we come to a tenement that was attached to Bill Fisher's shop. Up the stairs, there was a family there...the Burns family...one of the daughters was on the phone on Sunday night from Vancouver. We were talking about it...she was born up the stairs where Stenlake's offices is now. That was all houses up there...the next shop again was Annie Urquhart's and that was...a ladies' outfitters as well! ...The thing was their stuff wasn't expensive and in those days folk didn't travel. Everything was centred in your village. You didn't need to go out...there wasn't transport especially. Folk worked on a Saturday morning; they worked in the mill on a Saturday morning; they worked in the pits on a Saturday morning; they worked in the Bleach Field on a Saturday morning. Folk just didn't get away. The money wasn't there. You needed it. The odd time you'd maybe get on the bus and that would be a treat for you...*

So that was Annie Urquhart's. Then it would be...the Royal Bar at that time. Then it was more houses...you went further along and it was Tammie Elliot that was the school janitor that lived in one of the sandstone houses. It would be part of the pub noo. It's for let, but it's on this side when you go round the corner... Tam Elliot was the school janitor, and not that it affected us because it was a Mr. Dunsmuir that used to come out for the Catholic school...and if you weren't at the school your door got knocked! I mean that's how strict the janitors in the schools were in those days... Next to that was an office...it was the parish office...folk didn't have much money and some used to find it awful hard...say somebody had a accident in the pit or something like that, in those days you didn't get your wages...you just didn't...folk would maybe go into the parish for parish relief. And that's what it was in those days, parish relief...not that I...but I remember folk saying about they went in and the woman who run it wasn't very nice because she used to say about the wages that the miners had, but miners didn't have big wages. Miners were like everybody else; they just didn't have big wages...they didn't always have work. If you were a shot-firer in the pit, that's what they said a fireman aye, you did but you'd to go for training. But see the likes of my dad and most of the miners that were down at the coalface, they were only at the coalface if there were hutches on that day. When we were in Mill Street, if my dad had been on the backshift...they a' had their bikes, and we used to walk from Mill Street right up Whiteflatt, by the farm, up to the road-heid as we cried it and then my dad would go on his bike. We would maybe be just about an hour back in the house when he would come back. There wouldn't be any work for them that day. There wouldn't be any hutches and if there wasn't any hutches there wouldn't be any pay! I think a lot of folk used to think Oh, the miners had great, big wages, but the miners maybe didn't have big wages. If they weren't at the coalface which was awful dangerous and if you weren't a shot-firer, that's where the big money was really...okay they had their concessions, they had their baths...then they put on buses for the miners, but it was a hard life because...if there were no hutches there was no money... I can remember my mother telling me about this woman who had went in [to the parish office] *and she said, "Ohh, I'll have to look for a job because I'll never go back in to that woman!" Her husband was a miner. Aye, they maybe had a wee bit more than the mill workers had but they weren't flush with money I can assure you! We were brought up in a miner's house...so, that was where the parish offices was...then it was Park's the butchers...in where the Pit Stop is now...that was a top class butchers shop...then the shop at the corner where the florist is now was Robertson's the jewellers...I was actually speaking to the florist on Sunday and she was saying that when they went to get the shop painted outside o it they were scrapping the old paint off and it was Robertson's the Jewellers that come up. He came from Cumnock...the woman that worked there...she stays in Auchinleck...*

You went down Ford Street and that's where the start of the Co-operative was...you had the butchers which was Isaac Wallace, he was the manager...then you went through an entry, through the back and up the stairs at the back and that was the Co-operative offices. It was Jimmy McGavin in those days that was the store manager, the Co-operative Manager. When you came back down the stairs at the back was the cobblers. It was Davy Duncan and Bobby Cairns...you came out of there and the shop next to it was the drapery which was quite a place, the Catrine Drapery, the Co-operative Drapery...every six months...there would be what they called The Turn of the Leaf in Catrine Co-operative; in all Co-operatives. You could get goods, like dry goods, in the drapery but you'd to pay it...you'd to get it for six months, but you'd to pay it before six months. If you didn't pay it before that six months they took it off your dividend...there was always a dividend day...that was what they called The Turn of the Leaf. The shops were shut; the grocery was closed; the drapery was closed as well because they done their stocktaking. Then they opened again on the Friday morning and you started your slate off from scratch...and then your dividend got paid weeks after that. You went up the stairs to the Co-operative offices...it was great! The Co-operative had a bank there, also they had a dentist...but he only came about once a week. That was all in that one wee area. You went further doon, and...that was all houses. On the opposite side of the street was houses as well... The Co-operative dentist could give you your false teeth. When my mother died she had the teeth she got from the Co-operative dentist and my mother was 86 so that would be about 60 odd years, probably, she would have teeth. You didn't run around in those days and change your teeth for cosmetic reasons! Then across the road from there it was all lovely houses and everything else... The shops were beautiful! ...The main street was busy with shops as well...you had Paterson's...his first shop had nails and all these kind of things as well as what Fisher's had. Then you had the paper shop and the grocers shop further up. You had the Brewery Bar which was run by Mrs. Kemp...the Kemps and the Patersons were a' connected. Mrs. Kemp was a strict old woman, and she didn't allow women into her pub! In those days it was just for men. It closed at half past nine every night. Across the road from the Brewery Bar would be the Bazaar...it was a grocery shop and it was a really nice shop. Next to him would be...Bob Ferguson. He always got Sasta Ferguson for his nickname...I don't know how that came about...his wife Jean run the fruit shop, if you were lucky to get fruit in those days...he also ran the taxi...and he would be about the only person that would have a telephone. So you went to him and you got it...Mrs. Lorimer, Bessie Lorimer, bought the business after him but there were still houses up the stairs in those days.

Then you went further down and it was more houses and it was Nanny Murphy had the bakers shop. It was something! You could get wee gingerbread men, you could get miniature loafs. It was a beautiful shop. Ferguson the bakers bought it. Then it was the big Co-operative...where the Premier is now, next to the post office, that was the Co-operative. That was the grocery...up the stair it was Co-operative houses. You had to be somebody to get a house in the Co-operative building...you had to get somebody on the board speaking for you, they were lovely houses. It was a beautiful, big, sandstone building...that would be the main Co-operative then because the other one closed down during the war years...you went up the Vault and that was the Co-operative bakers. It was Willy Duncan that run it. He was a master baker...so you can see how the Co-operative played a big part in Catrine...I worked in the grocers [not long after leaving school]*...you were somebody to get into the Co-operative in those days. You had to be somebody...it wasn't everybody and anybody that got into the Co-operative. It wasn't the best of jobs. I got £2 a week...it was just a job that came up. You were glad to get a job in those days. I mean, you didn't get running the streets oh no, no way! Next to that was the doctor's surgery at that time. He had moved up there. That's where you went to the surgery...during the war there was this other shop...it was the first time in my life that I'd ever seen crinkle chips...it was Nanny Follie that had it and it was – ohh, you couldn't have light showing during the war years you would go in and this blue smoke! ...Nanny was always packed! So she had a wee chip shop in there. Then the next place was Annie Bryan's butcher shop... Everything revolved round Catrine. Catrine was beautiful. You can understand, when you think on it, why it was Queen of the West. So that was Annie Bryan's butcher shop...then*

there was the Burns Hotel...there are houses there noo...and then it was more houses. Then we had Tam Aitken's...you could go into Tam's and he was a lovely soul, a canny, canny soul. You would maybe go in for a size 6: "Miss Kiernan I couldn't give you a 6, but I could give you a 5". No wonder our feets as bad as they are the day! If it was a shoe we wanted we squeezed our feet into them! Some folk remember all this and they'll say, "Oh aye, that was the shop, I cannae gie you that but I can gie you another size"...and then it was the Royal Bank. My mother and them were all Co-operative folk in those days. The bank in those days...was only for business folk. It wasn't for the likes of us going paying things, paying accounts and that. They things just didn't exist...if you were saving you saved in the Co-op.

...I think it would be after the war years. Folk started getting that wee bit better off, getting better wages and everything else. Then that was it. The mill stopped working on a Saturday...they brought in a five day week. The same with the miners. The only way the miners would go out is if it was an extra shift on a Saturday. But the mill: that was it...it closed on a Friday. So folk was that bit better off and then they started going away on the buses, because petrol started to get that wee bit better. You couldn't have petrol during the war years, it was only for emergencies. So folk relaxed then and they went away to Kilmarnock and Ayr. Then, sadly, we had supermarkets come on. Folk used to say you could eat yourself out the Co-op, but you could eat yourself back into it. If you couldn't pay...them what you owed them when they said it was the Turn of the Leaf, they just took it off your dividend.

Evelyn Campbell: *That Square used to be flat, right. I had the tearoom just roon the corner there. There were no stones nor nothing. There were two big plots like that* [demonstrates] *wi flowers in it, and it was completely slabbed. In the summer, the fella that cleaned the streets...he had yin o the empty hooses up there and there were tables, chairs and umbrellas, and they used to get sat roon the Square in the morning, and he took them back in at night-time.*

Leisure & Recreation

John Johnston: *I didnae have a great deal o hobbies bar playing a bit of football, or something like that. Going to the* [AM Brown] *Institute. You could go into the Institute go to the boys' room, you see…you had billiards…table tennis…carpet boules…aye, you could win what they ca'ed the Jing-a-Ling. You went through everything and it a' depended on how far you could get. You could get put oot in the first…say you were playing billiards first if you lost at that, that was you oot. It was hardly worth going on cos you couldnae win it…I liked the billiards. We never played much snooker. Billiards. White ball, red yin. I never played in a team, or nothing. Just mixed games.*

…Sunday School…I never liked it either! It was teaching again. I wasnae daft in it. I went. I had tae…your folks were keen for you to go to Sunday School in thae days. Ma sisters went, but no ma mum and dad, no. I went from the Sunday School to what you ca'ed the Young Worshippers League. That's you a bit older then, maybe till you're about 16 years old. Then after that you could enjoy yourself! You could go to dances. My favourite bit was in Auchinleck, but you got good dances in Catrine tae. Town hall in Auchinleck…I left the school in 1936 so I would go to the dancing when I was about 16 years old, or something like that… The Savona, they came from Hurlford way, I think. I'm trying to think of the other one…they were the Scottish champions…there were some good bands in thae days… I never drunk alcohol then…I was never in a pub till I went to the soldiers. I didn't go to pubs, nor nothing, until I was about…till I came home from the war…you drunk a bottle of lemonade if you could afford it…it would be about fourpence. Well, it was [a lot of money] *if you hadnae got it in those days…when I started work…only four shillings a week – that was my pay serving my time as a mechanic!*

Robert Dalziel: *The Red Lion was very popular! As an inn in the village, or a pub in the village, it was mainly for old folks…Old Suck… My grandmother Archibald's maiden name was McDonald and he was a relative of her, a cousin…he had a beautiful singing voice and he was a great attraction at the Red Lion. He used to go down to the pub, drink and sing. He would sing, and I can remember the folk standing outside in the street listening to him singing, cos the pub was too full, you couldnae get in! He…had a dragon of a wife…he was once invited by Harry Lauder to go on a tour of Australia…because he was a lovely singer! I only remember him in his old age, he had a really good voice in old age, but his wife wouldnae let him go! I reckon she felt he would never come back, which to be fair to him, was true in those days, but he never got and he never became a professional singer…I just knew him as Old Suck McDonald…S-U-C-K, because he sucked on a pipe all the time! That was his nickname…I cannot remember his name…he died rather sadly and yet maybe it was appropriately…he was found lying just over the bridge one morning at…the bottom of the Whiteflat Brae…he'd obviously sat on the bridge for a rest and probably had a heart attack, or whatever, and toppled over and that's where he was found. In a sense it was quite appropriate because he was a great village character…but he must have been a great age, be 90 at that time I would have thought…he was in a sense, aye, aye, in the heart of the village.*

Alistair Plenderleith: *Aye, they had drama groups and that. The main interest in thae days was the Institute…they had billiard cups, reading rooms, draughts, snooker, carpet bowls. Thats where you came home from your work and went tae, ken…I came here wi two or three o the boys I ran aboot wi. We played snooker and that. I won the snooker cup. My name's in here* [opposite page]*…*

A photograph (illustrated below) of the gala day is produced and Alistair is asked if he was the winner...

Aye…I think that was George Roxburgh, Billy McDowall, Jim Waddle and the wee chap coming into the view there was Geordie Weir…they worked in the mill and the Bleach Field…that was the Bleach Field big lum… It would be late 49/early 50… That's Bob Melrose, he was a heid man in the mill…they took photos and they put them up in the post office window. Anybody that had their picture taken could go in and buy it…that's where I got that… Catrine Carnival 1948…there was a football five-a-side competition on that day. I think we got to the final but we drew or something like that…

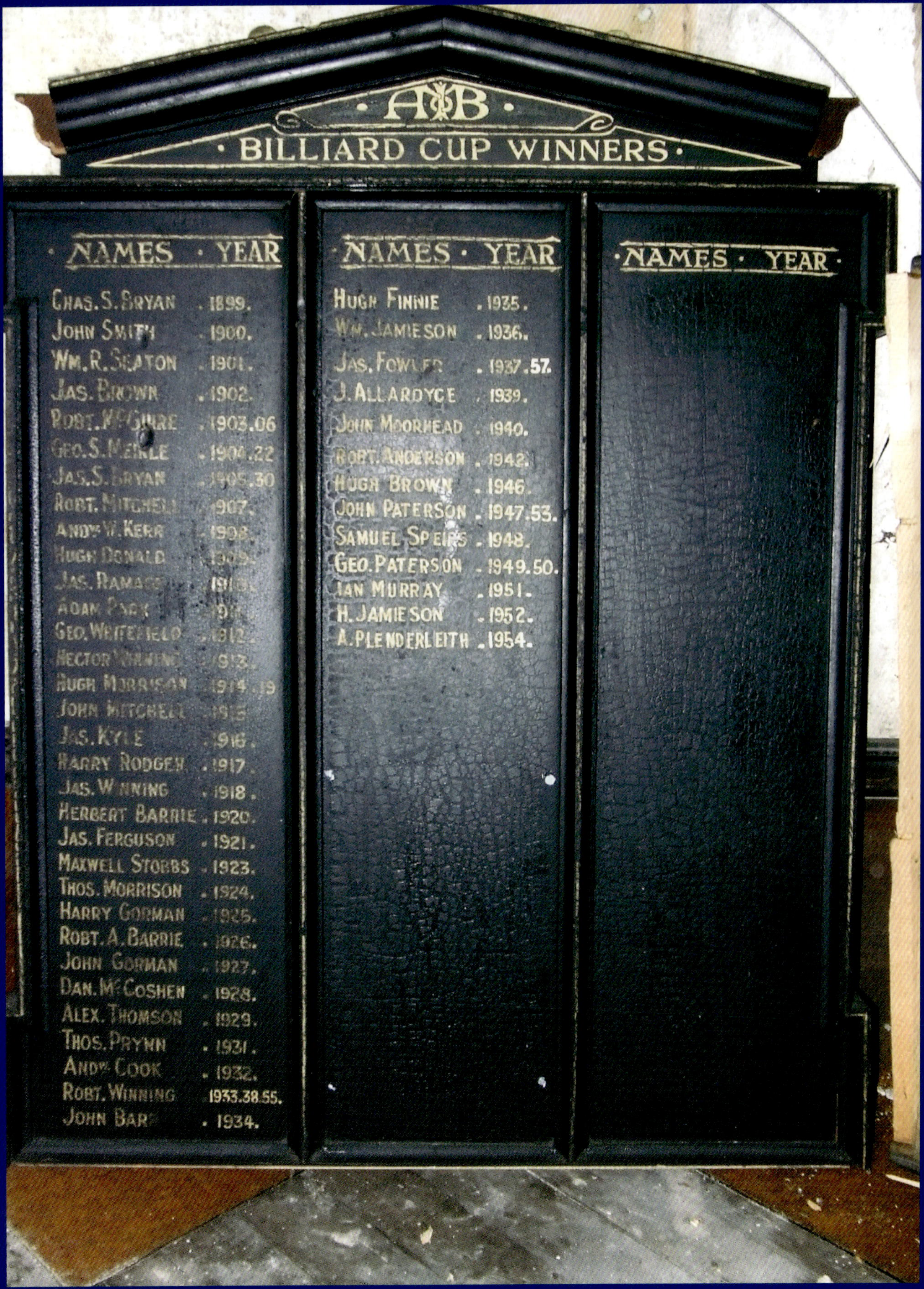
A B
BILLIARD CUP WINNERS
NAMES · YEAR
CHAS. S. BRYAN . 1899.
JOHN SMITH . 1900.
WM. R. SEATON . 1901.
JAS. BROWN . 1902.
. 1903.06
GEO. S. MEIKLE . 1904.22
JAS. S. BRYAN . 1905.30
ROBT. MITCHELL . 1907.
ANDW. W. KERR . 1908.
HUGH DONALD
JAS. RAMAGE
GEO. WHITEFIELD . 1912.
HECTOR . 1913.
HUGH MORRISON . 1914.19
JOHN MITCHELL
JAS. KYLE . 1916.
HARRY RODGER . 1917.
JAS. WINNING . 1918.
HERBERT BARRIE . 1920.
JAS. FERGUSON . 1921.
MAXWELL STOBBS . 1923.
THOS. MORRISON . 1924.
HARRY GORMAN . 1925.
ROBT. A. BARRIE . 1926.
JOHN GORMAN . 1927.
DAN. MCCOSHEN . 1928.
ALEX. THOMSON . 1929.
THOS. PRYNN . 1931.
ANDW. COOK . 1932.
ROBT. WINNING 1933.38.55.
JOHN BARR . 1934.
NAMES · YEAR
HUGH FINNIE . 1935.
WM. JAMIESON . 1936.
JAS. FOWLER . 1937.57.
J. ALLARDYCE . 1939.
JOHN MOORHEAD . 1940.
ROBT. ANDERSON . 1942.
HUGH BROWN . 1946.
JOHN PATERSON . 1947.53.
SAMUEL SPEIRS . 1948.
GEO. PATERSON . 1949.50.
IAN MURRAY . 1951.
H. JAMIESON . 1952.
A. PLENDERLEITH . 1954.
NAMES · YEAR

...You could take [jam jars and bottles] *to the Co-operative and they gave you money. You could always get a cheap fish supper tae. They werenae as cheap as they are noo! ...In that days too, on a Saturday and Sunday you went and played fitba' in the play-park. You would ha played a' day. You went hame and had your breakfast and your tea, and went back doon. It was a cock or a hen: whatever was the cock went to yin side and the hen went tae the other. I've seen aboot 50 or 60-a-side by Christ! Aye...and a lot o fishing...I never fished but I used tae go and watch it. It was a scream... I've aye mind of an old man you were talking aboot; Jimmy Mullen's faither, he did a bit o fishing and he lost a leg during the war. He had a wooden leg. He went fishing for salmon. He just gaffed them, ken. Whenever they hooked yin it run away doon the water and he was after it wi this wooden leg, ken! They caught huners o salmon that way. Up there where they went and fished, up Mortons, they had hens. They ran a' aboot. Naebody ever touched them or that. They had dugs...fox terriers and the hens were there a' day and naebody ever bothered.*

Harry Houston: *Basically we'd to make oor ain thing. We had nothin...money-wise we had nae money either. Things was hard after the war. If somebody got a ba in the street that was you; everybody got a game, you'd to go and play fitba. We tracked a' o'er the countryside gatherin eggs, that's birds' eggs...we went up to the seagulls colony up at Sorn and Blacksidend...when we went as boys we went for the day oot, and we always knew when to come hame because you could hear the mill bells and you knew the time then. You knew, pssht, thats dinner-time. So if you heard the 6 o' clock one you had to get hame quick because that's you, you were grounded after that. But, aye, we had oor ain thing. Up at the, what we cried the back lade, that's up at the weir, was where we used to go swimming when we were younger. You learned to swim in the back lade first and then you went on to the river. The other ones we went doon tae was the Black Horse. If it was a good summer day we went picnics. Whole families went doon there. That was another popular place...up the Kensie Burn. We used to go as young fellas. We used to say we were going camping up there and steal the tatties and roast them on the fire and things like that, ken.*

...When we were younger the gamies [gamekeepers] *used to hunt us from Daldorch. You couldna get up that way, but we used to go up in the summer and we were swimming in the water. There was an ongoing battle because their fence was back so many yards fae the river edge and we said, Naw, we go o'er there. Noo they had a bridge o'er there which was theirs, right? That was their story then and they locked it and we didnae get o'er. But when the water wasnae big we just crossed it and we went up that way and they used to try hunt you but we wouldnae go... Noo, when that bridge became obsolete and they needed a bridge o'er, they put a temporary bridge o'er. That bridge doesnae belong to them now. They say it's no theirs. But I remember when they wouldnae let us o'er there and it was theirs... Daldorch had a daffodil day the likes of Sorn Castle. It was a big hoose, really a nice, big hoose, but then it got left and it just went to ruin and at one time they had doon at the stable area they had an American cult in there. Teen Missions I think they called themselves. Then eventually this autistic school took it up. It's been a great thing for the area...*

John Fleming: *...In 1951...we came to Blackside End at Sorn. I attended Catrine School and left there in the Christmas of 1954 and started at Crowfoot Farm, just outside Catrine here, in 1955, was there two and a half years and then went to Hillhead Farm as tractor man which was for a handsome fee of about £7 a week. I was there for ten years and, as Anne has mentioned, we got married and that's where we got the cottage up there. The cottage we got at that time was the original Sorn Golf Course* [Clubhouse]. *It was a 9 hole course up there and my late father-in-law never forgave me because I ploughed that up...*

Anne Fleming: *Jack had a motorbike! You went walking really...if you were lucky your mum and dad went out and you got the hoose to yourself, but unfortunately fortunately or unfortunately my grandmother stayed with us at that time and she had her own wee room. So if we were left in thinking, Oh that's good, we'll get the hoose to wirselves tonight, you got about ten minutes and then Granny would knock the door: "I think you wanted to see these photies Jack!" "Damn!"...A chaperone!*

John Fleming: *The main thing was Mauchline Pictures, the Abbey cinema in Mauchline...permanent booking on a Saturday night and it was good. That was basically it...and the dances. At that time a lot of the dances were a whist drive first, then the dances would follow on.*

Anne Fleming: *You went to the herds dance at Sorn and things like that. I was a Sunday School teacher and they had things in the church hall. I was in the church choir and then there was another ladies choir called The St. Cuthbert's Singers. It was a Mr. William Gibb that was the conductor and we went out singing at different venues in the area. I have sung solo, and in duets, on one or two occasions but I was mainly a choir singer. My mother was in it as well...it was all types of music, from the shows and things like that.*

John Sharp: *The Target…it started at the Kenstey Farm. My father and uncle was in that. Brigend was where…it split between the two. You used to shoot fae the Kenstey on to Brigend and the Target was there…you used to shoot fae the top o Catrine…it was stopped in 1961. Brigend had complained that the ricochet was killing the coos* [although the main reason it closed was because the Ayrshire Rifle Association could not afford the rent and rates]!

…In that Institute…up the stairs…there used to be snooker or carpet bowls or somethin upstairs there years and years ago…and there's also the auld police door [opposite page]. *As you go upstairs…on the first floor there's an auld door wi big bolts on it and that used to be the police door. It came doon fae – 1800s or somethin they took the door aff…the police station oot the Mauchline Road. I remember the police station being there. The door was away in the mists o time. They've kept this door so its obviously of some significance cos it's still there…*

Ruth Sharp: *Well, it has been done up…part of it has been re-floored…they had a library in the biggest what I would call the dance hall now…the books came in in boxes from Ayr, the central library and they kept them for a couple of months and then they went away and filled them with different ones…*

Robert Dalziel: *…Every street did their own* [carnival] *float and dressed it. My grandfather Robert Dalziel also had a dancing school. He was the foreman in the mill, he had a dancing school as a side line. They gave dancing lessons in the house in the front room, or good room, of the house…one year…Ballochmyle Terraces as it then was – now the Mauchline Road – decorated their float as Dalziel's Dancing School and I remember being in that float, and then we did one as a wedding.*

…There were lots of competitions held over in the play park at the bottom of Co-operative Avenue: you had tug o war; 5-a-side [football] *and of course stalls. It was a big day's holiday. The only other big day in the village it compared with was the Cattle Show, which I remember being held in the Burnpark…we used to go and run aboot the tents when they were putting them up a couple of days before. Oh Suck McDonald used to give us a row! He was the watchman; he usually put* [them up] *two nights before as they set up the field. It was always a big event…everybody in the village would go across to the field. Again, there would be stalls and things and of course lots of competitions.*

Maggie Bunting: *Well on a Sunday night we used to always walk out the Mauchline road and we met the Mauchline boys and then the Mauchline girls met the Catrine boys out the road on a Sunday night.*

Robert Dalziel: *We were churchgoing people…Sunday was the Sunday School. You went to the Sunday School, you came out the Sunday School and you went down to the church. You were there for about 20 minutes and there was the childrens' address…then you got out. Now that was okay for me because my granny lived with us all my parents' married life, and she wasn't really fit to walk the brae to the church…a right problem for the elderly…relatively few people had cars so my granny didn't often get to church but if I wanted to go back to the house I would go back and she was there to look after me…if it was a decent Sunday…you would go for a walk if it was a decent day. Double Dykes walk used to be a great favourite…the Radical Brae walk, as well, was a great favourite…*

…This is…the building where I played with my first full-sized billiards table. I think, maybe, it was one of the billiard rooms that became the library. Apparently billiards was played in the Institute for a very long time. My father remembered playing competitions in there…there was also a very substantial library here. That's about early 1960s and the building was being transformed into the community centre…Mrs. Nisbet was the councillor at the time and I remember her taking me into the library and saying, "Robert, these books are going to get thrown away. If you could use some of these would you like to take them?", but I had nowhere to keep books like that. When I think about it, it was a great shame that happened because there were literally hundreds of books in the room.

…Catrine was a great place for walking…Jacob's Ladder could take you up to Ballochmyle and the ice house was just at the top…that's the ice house for the original estate…you could still look into the old ice house… There was the remains of the fog house where Burns reputedly saw the lass of Ballochmyle! That was a nice walk because you could go in at the gatehouse, the East Lodge gatehouse at the bottom of the Rabbit Warren Brae which was a right of way in those days, and you could walk along that path over the old Shepherd's Bridge where the original mill lade led the water around to the river. The Shepherd's Bridge is now gone completely but you could…go up the 'Ladder' walk round Ballochmyle Estate and come back down what we called the Ladies' Walk, which was through the middle of Ballochmyle Woods and back out the same gatehouse…or you could walk right through Ballochmyle and

go out at one of the other gatehouses that used to exist on the Catrine/Mauchline road and walk back down the Darkwood Corner, and down into the village of Catrine from the Mauchline Road…there were lots of nice walks. The Double Dykes walk went up Shaws Brae, right up to the back of the house and then there was a double pathway between two fields which again was an old right of way, which took you across onto the Gas Works Brae and you could walk down into the village: the Radical Brae, which brought you out at the voes, or you could go back into the village down the Gas Works Brae…the other great walk was down the other side of the river. For us to get to from the Mauchline Road you had to walk up, cross the timber bridge, go right across the wee footbridge towards the Holm Farm and walk right down the other side to the banks of the river…

…There was always church league football matches Saturdays…in the play park and the Catrine teams were quite good sides, some quite good teams…I remember the one…it might be the churches' league trophy in Scotland – we won at Townhead Park, one of the Catrine teams, the wee kirk teams we called them, and they were a better side at that time than the big kirk team…quite a lot of local people obviously played in them, maybe almost all local people…Matt Sullivan, the congregational minister from Cumnock, played for the congregational church team…never any swearing…out of respect for their minister, but he was a hardy player.

…The farmer McKerrow very kindly – having got frustrated trying to stop us playing football in his field at the Burnpark – decided it was easier to come to terms with it and allowed us to play football in the wee triangle, or corner, of the field which now is private housing. Just as you come in from Mauchline, on the right hand side, is a wee triangular corner by what we called The Puddock Burn and a wee stream that runs into it. He eventually said, "Tell you what: I'll let you play in there if you don't bother damaging the grazing,"…which was a very good deal by him, which meant we had a playground to play football. We had no reason ever to go anywhere else in the village except to play there, because you had the swings and things in the play-park on the other side of the road [Mauchline Road]*, so we very rarely went up the street in Catrine, certainly not up to the new housing estate… They came from all over the village but actually most of my friends would come out to the Mauchline Road to play because there was a football pitch…you could play there…used to actually get so many out there, really, probably too many! 15-a-side was too many for the area! It was the perfect playground and Ballochmyle Woods was another perfect*

Mauchline Road, Catrine PN3758

playground…nobody bothered about what you did up there. We used to go in, cut sticks and make pretend swords and bows and arrows, and we used to build huts and spend…half the summer in these places. You had a kind of idyllic childhood…the height of our challenges, really, we used to walk to Blacksidend and quite often we were too tired to walk up it when we got to the bottom! You could walk that far up and we would be away all day. We were away early in the morning you would be back about 9pm at night, when it was beginning to get gloomy, and your mother would say, "Where have you been? What you been doing?", but we would just wander away and keep wandering…nobody would let kids do that now…but in the countryside you were in no danger from anything.

Maureen Kiernan: *The Institute…had a library…in where the big hall is…there were seats all round about it. The alcove wasn't always there, that was just a straight wall…when you come in the main door…beautiful glass cases right along till you came to the bottom door and shelves and everything in below. They doors were only opened when the library was opened. It was Mr. Clark, Ducky Clark, and he was in charge of the library. He sat* [at] *a big desk and* [on] *a big, high stool. Then they had their billiards room and all this kind of thing in the Institute, but it was more a games kind of place, where it wasn't so much a social gathering place. Although folk were married in there, it wasn't so much that as what it would be the Wilson Hall… Of course the council decided that the Institute had to get done away with…and the council stepped in and bought it and…I think they wasted the actual building because there was a lot of…Catrine heritage went down the river, and I mean literally, down the river! We had a councillor at that time and she couldn't get the mill pulled down quick enough, she couldn't get the company houses pulled down quick enough or anything like that and then she started on the Institute… I can remember when it was the hall bicentenary down there and there were two big paintings in that big hall. See, that hall was separated…see where you come in the bottom door, there was a partition right across there…and at the back o that it was what they called the ladies' reading room. Ladies could go in there and read. So you can see the hall wasn't as big then as what it is now. Because of the war years petrol was short, and we could only go to the church once a month up at the Birnie, up at St. Patrick's. The priest at that time was Father Maxwell…priests and doctors got a special allowance for petrol…he would come down the rest o the time and he would actually say mass in Catrine Institute…and where it was partitioned off there were two paintings. One was Mr. Brown and the other was Mrs. Brown, and she was sitting and she had her fan…and I used to think, well when you were younger let's face it, you weren't interested in sermons…your mind was away in a hundred different places. I says, I could tell you every bit of lace that was on that woman's hat!*

…Daldorch was a private house at that time…Daldorch was really private…you didn't get on to the grounds at Daldorch… When we were younger, as I say, money wasn't plentiful. We just didn't have it. If it was a nice day you went a picnic and my mother used to make us a lemonade bottle of Boston Cream. They'll not be many folk will ken what Boston Cream was! It was like eggs and baking soda and other things. I think my mother used to boil it and then when it was cold you used to shake it and it was terrific! Absolutely terrific! You put a wee bit of baking soda on top and it fizzed right up! You would take your picnic and go up there, but you were only allowed up a certain bit o that river maybe where the fish pass is. That was all. You didn't get any further. They wouldn't let you. They sent the dogs on you! I think it would be Campbell…I think he was to do with the ship building…he had a chauffeur who drove him up to the ship building…peacocks used to come down, so that'd be why…when you went round the river you weren't allowed any further than that. You'd to sit there. The other place we went for picnics would be down to the Black Horse…you went picnics there and the other places you went…by the farm and through another gate you were leg-weary by the time you got and it was the Target. Now, there used to be a shooting target up there…and auld Jimmy Campbell and some more of them used to go up there and practice and…they went to…Bisley down in England and it was the British competition, and they won that competition. That was something to come back to Catrine with… That's what the army used to use…you didn't get up if the red flag was going because that was the army up there…

The Wilson Hall

The Wilson Hall was in Bridge Street on the site where the day centre is now. Opening in 1882 it quickly became the venue for all sorts of concerts and public meetings. In 1896 a concert was held there with music being provided by the (then) new-fangled phonograph. When moving pictures came along it was used as a cinema and had 500 seats, an impressive size for a town with a population of about 2,200. The cinema was latterly operated by F Palmer of Lesmahagow.

Wilson Hall

Mary McCluskie: *It was hard seats…it was an Italian man that came from Lesmahagow – Palmer, you called him. He used to say, I've been aksed to tell you…; we always laughed when he came out and said that, I've been aksed to tell you…we've had a bother with the…projector…we used to laugh at this! Pearl White: that was yin of them, lying down in the railway, you know, silent movie types. Oh aye, and two or three of them…Mr. Gibb, he had a social thing that took up. It was Esmeralda; that was the play we made and I was in it…my granny and my mum came to see it and she says she wouldnae come back and see me – she thought I was going to faint!*

Robert Dalziel: *…The cinema…was the Wilson Hall. Two or three days a week. I can remember on Saturdays waiting – clutching, actually I clutched a shilling – waiting for Palmer coming to open up the cinema! To get in it cost you thruppence; to sit in the three front wooden benches it cost you sixpence; a carton of Kiora Orange and a thrupenny bag o chips out Sisi's…then going doon the road back to Mauchline on our way home and that was my Saturday afternoon entertainment. I think it was one* [shilling] *and six pence to sit in the seats in the balcony upstairs…my family used to have three seats booked for Saturday nights! That was when I was a bit older and we used to go to the cinema – that was our entertainment on Saturday nights. It was popular. I mean, up until the mid-1950s televisions were still fairly scarce in homes. A lot o folk got their first television, as we did, for the Coronation in 1953 and up until then the cinemas were probably the main source of entertainment… It wasn't on every night, it was something that only happened two or three nights a week…he* [Palmer] *did go to different villages usually on different days and that's how he made his living, taking a travelling cinema to different places… The Wilson Hall is away. It burned down as well and that was very much a central part of village life, because lots of things happened there. Not only did the cinema get held there but shows used to get put on there…and they would put on wee concerts there as well.*

Evelyn Campbell: *...We stayed here and see on a Monday night...you'd to queue to get in the dancing there. They came fae a different places to go there and then twice a week they* [had] *bingos and things like that...but before that it was the picture house...there was aye a queue to get in. I think it was thruppence. We had the sweetie shop at the time...we selt the sweets before they went into the pictures. It was wooden benches... It was an uncle of mine* [Wullie Thompson] *that was the hall keeper...*

Sean Campbell: *...And see when we'd nae money, see the wood up there, we used to walk wi a wee rake and dig up the ground nuts washed* [them] *to take to the pictures... A wee spade a wee, totty spade and dig up the ground nuts, then took them doon to the water and washed them...then put them in a poke and ate them.*

Evelyn Campbell: *He...he done Bottle Kate oot a job!*

Sean Campbell: *Auld Kate Beer Bottle was off rich, rich people, but her man wasnae guid tae her. Me, being a character...I used to go aboot the doors chappin for beer bottles. So auld Kate came to ma mither's door and she gave ma mother* [hell] *for me no to go back for the beer bottles... Pair auld soul she got killed by a horse...she was lying behind a hedge and she could have moved, but this horse killed her, kicked her.*

Alistair Plenderleith: *They used to say he stayed in a hotel up here...Palmer. He came fae...Lesmahagow, aye...they were on three days a week...there were matinees tae, ken. They actually had three on a Saturday. You had the matinee, the first hoose and the second hoose.*

Harry Houston: *It was a guy cried Palmer that come wi the pictures. It used to be on a Monday and a Thursday and a Saturday...it was always John Wayne...Tarzan films...Randolph Scott...Laurel and Hardy...they changed it from a cinema to...it was the Masonic Lodge that ta'en it o'er into a big sorta hall/social club, then it disappeared as well.*

Five time Olympic gold medallist Johnny Weismuller as Tarzan.

Laurel & Hardy

Ruth Sharp: *...They had lots of wee concerts and things like that, local talent. My grandfather, actually, he had a dancing school and he had a big concert every year...in the Wilson Hall. We all had to dance, you know!*

Maureen Kiernan: *That was the picture house, and the pictures would be Monday, Thursday and Saturday. It was a man from Lesmahagow...that came to show the pictures. It was Palmer that was his name, but he got Peddler Palmer. He got Peddler Palmer and as often as no you could be standing, frozen, waiting on Peddler Palmer coming down from Lesmahagow if his motor didn't break down, there was snow on the roads or something like that. It was thruppence for the matinee and ninepence for the first house of the pictures. There was a matinee and a first house. It was all wooden benches but it was always packed. If you were that wee bit flush of money you could go up the stairs...and watch it. If you couldn't afford thruppence – thruppence was thruppence in those days! ...You would maybe get a lemonade bottle and a jeelie* [jam] *jar* [laughing]*, and you could get tuppence for a two pun jar, and a penny for the pun yin, and a penny for your lemonade! ...So you managed just to juggle as much as get you into the pictures! And it was only thruppence, but ohh, you got your ticket there was a ticket box and everything and you went in there. But as well as that the Wilson Hall was used for functions. There were a lot of weddings...folk getting married in the Wilson Hall... The Masonic Lodge at that time used to hold all their Masonic balls. It was well, well, used was the Wilson Hall. Then later on the Masonic Lodge bought it and that's where the Day Centre is noo. That was the Wilson Hall and then the Masonic Lodge bought it because their lodge was up Chapel Brae up beside the Gas Works...so they bought the Wilson Hall and it went on fire and then they had to get other premises. My Dad was one of the trustees. It was run by a group of trustees and there was money left by Mr. Wilson. Once the Wilson Hall went that money was there and they couldn't do anything about it. They couldn't give it to groups. It had actually to go to Edinburgh for the trust to be broken before they could distribute it to various charities...it was a fantastic place. The concerts and everything that used to come there: Friday night dancing. Especially when the war was on. A lot of soldiers were billeted up on the hilltop up there...across from the War Memorial. The Canadians and quite a lot of soldiers were billeted up there. They came down into Catrine. It would be mainly Canadians because folk took the soldiers into their house in those days, just for to give them comfort. We would be in Shawlands Street at the time and there were two Canadians came to our house. I can't remember one of them but I know one of them* *was cried George Reader. He was from Gasbeau village in Quebec. His wife used to write – obviously they'll be away now, but they used to write and keep in touch with my mother and that. They always had chocolates and meat and everything. They used to bring it to some of the folk and that. So it was a busy, busy hall that on a Friday night. Even after the war years you got these big bands coming from Darvel and everything coming to play in the actual Wilson Hall. On a Friday night it was really, really busy…*

Randolph Scott

Buses

Jim Bunting: *Of course in these days there were no supermarkets or anything like that. You went to Kilmarnock on a Saturday on the bus. We used to go on the bus, and it was always Kilmarnock we went to rather than Ayr, wasn't it? …I think because it was a half hour service on the bus to Kilmarnock and it was an hourly service to Ayr, wasn't it?*

Maggie Bunting: *…It was one* [shilling] *and sixpence a return on the bus to Kilmarnock. It was one* [shilling] *and eightpence for a return to Ayr…aye the tuppence made the difference!*

Robert Dalziel: *…There was always a regular bus service to Kilmarnock…the bus came at 10 past the hour and 20 to the hour, so you had an half hour service and the Ayr via Mauchline bus came at 25 past the hour. I'm quite precise with that because my parents' day out on a Saturday…was to go and catch the bus either to Ayr or Kilmarnock for the Saturday afternoon…my father would get in probably back of 12, have our lunch and they would be ready in time for the 10 past 2 bus to go to Kilmarnock. The idea would be you could go to Kilmarnock to the cinema and you would maybe have a bit to eat when you came out of the cinema. Then you would get back mid-evenin, sort of 8.30 maybe 9 o' clock at night, but…the 10 past the hour bus…they were quite often full. If it ran by you, you would only have 15 minutes to wait till the 25 past and you went into Ayr instead! …What bus you could actually get on – quite often it was decided for you. The other way was a pretty regular service: the same way to Muirkirk and New Cumnock… Sorn had a less frequent bus service though…to go to school in Cumnock in the mornings I always used to walk from Mauchline Road round to where the mill was, and the old post office building at the corner where the buses turned, I caught the Sorn bus that brought down the mill workers from Sorn to start the mill in the morning. We called that the wee Sorn and that was the bus we always got to school. We came back in it at night and walked back down the road. There was no real logic to that except that everybody from Catrine got on that bus, so I liked to do the same as the kids from the Mauchline Road.* [They] *used to walk round and catch that bus so all the Catrine kids caught the same bus… There were a lot of buses came in to the village in the morning at that time, they all pulled into that bit. You could turn buses in that corner at the time – there's now new housing been built there – but they used to come down from New Cumnock, places like that, bringing the mill workers down from Muirkirk. They were bussing them in from all over the area for the mill which employed an awful lot of people… They always had these turban things on their head to stop the dust getting into their hair!*

The Bonnie Jean

Jim Bunting: *...The Bonnie Jean, that was the ambulance. That was named after Jean Armour of course. You know, the Burns connection...*

Maggie Bunting: *It was Ferguson down on the corner that drove that.*

Jim Bunting: *...And did all the workers not contribute a penny a week or something, to the upkeep of it? Out their wages?*

...I think it would probably be the 50s that that stopped: the Bonny Jean.

Maureen Kiernan: *...It was Bob Ferguson's brother that drove the Bonnie Jean...they lived down past us in Mill Street. Do you know where Ayrbank big house is? Well the house before you come to Ayrbank that was a company house again. It was Mr. Ferguson's. The miners paid for the Bonnie Jean...there was so much came off the miners wages every week for the Bonnie Jean, because they used the Bonnie Jean a lot if there were accidents. It was green and white...it was a beautiful shade of green...but when Finlay went out of Catrine that's when Catrine went haywire. Finlay let them be what they liked and poured a lot of money into this village. Finlay preserved this village...do you know there was a Bonnie Jean trust fund? That was money that was put to the side for the Bonnie Jean. Then NHS came in in 47, 48... When the NHS came in this money was in trust and there were trustees distributed that money. One of them was Dr. MacCrae...a lot of folk used to go to Dr. MacCrae and he would give them a slip maybe for £5. Now £5 was a lot of money. Some of them played on it...and they would jog away with it. Well, there wouldn't be any money left noo in the Bonnie Jean fund...the Bonnie Jean was funded between the mill and the miners, but moresay Finlays, aye.*

The "Royal Visit"

Harry Houston: *I was born 5.1.39, lived a' ma life in Catrine... My first teacher was a lady cried Miss Begg...she was one o the real old ladies of the school. She was tall, thin sort of woman. She was very good wi kids. One of the first memories I dae remember of the school was, we were a' ta'en up what we cried the School Hill, which was just next to the school; lined along there and waiting for the train to come into the station which was the overnight...the train was stationed there overnight where the king and queen were on board. But, eh, when the train went by naebody waved oot tae us. The other one was at the same time, or same era, I always remember being up the School Hill and eh, we were watching the paratroopers dropping onto the Sorn hills.*

Maggie Bunting: *...The station was up there and they slept down at the corner just where you go to go up the Lambeth Walk...the railway line came right in to just about the bottom of that...the station was further up...when we came back from – I was working at Bowhouse at the time. At that time...you were all shifted for the war effort... Came home from work at 6 o' clock in the morning...we went up to the station, but no, we never had a glimpse of them at all! My dad was working at Bowhouse at the time too, and he was on the day shift, and he saw them go through the railway line down there. We had went up there and stood all that time and saw nothing!*

Wood Street

Sean Campbell: *...There was more folk stayed there than the rest o Cotirn...it was a combination of mill workers and miners...they had big families...in thae days.*

Evelyn Campbell: *The houses up there was like what these were: entries. And maybe on one side there would be a couple wi six or seven kids, ken, and maybe like four houses.*

Maggie Bunting: *Oh aye, Wood Street was a very* [dirty?] *place. The top, this end here, they called it the Tramps Lodging House. Where the tramps stayed when they came around looking for money. They chapped the door for a penny. It was* [Rodden] *the people, I think, that had the lodging house, the tramps lodging house at the end of Wood Street...there were a lot of folk in it, in those houses.*

Jim Bunting: *They say in the olden days that the milkmen used to race to get to Wood Street first because there was so many people there, you know, the first one there sold the most milk! ...It was a kind of rabbit warren of a place...*[the hosiery]*...it was a private enterprise. Eldorado, the new houses that are built in Wood Street, what they call Eldorado was exactly where the hosiery was...*

Robert Dalziel: *...Earlier in his* [father's] *life he was a worker in the Holm Farm in Catrine and in his early 20s became milk roundsman for the Holm Farm, and there were four or five milk roundsmen working in Catrine... My father used to say he had to get into the Wood Street in Catrine by half past 5 in the morning and if he wisnae first in or close to first in milk roundsman, he wouldnae sell half his milk round because there were so many people living in Wood Street. It was one of the most densely populated and indeed one of the poorest parts of the village, but they all needed milk and so it was a kind of a race to get there for early in the morning; the milking by 4 o' clock in the morning...* [Wood Street was] *mostly mill workers, aye, mostly mill workers.*

203/105

Wood Street, Catrine.
Mrs Rodden
Willie Cree

Jacob's Ladder

Jim Bunting: *...250 odd or even more* [steps]*! I used to walk up and down it every day to my work...it was quite an effort to get up... A lot of people used it. I remember Wullie Buchanan who was one of the gardeners at Ballochmyle, he lived up St. Cuthbert Street. He biked to his work. Wullie would bike to the bottom of Jacob's Ladder and carry it up the 'Ladder' to his work in the morning! The best of it was when he finished at night, instead of coming back down the brae on the road, he came back to the 'Ladder' and carried down the 'Ladder'...Wullie never missed a single day at his work in all his life!*

The Scheme

Harry Houston: *...We stayed at that time in Somerville Street. Actually, I was the first born in that new scheme which was Shawwood Housing Scheme...it's huge noo in comparison to what it was then...it was just a few hooses up there. There was also a field which was next to it and there was a family, the Innes's, and they used to stay in a hut...I used to think, Geez. Look at that! Ken, here's these folk stayin there and a' they've got is a fire, a wood burning fire; nae toilets; nae nothing. They kept hens. But they were a guid family, ken. That's always a mindin I've got o that...*

Anne Fleming: *I'm Anne Fleming. My own name was Hastings and I was born at 16 Park Terrace in Catrine in August 1939. Then the war broke out! My dad was away in the Air Force, so he was away for the first five years of my life...mum and I stayed with my gran – she was on her own at Park Terrace – till my Dad came out the Air Force and I went to primary school across the road, so I hadnae far to travel. ...Then we were lucky enough to get one of the new built prefabs* (shown below) *in 1946; we moved up there, my mother, father and I. This was great, to have your own house, a fancy kitchen and you had a fridge which was an American idea and had never been known in Catrine! You had your separate toilet and bathroom.*

Sean Campbell: *Aye, born and bred, up in Wood Street, number 1 Wood Street...the hooses got built in 39. I moved up there when I was aboot two year auld, up to Sorn Street...you were getting inside toilets, you could get a bath, instead o folk sharing it.*

Evelyn Campbell: *Well, we were in business so it suited us, ken, cause there were an awful lot more people in the village. Aye, it was a good thing. The old scheme went to about where the shops is...and then they started building on from there...when you think, in Wood Street, there were maybe about six rooms and kitchens. When yous moved up the scheme, yous had two rooms then...see doon this street here, maist o a' the hooses even o'er* [by] *the village hall* [Institute] *belonged to the mill company. More or less the hail o Catrine belonged to the mill company then. Then it was council houses...St. Cuthbert's Street? They a' belonged to the mill and if you got a job wi the mill, you got a hoose...there were quite a few people came fae...Deanston to come here to work...they got mill hooses...there was a lot of work here. It was shift work...fae Muirkirk they used to travel...*

Anne Fleming: *...A lot of the people that lived in Mill Street, they all came up here to the prefabs...there was gas in the scheme up to the back of Shawlands Street there, but the rest of this bit didn't have gas up to, oh, not many years ago, because so many people got the pit coal...they deemed that they didnae need gas. Before you had double-glazing and all that, this was a really cold house...*

Catrine Today

Robert Dalziel: *As a child I can remember the village very much dominated by the two mills…dominating the village main street. The open square is really quite new to me cos although I was in the village, till I was 23 I went to university in Glasgow for five years and consequently left the village in a sense at 18, which is just after the Mill burned down. Therefore it's a big change and just seeing the open square it's in many ways better. It's a nicer looking centre to the village than the Old Mill… I still think I'm coming home when I drive down that Mauchline Road and come in, down all these winding bends, that were of course made to help the horses drag their heavy loads up the hill. I still think I'm coming home. I still think of the village as home…the Catrine I'm remembering, of course, doesn't exist but then that's probably how anybody is where they were brought up when they were young, and I still think about…I quite often just drive through the village…just have a wee look to see what is like. I find it quite impressive that there's new houses in the Burnpark, which I still find quite surprising cos we played football there, but it's still nice to see them there. Nice houses, or they look nice houses to me passing through the village, but it's an enormous change in the village and there are lots of changes: lots of new buildings and new houses and of course lots of the old ones have disappeared the big thing being the mill having disappeared. That transformed the village. Driving, just the ability to drive straight through the village, still takes me by surprise. When they built the mill, of course, they were only worried about bringing things in from the Mauchline side cos that's where they were coming from. They were coming from Glasgow, from the docks, so they never bothered about the idea of building the mill with prospect of a road going out to Cumnock at the back of it, so it didn't matter because you were stopping at the mill. Obviously as time went by they were developing that road and then you had the problem of 1, 2, 3, 4, right-angled-turns to get round the mill. It was much more sensible to build the mill round a different way with its back to the river, but that's not how they did it! There's an engraving by Black circa 1820, a picture of…how the wagon loads are being pulled up right to the front of the old mill, and that's where everything was focused, to the front of the mill, and the streets were just built round about it to house the village workers. That remains the heart of the village. What's happened in the last 50 or 60 years…is that central part of the village, where so many houses were crammed in, has vanished and it's opened out the Mauchline Road council houses as they then were…but instead of developing that area after the war they moved to the other end of the village and built the council housing estate up at the top end of the village towards Auchinleck, and they didn't develop the Mauchline Road end with council housing. There's an awful lot of better housing there now than there used to be, although having said that, some of the original mill houses were quite good…*

Lara McPyke (*neé* Bunting): *When you go to New Lanark, we went years ago, and that was the first thing my dad and my mum said how similar it is…obviously David Dale was one of the partners that established here as well, so it's a bit like New Town idea… The thing that amazes me when you look back at how Catrine was designed was the fact that they're now talking about this new thing that Prince Charles is trying to do, this new community* [Knockroon] *where everything is within five minutes of everything else…Catrine's really like that, really, compared with any other village round about. It was built on quite a tight grid so it was obviously planned, and planned quite well…*

Jim Bunting: *Just the old home town…at one time you knew absolutely everybody in Catrine…it's changed a bit now…it's a great wee place!*

Alistair Plenderleith: *Down to earth. You've a wheen o rogues and that ken, you've got to watch… There's a lot o genuine folks.*

John Johnston: *…Oh I love Catrine! Love it! You were born and bred in it. It's never done me nae harm. I love Catrine. Always did.*

The Interviewees

Alistair Plenderleith

Linda Smith (*neé* Wilson)

Jack & Anne Fleming

Ruth Sharp

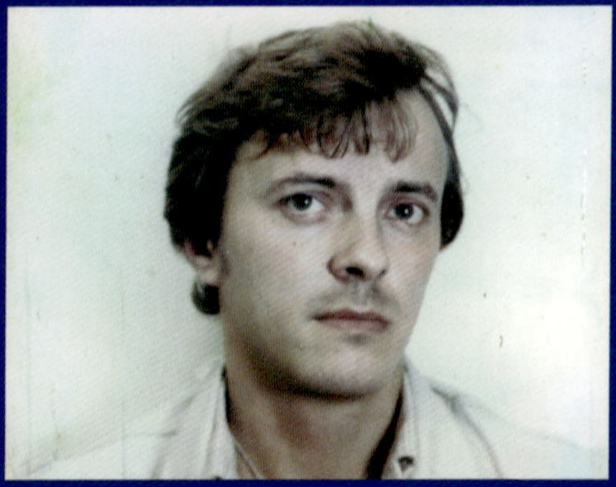
John Sharp

Harry Houston

Mary McCluskie (*neé* Spiers)

Maureen Kiernan

Maggie Bunting

Evelyn Campbell

Jeremy Lloyd

John Johnston

Interviewees not pictured: Jim Bunting, John (Sean) Campbell, Robert (Bob) Dalziel, Billy & Margaret Dick, Lara McPyke (*neé* Bunting). Nessie Henderson is pictured on page 24.

Picture Acknowledgements

Catrine Community Trust: 113

Dundee Art Galleries and Museums: 4 left

Finlays PLC: 22-23, 24, 27, 28, 39, 40, 41, 46 lower, 47, 48, 50, 60, 61, 62 both, 63, 64, 68-69, 72-73, 76-77, 78, 79, 103, 120 upper

Anne Fleming: 58, 59, 125

Terry Harrison Collection: 32

Johnny Johnston: 38

Alistair Plenderleith: 104

Royal Commission on the Ancient and Historical Monuments of Scotland; Licensor www.scran.ac.uk: 1, 92, 94, 95, 96, 97, 121

Ron Scott: 36

Ruth & John Sharp: 33, 55, 56, 57 upper, 109, 114, 120 lower

Sotheby's: 6

Richard Stenlake Collection: 3, 4 right, 5, 8-9, 11, 17, 18, 20, 21, 25, 29, 30-31, 34, 37, 42, 44, 45, 46 upper, 51, 53, 84, 85, 87, 88, 89 both, 91, 101, 107, 110, 111, 115, 116, 117, 118, 119, 122-123, 124

Richard Stenlake: 13, 14, 15, 52, 57 lower, 80, 81, 82, 83, 98, 105, 106, 108

Whiteholme Ltd: 102

Modern photographs of interviewees by Colin McGilvray & Richard Stenlake.

Sources Consulted Not Referenced In Text

Mills and Millwork, William Fairbairn, 1864

The Arkwrights 'Spinners of Fortune', R.S. Fitton, 1989

The Life of Sir William Fairbairn Bart., 1877

Scottish Banking A History 1695-1973, S.G. Checkland, 1975

A Short History of Slavery, James Walvin, 2007

King Cotton and the Abolition Movement, the role of David Dale of New Lanark, David McLaren, unpublished paper, 2010